Blackouts to
Bright Lights

CLASS CODE: 13261.

E.K.I.D. 83. 4

WADDY. Audrey R.

PHOTOGRAPH OF HOLDER

Signature of Holder

Audrey R.F. Waddy.

Blackouts to Bright Lights

Canadian War Bride Stories

edited by

Barbara Ladouceur

& Phyllis Spence

RONSDALE PRESS

RONSDALE PRESS LTD.
3350 West 21st Avenue
Vancouver, B.C., Canada
V6S 1G7

Set in New Baskerville: 11 pt on 14
Typesetting: Julie Cochrane
Printing: Hignell Printing, Winnipeg, Manitoba
Cover Design: Cecilia Jang

The paper used in this book is Miami Vellum. It is recycled stock containing no dioxins. It is totally chlorine-free (TCF) as well as acid-free (therefore of archival quality). The paper is made from at least 10% post-consumer waste.

The publisher wishes to thank the Canada Council and the British Columbia Cultural Services Branch for their generous financial assistance.

CANADIAN CATALOGUING IN PUBLICATION DATA

Blackouts to bright lights

ISBN 0-921870-33-7

1. War brides—Canada—Biography. 2. World War, 1939–1945—Women.
3. World War, 1939–1945—Personal narratives, British. 4. Canada—Emigration and immigration—History—20th century. I. Ladouceur, Barbara, 1949–
II. Spence, Phyllis, 1943–
D810.W7B52 1995   306.84'5'0971   C95-910077-6

DEDICATION

This book is dedicated
to the war brides who were not able
to record their stories for
Blackouts to Bright Lights.

ACKNOWLEDGEMENTS

The editors wish to express our heartfelt thanks to our families and friends for their ongoing enthusiasm and support—especially Peggy Maurer (whose proofreading skills proved invaluable), Alicia Ladouceur, Jeffrey Ladouceur, Maureen Davis, Bill and Kelly Brimacombe, Kathy and Gerald Watson, Judy Laviolette, Kathryn Maurer, Dawn Campbell, Stanley Spence, Marilyn Roodbol, Penny Beckett, Bradley Spence, Allison Spence, Liz Ciocca, and Sue Harvey.

We also very much appreciate the early interest and encouragement of Dr. Jennifer Waelti-Walters, Director of Women's Studies at the University of Victoria and Dr. Tanis Doe, Research Director at the World Institute on Disability in Oakland, California.

We are grateful beyond words for the skilled editorial assistance of David Burton and Donna Spence.

A special note of appreciation to Ronald Hatch for believing in the power of these war bride stories, and for sensitively and expertly bringing the editors and thirty-six war brides to the completion of a most exciting and worthwhile project.

And most important of all, we are deeply grateful to the war brides who participated in this book for sharing their compelling stories, photographs and mementoes, and a special thank you to Eve Mitchell for the gift of this book's concept and Rosemary Bauchman for the gift of the title, "Blackouts to Bright Lights."

CONTENTS

Personal Narratives:

PROLOGUE

The stories in this book offer a passport to another time and place through the eyes of World War II war brides. Their stories describe how it felt to be a young woman coming of age during a war that resulted in a level of destruction and suffering never before experienced by a civilian population. They also demonstrate the conflicting emotions of fear and pride, the dark memories of bombings and deprivation along with proud recollections of the important work they accomplished as part of the war effort.

The war brides' stories point to the vital new roles and responsibilities that women assumed to assure their nation's survival in the midst of war. Before and after meeting their future husbands, these war brides were ambulance drivers, balloon barrage workers, nurses, fire fighters, air-raid wardens, factory workers and members of the armed forces, including the ATS (Auxiliary Territorial Service), Land Army (farm work) and Air Force.

Some of the war brides were as young as twelve or thirteen when the war began, but their childhoods ended abruptly as the bombings began and the harsh realities of blackouts, rationing and civil defence preoccupied their lives. These young women met and fell in love with Canadian soldiers. In doing so, they encountered a whole new set of problems: first, the lengthy bureaucratic procedure required before approval was granted to marry a Canadian soldier and emigrate to Canada; then the emotional turmoil of saying good-bye to family and friends before embarking on a journey to a strange new country.

Over 48,000 war brides came to all parts of Canada during and after World War II. With them they brought their children— some 22,000. Many of the war brides settled in cities or towns where they coped with postwar housing and furniture shortages. Others travelled to remote regions of Canada that placed them in the midst of isolated living conditions and long cold winters. Wherever the war brides went, they displayed a pioneering spirit that grew from the determination and creativity they developed during the war years. And throughout their stories these remarkable women—whether they wrestle with balloon barrages in the United Kingdom or wood and coal stoves in Canada—display great courage, spirit and humour. The narratives of these extraordinary war brides are histories which have become an important part of our Canadian heritage.

The concept for this book began with Eve Mitchell whom the editors first met in 1993. As President of the Vancouver Island War Brides at the time, she invited us to record the war brides' oral histories and publish them in book form. During the past year the editors have had the pleasure and privilege of listening to war brides as they remembered times past. We tape-recorded their reminiscences of participating in the war effort, meeting their Canadian husbands, leaving their home countries and adjusting to life in Canada. We then transcribed their spoken words into written life histories that highlight their individual voices.

The war brides featured in the oral histories of this book have played an integral role in the proofreading and editing of their stories. The editors thank them for their invaluable assistance and generous sharing of their experiences as well as the photographs that enliven each of their stories. Five of the war brides chose to write their own stories, and these narratives are presented in the final section of the book.

These stories are truly representative of the war brides who emigrated to Canada during the 1940's. Although all the war brides in this book now reside on Vancouver Island, most of them initially lived in other parts of Canada, including the Maritimes, Ontario, Quebec, the prairies and the Yukon. Thus these women's stories reflect the Canadian war bride experience from coast to coast.

This year marks not only the fiftieth anniversary of the end of World War II; it also represents fifty years of memories for the war brides in Canada. Many of them have recently celebrated their fiftieth wedding anniversaries or are about to do so during the forthcoming year. Their memories will always be double-edged with joy and sorrow, because their promising partnerships with their new husbands began in the tragic context of World War II. The life stories of thirty-six of those war brides are recorded in this book for future generations to cherish.

Barbara Ladouceur and Phyllis Spence
January 1995

Three war brides with children arriving in Halifax at the end of World War II.

Betty Patriquin

"MY DEAR YOUNG LADY,
DO YOU KNOW WHAT
YOU'RE DOING?"

---

*Betty Patriquin was born in Croydon, England.
At the age of sixteen, she attended an art college
to study dress design for two years. She was
nineteen years old and still living with her
family when the war started in 1939.*

You really can't explain how bad it was. It was very serious, really. But I think when you're young—eighteen or nineteen—you think the war is all sort of a lark. It's an adventure. My mother would say, "It is not funny—it's very upsetting and worrying." But there were all these troops around, and young people had lots of fun.

At this time, the air raids took place every night. It wasn't just the bombs but the shrapnel from the guns as well that was dangerous. It was a funny sort of life but when you're young, you adapt more easily. My brother and I used to sit up and play cards in the air-raid shelter in our garden. We had lights and a radio down there as well. We used to take a little hot plate down too so we could make tea. If there was a lull in the air raids, one of us would run up to the house if we needed anything or had to go to the bathroom.

If we could manage to go to dances, my friends and I would do so. When the air raids were heavy, of course, we couldn't go. But anytime there was a few days respite from the bombing, we would go to dances. Otherwise, the bombing was so heavy that you couldn't go anywhere. It was a difficult time for everybody. You look back now and you're amazed that you survived it so well.

In 1941, I was to be called up because they now had conscription for women from the age of eighteen to thirty. They said that I could only go in the Army or into munitions at that time. I moved with my family down to Bognor Regis which is on the south coast of England. We got the upper unit of a furnished duplex right on the seafront, which during peacetime had been a very, very good area—usually very expensive. But, of course, most people had gone from the coastal towns by this time.

My father continued to go back and forth by train to work in London. I went to find out what kind of work I should do, and I was told that I could go in the Land Army because they needed girls for farm work all around there. I thought, "Well that would be better than being cooped up in a factory." They sent me to this place in Sussex, but it was twenty-five miles away from where we now lived. So I had to live there during the week and go home on the weekends.

I was billeted in a little cottage in a village. It had no lights and no toilet. I was staying with a young couple, and the wife was very kind to me. She did her best for me. But it was lonesome for me because I'd always been with my family. This was the first time I had ever lived away from home. At night, I had to just sit in the kitchen with the young couple or go to bed. During this time, I went to bed earlier than I ever had in my life.

On the farm, another girl and I spent most of our time planting vegetables and digging up potatoes. We worked at a market-garden farm, and our main task was to bed tiny plants in the greenhouses. We also had to clean out the barns which were where the farmer kept his cattle. The cattle were kept mostly for the manure they provided. We did all sorts of dirty jobs, and all this work got to be rather boring. Then one day, the farmer asked us, "Which one of you girls knows how to drive a horse and cart?" So I said, "Oh I do!" I was thinking it would be a nice change, but the problem was that I really didn't know how to drive a horse and cart. I just decided that there couldn't be much to it.

The farmer took me around to the barn to pick up various things that had to be delivered to other farmers. When he showed me the horse and cart, he did try to explain that "you do this and you do that to start and stop the cart." "Oh yes," I said. He piled up the back of the cart with all these big boxes of little chickens and what I think were sacks of flour. Then I set off in the cart with a list of the places to which I was to deliver the various items.

I would get the horse and cart into a driveway, and then I would say to the farmer, "Could you turn my horse around, please?" Because I really didn't know how to do it. The farmers would look at me as if I were a moron but they were all nice enough to say, "Oh yes, sure I'll turn it around." Then there were Canadians everywhere along the roads, and some of them asked me, "Could we come for a ride with you?" I had to reply, "No, you couldn't." Then they asked, "Could you go out with us this evening?" I answered, "No, I couldn't."

The next thing I knew, one of the Canadians fed the horse some candy which I could have drooled over because it was such a rare treat in wartime England. Then when I tried to go in a different direction, the horse started to follow the Canadian who'd fed him the candy. Suddenly the back of the cart went down in a ditch, and the Canadians had to help me pull the cart out—with all the chickens squawking hysterically.

On the way home as I was going around a corner, the vicar was coming from the opposite direction on his bicycle. I caught the side of his bicycle on the cart wheel, and he fell into the ditch. I was very upset. He didn't hurt himself but I was just horrified that I had knocked over a minister. He looked at me and inquired, "My dear young lady, do you know what you're doing?" And I assured him, "Oh yes, I do. It's the horse that doesn't know!" Then he got up and he was alright but I thought that I better get back before anything else happened.

After that exciting first ride, I took the horse and cart out whenever I was asked to do so, and those outings gave me a much needed break from the usual chores. Obviously I got to know what I was doing. And as I drove the cart around the countryside, I found it both fun and interesting to meet other people, including the other farmers in the area. It was great to do something entirely different from the other responsibilities I had. But then I suppose most of the girls in wartime did different jobs from what they were used to.

I went home on weekends, and eventually I met my husband, Pat, at a dance when he asked me to dance. He asked me where I lived, and I said, "Well we really live in Croydon. Do you know where that is?" He answered, "Oh yes, I've been up there on a course." I explained that we'd moved here because the bombs were so bad in Croydon. Then he declared, "Well, when we're married, we'll live in Croydon, and we'll spend our holidays here." I really didn't take him seriously but I agreed to go out with him on Monday night.

The next day, Pat came marching along the seafront with this group of soldiers. I think they were marching to the cookhouse for dinner. My mother and I were walking along, and Pat said to the troops, "Eyes right." My mother asked me, "Do you know that man?" I said, "Yes, I do." So she remarked, "Well, he's a nice healthy looking boy," and I responded, "Oh yes, I guess so."

Come Monday evening, it was pouring with rain—just pouring. My mother told me, "You're not going out tonight, dear." But I said, "Yes, I am. I'm going out with that nice healthy looking boy." She protested, "Not tonight!" I assured her, "I really don't think he'll be there." I was thinking to myself that he'd had a few beers the night he asked me out, and he'd probably forgotten about tonight. However, I thought I would go along and see if he did show up. I told my mother, "If I don't come back, you'll know he was there and we've gone to the show."

When I reached the corner where we were to meet, there was Pat waiting for me with the rain dripping off him. So we went to the show and then for a drink afterwards. Of course, in those days, nobody had cars. You had to walk everywhere. He asked me if I would go out with him again. A couple of days later, he told me, "I'm going to London for seven days' leave. I wish I didn't have to go there now that I've met you." But I just said, "Oh well, that'll be nice for you." Then he said, "Oh I do wish you could come too." I informed him, "I couldn't do that—my mother wouldn't let me!" For one thing, she wouldn't let me go to London with all the bombing, and for another thing, girls just didn't run off for a week with their boyfriend in those days.

Finally Pat said, "Well I'll see you when I get back, so don't forget me." When he came back we went for a walk and he asked me, "When are you going to marry me?" I quipped back, "Oh tomorrow!" I thought it was ever so funny—a joke—although I really was very much attracted to him. He was a nice, tall, healthy man. But I didn't know anything about him.

When I returned home, my mother and aunt asked me, "Did you get along alright with Pat?" I answered, "Oh yes, I sure did." Then they asked me, "Does he like you?" I said, "Yes, he's just asked me to marry him!" They laughed and laughed. They rolled on the bed with laughter. My mother said, "You've only known him a week!" I declared, "Well, that doesn't make any difference." I was so young and very clever. "Love at first sight," I said, "You've heard of that."

My mother went and told my father, and he just about hit the roof. "I never heard such a lot of rubbish," he said. "That girl doesn't know what she's talking about. She's *certainly* not going to marry him!" And so on and so forth—I could hear him going on and on. I thought, "Oh dear!"

The next night Pat came around to the apartment and we went out. He said, "I went to my Commanding Officer today, and I put in an application to be married." "You did *what?*" I asked. He explained, "Well you have to ask for permission, and you have to wait so long. And I didn't think we wanted to wait so I put in an application. When they asked me how long I had known you, I said ten months. I was up in the Croydon area before and I *could* have met you then." But, I protested, "That wasn't true." "It doesn't matter," he assured me.

We got married on March 14th, 1942, and then went to Bournemouth for a week-long honeymoon. While we were on our honeymoon, I got this terrible tonsillitis (it was very wet in March). I was awfully sick. I went home, and Pat went back to his station. I had a high fever so my mother sent for the doctor. He said, "Well you won't be going back to work for awhile. You're going to have to stay in bed for a couple of weeks with that." I ended up in the hospital to have my tonsils removed, and for some time after I was very weak. So I wrote the Land Army a letter, and they said they understood. If at any time I felt well enough to go back to work, they would be glad to have me.

The war certainly opened up different work opportunities for people like me. You could see that the class system was breaking down in England. Before the war, the upper class hired members of the working class to be maids, gardeners and butlers. After the war, both men and women had higher expectations. I think that the war made women much more independent. A lot of them didn't want to go back to the same life.

I returned home and went back to my dressmaking. I had piles and piles of work. I could have worked twenty-four hours a day because all the different seamstresses and dressmakers were called up during the war, so there weren't very many that could provide such services. It wasn't exactly what you'd call war work, but still women needed things to wear. It kept their morale up. I also sewed children's clothing. During wartime, there were so many alterations from old clothes to make them do, because clothing was rationed as well as food. In any case, I could have had much more work than I wanted.

In 1944, Pat was sent back to Canada on leave because he had been one of the first ones in England, and he was due to go back. I would have been allowed to go, too, but I didn't want to go. It was 1944, and I said, "I won't leave my family in wartime while there is still danger from the bombing." My family had returned to Croydon but now the Germans were sending over doodlebugs and rockets that they shot over from France. You had no warning, and it was very, very nervewracking. So I couldn't leave my family yet.

You put out of your mind how sad you are about leaving your family. Part of you wants to go so badly to see your husband again but another part of you doesn't ever want to go. You're very torn, and I think with all the war brides, this has been a common dilemma. Some of them settled down in Canada immediately and never worried about England again. Others never really adjusted to coming here. They'll always have one foot in England and one foot here.

When the war was over, I put in an application to go to Canada. I had to wait a whole year because they took all the troops first. The women were getting very fed up. There were many articles in the paper about it. Finally, the war brides marched with banners to Canada House to protest the long wait to get to Canada. I had gone just to see what was going on. Then they started to take wives but naturally they gave priority to women with children and women who were pregnant. They also took women whose husbands were ill and in other situations like that.

Eventually I did get to go. First I had to go up to London to
Canada House. I had to have quite a strict medical examination to
prove that I was fit to travel. Then I was interviewed as to where I
was going. I think that the Red Cross in Canada went to wherever
you were going and met your in-laws just to see that there was an
adequate place for you. They did all this before they sent you.
Then we just simply had to wait until our name came up.

We were told that we were to go to London on a certain day. I
remember my mother and father took me to the station in
Croydon where I was to catch the train to London. It was so hard
to say goodbye to them. They wanted to come up to London with
me, and I said, "I wish you wouldn't." I knew all the girls would be
taken away in a hurry, and I wouldn't even have time to spend
with them. So they just took me to the station in Croydon.

When we reached London, they took us to this great big house,
and it was awful. There was no furniture in it. It was being used to
move troops or war brides through London. It was all bedrooms
with bunkbeds and washrooms with rows of sinks. In the eating
areas, there were old trestle tables. It was very, very primitive—just
horrible. That night as we were waiting to go to Liverpool the
next day, there was a line-up of girls to use the two phones to say
goodbye once again. It was heartbreaking and everybody was
crying.

Our ship, the *Aquitania*, left Liverpool in the last part of
February 1946, and it landed in Halifax in the first week of March.
Pat was to meet me there. I had been with a group of about five
war brides from my area of England, and I was the only one whose
husband was going to meet me in Halifax. So they were all quite
intrigued about him. I thought he would arrive in his lovely officer's uniform but he was in civilian clothes with a big fedora on,
which they liked to wear in those days. And I thought, "My goodness, doesn't he look funny!"

I guess we all thought that our husbands looked strange when
we first saw them in civilian clothes. It was not just seeing them
out of uniform; Canadian men dressed differently from British
men. They dressed more flamboyantly. British men were more

conservative. My father always wore a dark suit, a white shirt and a bowler hat to go to work in London. In the winter, he would wear what were called spats. He was immaculate.

Pat was on leave so we went to visit his parents, and then we went up to New Brunswick to visit his sister and her family. Pat's parents were very nice and kind to me. I'm sure they wished their son had married a Canadian girl as I'm sure many in-laws of war brides wished, if they were honest. Pat's parents were strict Baptists, always going to church, which wasn't my way. I was an Anglican. As Anglicans, we went to church on Sundays but we didn't go two or three times during the week and two or three times on Sunday. My mother-in-law was a very devout Baptist.

When I met people at church, they made such a fuss, and they wanted to know who I was and where I was from. And did I like Canada? It was strange to me all around. I did my best when I was with my in-laws but I didn't have to live long with them as was the case with many war brides. Some had to stay with them for years until they got on their feet. I didn't have to do so, and in that way I was lucky.

We were in Nova Scotia for a couple of years. We stayed in Kentville, Nova Scotia, which was outside of Camp Aldershot, a big military camp where my husband was stationed. Pat found a boarding house in Kentville, and there were three Army wives at that house as well. They were Canadian women married to Army officers. There were also four young men who were at the agricultural college in Kentville. They were nice and very kind to me. The landlady was lovely too and took me under her wing. She invited Pat for dinner on the first Sunday I was there. That Sunday, we had dinner, and we were all sitting around this big table. After dinner was over, my husband asked, "Do you mind if I smoke? If you don't mind, I'll go and get my pipe." One of the Canadian Army wives asked me, "Why don't you go and get it? We understand that English girls wait on their men hand and foot." I protested, "Oh no we don't!" I felt very hurt and realized how much they resented me.

Later, the Army wives were talking to each other, and they said,

"The weather's so nice, we must go for a good walk tomorrow." It was springtime you see. Then they asked me, "Would you like to come?" I replied, "Well yes, but I didn't think Canadian girls walked." They looked at me and I said, "Well the Canadians always told us that Canadian girls had to be driven everywhere, and they all had cars." Of course, we never had any cars in England, especially in wartime. We had to walk everywhere.

The next day, they walked me for miles—five miles I think! But I didn't give up, and I wasn't in a good state of health, I must say, when I first came to Canada. I suffered from malnutrition, and I was very, very thin so I got tired very quickly.

When I first came to Canada I used to walk downtown and see the little shops. Kentville wasn't a very big place but they had the most gorgeous ice-cream parlour in the drugstore, and everyday I used to go and have a great big ice-cream sundae. Sometimes in the evening when Pat came over, we'd go again, and I'd have a milkshake because I enjoyed all these lovely things. I suppose because I was so thin, milkshakes didn't do me a bit of harm. They were probably very nourishing.

Afterwards, I got to know those two Army wives, and they were lovely. We got along just fine. And Pat took me to the officers' mess where I was one of the first British war brides there, and most people were nice to me. The Commanding Officer's wife took me out in the car with her for lunch several times. It was very pleasant—people were good on the whole. I was surprised there wasn't more resentment. I do think the Canadian girls were rather upset that so many of their best men had gone to the war, and then came back with wives!

Canada is a wonderful country—one of the best in the world. And I think we're so fortunate to have what we do have. Since we moved to Victoria twenty years ago, I have felt more settled than anywhere else I've lived. I've developed a stronger feeling that Canada is the place to be, and after all our moving around, Victoria is the first proper home we've had.

Connie Rust

"MOTHER WAS HORRIFIED, SHE REALLY WAS"

Connie Rust was born in Wem in Shropshire.
As a child she made her own fun, playing
with her dogs, climbing trees and
taking music lessons.

I had arranged with my skating instructor to go up in his plane the morning war was declared. He was to give me my first flying lesson. But I had to listen to the radio first. We all sat and listened; they said all planes were grounded, so that was the end of that, no flying lesson. I never did learn to fly. I used to lie on the ground and watch all the dogfights. There were many because we lived in a triangle of three air fields and we were one of the worst bombed areas. I used to lie outside sunbathing in the summer, and all these fighter planes would come over. The sirens would go off, but I didn't care. Then all of a sudden the planes would start peeling off, and I was there watching the fighting.

Since we had to have an air-raid shelter of some sort, we cleared out underneath the stairs so we had somewhere to go. I had a Scotch terrier and she was always the first under the stairs, and my mother was the second. I hated having to go in there. If we were at work and the siren went, we all had to go down to the basement of the store. This is what we did on the morning they dropped a land mine. It didn't go off so they had to defuse it, but it dropped back in the hole and all the crew were killed. I was standing in the candy shop downstairs, and the mirrors bulged right in and then went back out. It was amazing, as if they were elastic.

I was nineteen when war broke out. But I had to wait until I was twenty-one before I could join the Air Force without my mother's permission, because I knew she wouldn't let me go. I decided that I didn't want to be pushed into the Land Army or a munitions factory. I wanted to be in the Air Force and that was it. That's why I dashed up to London the minute I was twenty-one and signed up. I was notified within three weeks to report. Mother was horrified, she really was. But I said that was what I wanted to do, and that if I didn't, the authorities could send me up north to a munitions factory. She got used to it. After my training, I was sent down to Colerne, Wiltshire, and this is where I spent the whole four years. It was only a little village with a few houses, a bakery and a large wartime Air Force Base. I ended up as a physical training and drill instructress, which I just absolutely loved. I loved the service life altogether and I ended up as a sergeant. As new girls came into

Physical Training session during "Wings for Victory" week, in Bath, Somerset, 1943. Connie with her back to the photographer.

the Air Force, we older women would look out for them. Some of the girls were only seventeen or eighteen, and it was the first time they had been away from home. I was only twenty-four but I would kind of mother them up a bit until they got on their feet. I was in charge of the barrack block and there were seven rooms with twenty-eight women in each room. I used to have to inspect the rooms every day to make sure they had mopped under their beds. Apart from taking daily drill and PT (physical training) sessions, I used to head up a lot of parades and put on PT demonstrations.

I met David, my future husband, in September of 1944 at the coffee urn in the sergeants' mess. My friend introduced me to him. He asked her if she would find him a nice girl with money and she said, "Yes, here's Connie!" I knew the minute I looked at him that this was the guy I had been looking for. He told me on our honeymoon that he felt the same way when he met me. David was an instrument mechanic in the 406 Squadron, and he had been a watchmaker and jeweller in Canada before he joined. He went over before the main body of the Canadian Air Force did, so he was attached to a Royal Air Force squadron, and this is where he got the nickname Rocky.

David and I went out together for about two months, when he asked me if I would marry him and go to Canada. But then when he was sent to camp to go back to Canada, he said, "Let's get married before I leave." He went off to report to Warrington to see if he could get off the draft to get married. I stayed behind and planned the wedding, never knowing if I would ever see him again. I planned it in five days. I horrified my mother because I had only mentioned his name once to her in a letter saying I had been out with him, and then I phoned her up and asked her to come to my wedding next Saturday. My mother asked why I didn't fall in love with an Englishman; she was afraid I was going too far away. In England, Canada is the back of beyond. I said, "Oh well, we won't be going that soon." But of course, three months later we were gone.

David had to get permission from his Commanding Officer to marry. In fact one morning when he met me in the mess, he pushed this piece of paper across the table. I opened it and read that "Sergeant David Rust has permission to marry Sergeant Constance Morgan," and that was what we had to have in order to get a marriage licence. We had to take it the next day to the registrar at Chippenham to make the arrangements to be married. We could have been married on the Friday, but I knew my mother wouldn't come if it was a Friday because she was very superstitious. I went and stayed the night before the wedding with my girlfriend and I was just terrified that David wasn't going to turn up the next morning—that he would get cold feet and wouldn't come.

We were married in December 1944 in the registrar's office. It was a very simple wedding with just my mother, my sister and my girlfriend, who stood up for me, and David's friend, for him. Afterwards, we went for lunch. We took off to Stratford-upon-

Avon for a week's honeymoon. We had to report back to Warrington near Liverpool, and that was when they told him he could stay back and wait with me to go to Canada. Before we were married he thought he should go home and get a house, but once we got married that was it, no way were we going to be separated. In the Air Force, they had what they called an AMO (if your husband was on leave they had to give you leave at the same time). After we were married, we were both on indefinite leave, drawing full pay for three months before we came to Canada. So we went down to Cornwall where my mother was and lived in this fabulous hotel right on the waterfront, until they could get a passage for the two of us.

We left England on March 1, 1945. The war with Germany was nearly over but not with Japan. When I went back to camp for my discharge, they took my uniform because they wouldn't let me bring it over to Canada. Anybody who got out after the war was completely over was allowed to keep their uniform. That always annoyed me as I would have loved to have kept my cap and things like that. I only got to keep my badges.

The Air Force arranged our passage, but I had to go to Canada House in London and sign things. They told us what kind of weather we would encounter and that you would need a warm coat and boots in Canada. We were given coupons to go out and buy the things in England. We also were told not to talk to anybody about this, and when they sent for us we weren't to tell anybody where we were going. It was very secretive, so my friend and I had this little deal cooked up that we would phone each other and just say something to let each other know that we had been called. When they sent for David I knew that we would be going in a few days. Then I got my notice to report to London. He left independently and the brides all left together. We all went to a hostel in London, then we were taken to the docks the next morning, and we didn't meet our husbands until we boarded the ship.

The men were mostly together below deck; some actually slept in hammocks on deck. The women were all in large cabins (they had knocked the small cabins into larger cabins). There were thirty women in my cabin. There were three-tier bunks and I drew a lower bunk, but I traded with another woman and I got the top bunk. We were the first ship of war brides that came over without an escort. There were no children on the ship so that was why we were allowed to travel without a convoy. It was called the _Louis Pasteur._ It was actually a French luxury liner, and we made it over in five days. Some of the girls were seasick before we left the dock. It was terrible coming out of the North Sea. It was mined so badly that we changed course every five minutes, and the ship was tossing up and down. Out of the thirty women in my cabin, there were only two of us who weren't seasick. They were all moaning and groaning, so we took our pillow and blanket and sat in the shower all night.

It wasn't bad, five days. Some of the ships took two weeks in convoy, they travelled so slowly. We couldn't believe the food—white bread and bananas! Things we hadn't seen in so long. I did not miss a meal. I could get together with my husband during the day, if he wasn't on watch. We were allowed to be together until sundown; the minute they had to blackout the ship, we had to go to our separate quarters.

When we docked in Halifax our husbands had to go off separately again and we met on the train. My first impression of the houses in Halifax was that they looked tall and narrow. As we came across Canada, we dropped people off, and as the train emptied we also left train cars behind, so the train grew smaller. It was comical because there were quite a few wives, and the porter would make all the bunks up, but nobody ever used the top ones. So after a few days, he didn't bother to make up the top berths.

When I came to Edmonton, I thought it was a dreadful place because it was so dull. I had lived just a half hour from London, and had done things, like going up to the London Palladium and hearing Kate Smith sing "God Bless America." And then I came to Edmonton and there was nothing.

My husband had said not to bring a lot of stuff because I could buy everything I wanted in Canada. So of course I hadn't brought a lot of stuff. I thought why trail it over there; I can buy new clothes when I get there. In England I didn't have what you call a bottom drawer, collecting linens and things, because I hadn't any intention of getting married. We didn't have a lot of wedding presents because we didn't have a big wedding. So I had to go out looking for things to start a household. When David went to work, I would go into Edmonton with him and shop for the day; then I would go back with all these packages. For six weeks we lived with his parents until he received his discharge. I had money my grandfather had left me, an inheritance which I brought with me. So I went out and bought our first house. It was fun fixing up the house.

I was so newly married and so crazy in love with this guy that he was the main person in my life. But I did miss my family when I came over to Canada, and I resented the way everything centered on my in-laws. The first argument my husband and I had was over going to see his parents every Sunday. I said if my family lived here we would have to go visit my mother every other week, so the weeks I should be visiting my mother, I wanted to go somewhere different. I didn't want to have to go visit his mother. I won the argument, and we used to go off to visit friends and do other things every other week. We wrote long letters to my family telling them everything about Canada. They thought we were crazy, as we used to drive a hundred miles to go fishing on a Sunday and a hundred miles back. That's half way up to Scotland; they couldn't visualize the distance here at all.

We moved into the house in the summer. I can remember the next winter I was out sweeping the sidewalk in bare legs, and my neighbour called to me, "Have you got bare legs?" I had a dress on, so I said, "Yes." Then she told me, "It's twenty below." I guess my blood was so thick I didn't mind the cold weather. I bought a fur coat and boots with fur on them. I loved to skate, and we often went skating. When our oldest daughter was about three, we flooded our back yard so we could teach her.

A few years later we bought a jewellery store up in Whitehorse, in the Yukon, and I always said, I think if I had gone from England straight to Whitehorse I might have been one of the ones who didn't stay. There was nothing when we went there; there was no pavement or anything. We drove up to see the store, and it took us three days to reach there from Edmonton. It is a beautiful part of the country, it really is, and everyone is so friendly. We were square dancers so we joined a square dancing group as soon as we got up there. We had also bowled in a jeweller's league in Edmonton, so when we got to Whitehorse we also got into bowling. We would get a sitter for the kids and off we would go.

My husband was up there for ten and a half months without me. I became pregnant just as we were going to move up and the doctors wouldn't let me go. I stayed in Edmonton with a six-year-old and a three-year-old and very pregnant, all on my own doing everything. I was also caring for a big garden and big house. David went up in October and came home for Christmas, and again in April. Our third daughter was born in July, and he couldn't come home because he was on his own in the store. I had to send him a telegram to tell him he had a new daughter. She was two and a half months old before he even saw her. We were in Whitehorse for twelve years, but I wouldn't agree to buy a house because I was afraid we would get stuck there forever.

From Whitehorse, we came down to Sidney, near Victoria, BC. The store we bought in Sidney belonged to a jeweller friend of ours from Edmonton. We had kept in touch, and he wrote to ask if we were interested in buying the store. His eyesight was going, and they would have to get rid of the store. We received the news in a Christmas card. When I read the card, it said, "Do you want to buy a store in a warmer climate? Ha! Ha!" (everyone always joked about us living up north with the Eskimos). I had been out to a conference in Kamloops the year before and had just totally fallen in love with BC. When I returned home I said to my husband, "Why do we live up here when there are these gorgeous places down in BC?" So we came down, looked at the store, and decided to buy it. I ran the store for fourteen and a half years after my husband died, and sold it in 1991 when I retired. My interests now include line dancing and travelling.

Joan Brace

"BLACKOUTS AND NO MORE LIGHTS!"

Joan Brace was born in Darlington, Durham. She was an only child who grew up in a large extended family with many childhood friends.

It was a gorgeous Sunday in Darlington, and my friend and I were coming home from church. I remember our parents and neighbours were out in the street, and I could hear them saying, "Not again! the First World War was the war to end all wars." I can see us coming down the back lane and all the people were shaking their heads, and saying, "Blackouts and no more lights!" They expected to be bombed immediately. It was an awful feeling. We did not fully understand at first, although the adults did. I was thirteen at the time, and we thought this was going to be the end of the world—the way the adults were talking.

In 1939 we transferred to York from Darlington where I sat my high school exams. I wanted to go to work and do something, and there was an opening in a hairdressing shop near us. A sign in the window read, "Apprentice wanted." So I said to mum, "I am going to apply for that." She was surprised and asked, "Oh, did you always want to do hair?" and I said, "No, not always, but it's a job." Well, you only got pin money in those days, and you were at the beck and call of everybody. You had to watch and learn how to shampoo and set hair. The lady who managed the hair salon was conscripted into factory work for the war. The owner at that time didn't want to close the salon. So he asked me, "Do you think you can handle it?" and I said "Sure." So within a year of becoming a hairdresser, I took over the shop. Eventually my father bought the shop for me, and when I met Bert and married him, I sold it. I worked for the person who purchased it from me until two weeks before I came to Canada.

We all received gas masks in 1940 and were fitted with them because of the gas attacks during the First World War. We had to queue up for the gas masks. The babies were put into these things that were like a big bunting bag, but the air was dependent upon the mother pumping it in. If something happened to her, the baby would have smothered. The little children had masks with Mickey Mouse faces, and every time they breathed, it would flap and whistle, and that was supposed to make them happy.

In 1942, York was bombed and the gas works were destroyed. Quite a bit of the railway station was bombed, too. I went to work that morning, not knowing whether my place would be there. Fortunately it was, but there was no hot water. At the time, I thought no one would want their hair done, but sure enough, in they came. It was a morale booster, anyway. My hands were like a couple of lobsters, doing cold water shampoos. All the electric heaters had been bought up in town.

During the air raids my family and I went down the street to the underground shelters at the school every night. We didn't get much sleep, as there were only wooden benches, but we stayed there until the "all-clear" sounded. The siren would go and I would say, "I don't want to go." Then dad would say, "Come on, Come on, were not going to leave you here." That was when the siren suits were invented, the kind we put our feet in and zippered all the way up. My mother was a seamstress so she made ours and they were cozy. I remember one night in the shelter we could hear the thump, thump, and the men saying, "That's pretty close, oh that's pretty close, I bet so-and-so got hit with that one." When we came up the steps there was a ring of fire around York, from the incendiary bombs. It was referred to as a "Baedeker." The British had bombed Cologne where there was a large cathedral and the Germans in turn bombed York, trying to hit the cathedral, York Minster. It was such a gorgeous moonlit night and York Minster stood out because it is made of limestone. Yet they never hit it.

I met my husband on June 18, 1944. Mrs. Chalk and her daughter Eva were customers of mine, and she used to entertain the Canadians quite a bit. I happened to introduce Eva to her husband, because he was with a young man I was going with at the time. Later they introduced me to Bert. We were engaged September 13, 1944.

I remember the night that peace was declared. Bert walked in to my shop and he said, "Haven't you heard, it's peace." I said, "No, I haven't got the wireless on, I'm too busy," Everybody in the shop said, "You mean it's actually signed," and he said, "Yes!" The street lights went on that night and all the church bells started to chime again. They had been silent since the beginning of the war. That night the streets were packed, and they ran out of beer.

Bert and I were married June 5, 1945, at Edward the Confessor Church, in Dringhouses, York. My husband sailed for Canada the Christmas of 1945 on the *Queen Elizabeth I.* I went through all the paperwork to come to Canada. We war brides were never issued passports, but were issued permits. As soon as we docked in Canada they took the permits away from all of us.

On April 15, 1946, I left York for Liverpool, where we stayed in a hostel overnight. My father was only able to see me to the Liverpool station. Then an escort from the Army met me and took me and my luggage on the bus to the hostel. It was all very secretive. When I wrote to my mum and dad that night at the hostel, I put "somewhere in Liverpool" for the address of the hostel, as I didn't even know the address of where I was staying. The beds were like boards and none of us slept a wink, so we talked and read books.

We were put on a bus the next morning and taken to the Princes Dock, where we got our sailing papers and boarded the *Letitia.* The soldiers and Red Cross nurses met us and took us to our cabin. They had taken the cabins and made them into big dormitories, with sixty to a hundred women and children in one long corridor. There were three-tier bunk beds lining the walls and I was on the top bunk because the women with babies were on the lower bunks. When I slid into bed, I had the pipes right above my head, but it was a lovely soft bed when I finally got into it. We had only salt water to wash in and you couldn't possibly get suds on it no matter what you did.

Our lunch was one of the fanciest lunches I'd had since before the war. There was a young steward serving each table, which consisted of six girls, so we had no time to wait between courses. We had pea soup, with pure white bread, beef, mixed salad, creamed potatoes, blueberry tart with custard, followed by biscuit and cheese and coffee. So I was quite full.

We were all set to sail at eight o'clock that evening, when the stewards went on strike. They felt the ship was understaffed. It was agreed to let them go on an evening leave and some didn't come back. But nevertheless, at ten the next morning, they just pulled up the gangplank and left without them, and then they were even more understaffed. The strike came just as we went down to dinner so we had to help ourselves. They didn't take it out on us as we were still looked after very well.

There was a canteen on board where we could buy different things; we could buy as much chocolate and sweets as we liked. We could also buy cigarettes. Two hundred was the limit we were allowed to take off the boat. When the canteen opened we queued up, and I bought cigarettes, Revlon face powder and some other things. They had soap and Lux flakes—in fact everything we hadn't been able to get—and most things were cheap.

During the voyage there were bingos and sing-songs. I won at bingo a few times. The prizes were cigarettes and chocolate. Every day there was something to entertain us. We went to the picture shows. One picture we saw was *Her Highness and the Bellboy* but the film broke down five times.

I never saw so many children in my life, and I will never forget the smell of the disinfectant. What with the children's screams and the noise of the engines, it was noisy on the ship. Fortunately for me I was lucky, I can sleep through anything. The old boat certainly could rock but I only missed one meal from feeling sick.

At last we arrived in Halifax on April 25th. The band was out to welcome us and they played "Here Comes The Bride." It was really touching. I thought Halifax harbour was a picture, because all the green and white wood houses resembled the calenders that I had seen, and everything looked so clean. There was a reception for us on the train station platform and the Red Cross handed out magazines. We boarded the train, and I was on my way to Kirkland Lake. The soldiers helped to take our luggage on and off the train and helped every step of the way.

Our first stop was in Quebec, where we bought our first pair of nylons. They were even rationed here, but they had a few in the store and they sold them to us for two dollars a pair. It was interesting to see how the trains passed through the main streets at street level which amused me, as in England you always went onto platforms at the stations and you never passed through the streets. Stopping right in the middle of town—I thought this was really different. At all the stops, people came out to view our war bride train.

Three of us left the train at North Bay, Ontario, at two in the morning; they put us up at the Empire Hotel. Did we ever enjoy our bath, because that was the first time that we could get suds in the water since leaving England. We had to be up again at six o'clock to catch the Ontario Northland to go north to Kirkland. I knew this was a vast country (we weren't totally ignorant), but I thought, "Here we are in North Bay, and Kirkland Lake is only just a little bit further north." Being so familiar with British travel and the time spent, I thought it wouldn't be much longer. So when I got on the train I expected to arrive in maybe an hour or so. They gave us tickets for breakfast on the train, but I didn't dare go as I was so afraid I was going to miss my station.

Eventually we arrived at three o'clock in the afternoon. There was my husband, looking odd in a nice tweed sports jacket, but oh those striped flannel pants that he had on. My husband's family were all delighted to see me, and I received a very warm welcome from my father-in-law who is also an Englishman. The rest of the family were back at the house waiting. At my father-in-law's house there was a big sign that read, "Welcome Home, Joan." There were so many friendly faces and a beautiful meal; it was the first time I had peas in cream sauce and pumpkin pie—I had never had pumpkin pie before.

Bert had already found us a lovely furnished apartment, so we started out on our own. We even had our own phone, but the bad part was that it had a coal and wood stove for cooking and also for warmth. I never did master the stove; I never could get it to go. I had two very well-attended showers, and I still enjoy the different pieces of china and glassware that I received. Slightly worse for wear are the cookbooks that were mailed to us by the Canadian government. They explained the different measures and the names of different products. We always cooked by pounds and ounces in England and here it was cups and spoons. At the little corner store, the clerk was puzzled when I requested a stone of potatoes, which is fourteen pounds.

From Kirkland we moved to North Bay, where we stayed for just over a year when Peter our son was born. Then we were moved to Sudbury, where our daughter Pamela was born. While we were there, we purchased a piece of land. We built the little house ourselves, and then we kept adding on until we ended up with a seven-room home. We moved in around Christmastime but we had to wait until the next spring to drill for water. We had great neighbours and they said, "Come and take what you like." So we carried the pails of water and that is how we managed.

When we needed washing water, we didn't like to bother the neighbours for that. What we had to do was quite humorous. We would go down to the lake, which was about a mile and didn't seem far. I had Peter as a baby and I would put him on a toboggan with this great big square tub. I would take it down to the lake, break the ice and fill up the tub with water. Then I'd take it back, put it on the stove and fill up the washing machine. When I only wanted a little wash water, I would go out and get snow and put it on the oil stove and melt it down. From a big square tub of snow you would get about three inches of water. I had this all down to a fine art. When I mentioned this to my family back home, they couldn't believe that I would be doing those things. Many of my relatives thought I was spoiled, that I would come running home in no time, but I didn't. I thoroughly enjoyed it.

In 1966 we went down to California to visit friends who had moved down. My husband had been in a plane crash during the war, and ever since he has had a back problem. We thought the warm weather would be more conducive to his health. Also I had had arthritis as a child, so we thought we would move down as a trial. We went down first to see what it was like; then we came home and sold up everything. We had to apply to get a visa. That was a four month's wait, and they told us not to sell the house or anything, that they would give us the time to do it. Everything went off well and we sold the house. We didn't have any mortgage—it was free and clear, so off we went to Oxnard, California, and my husband went to work as an electrician.

Later I went into apartment management. We had invested in

an apartment block, so some of the other owners said, "You are part investors so why don't you manage it?" It was a lovely little place, fifteen units around the pool. Later on, I had four others that I directly managed. Once again it was a wonderful period. We really enjoyed ourselves, it was a once-in-a-lifetime experience. We also moved to the desert, where my husband was offered a job at the Roy Rogers Apple Valley Inn. So we moved to Apple Valley. It is a beautiful place, also in California, but in the high desert below Big Bear. Just before the recession in 1975, the inn was sold to another group who brought in all their own people. My husband could see the writing on the wall and we left. He was offered his job back at the place we had previously been, but we moved to Camarillo, north of Los Angeles, where I found another job as an apartment manager. It was around that time that my husband needed some attention from the DVA (Department of Veterans Affairs) and we thought it might be time for us to return to Canada.

We had been up to Victoria a few times, and we said that if we went back to Canada, we were not going back to Ontario. We would move to Victoria. So we did, and Bert started working at the shipyards. Until five years ago, I was an apartment manager. Then we bought this condominium, and it was the right time to do so, before the prices went sky-high. Our daughter married an American, and lives in Florida. Our son lives in Ontario, and our granddaughter and grandson both live here in Victoria. We are both retired now and in June this year, we will celebrate our fiftieth wedding anniversary.

Hilda Ross

"I'VE NEVER GOTTEN OVER THE WOODEN SIDEWALKS"

*Hilda Ross was born in London
and grew up in a little village twenty miles from
Manchester. At school she trained in
dressmaking, but her dream was to be a nurse.
Then the war intervened.*

I n England when you were going to be a nurse, you had to put in a thousand hours of voluntary service in a hospital. I was working at a place called McCorkadale's, and they made beautiful books, bound books and printed books. On a Friday night, I used to go to Warrington, which was the closest town that had a big infirmary, and I did nursing Saturday and Sunday. We did all the dirty jobs in the hospital.

Then the war came along. I was coming up eighteen by this time, and they conscripted girls at eighteen. The only place that you could go when they conscripted you was either in the Land Army, which was working the farms, or down on the ground making the gunpowder for the arms and guns and things. I didn't want to do either one of those things. So I went and joined the Air Force much to my father's dismay. He asked me why I didn't join the navy like my two brothers. I explained that I had tried to join but couldn't get in.

So three months later, I was called up to go into the military. By this time, the war was well on its way. The only place that could be found for me was on the balloon barrages. Women were now being trained to replace the men in this work. They doubled the number of women for the number of men they were replacing. For instance, sixteen women would take the place of eight men. We would be stationed in a field or on the docks.

There would be ten of these balloon barrages in a particular area. When the siren went, it would mean that aircraft were coming in over the low clouds, so we were given a signal to put the balloons up so many feet. Sometimes it was higher or lower. You never knew what height they would have to go up. And there was a bomb on the cable. You used to have to take the pin out of the bomb, so that once the enemy aircraft flew into that maze of balloons, it would never get out. It would hit the cable underneath the balloon and be blown up. That was the point of having a balloon barrage. And they were huge.

There were girls on duty around the clock. Teams of two girls would do duty for two hours at a time, just walking around, and this would go on all through the night. We were mostly on the docks or in the middle of the city. It was very dangerous actually. You had to learn how to patch the balloon, because a quarter of a mile down the road from each balloon site, there was an anti-aircraft gun site. They would, of course, shoot at the aircraft, and the shrapnel would hit our balloons. And there were girls in the Army on the anti-aircraft guns too.

We had a meter on the cable that would tell if the balloon had been hit and gas was coming out. I don't know what kind of gas it was, but we had to pump it into the balloons. If we saw this gauge going down, we knew that there was a hole in our balloon. Then, it didn't matter what time of day or night, we'd have to bring this balloon down, and we'd have to roll it over. We had what were like geiger counters, and we'd have to go all over the balloon to find the hole. And then we had huge tall ladders. We had to climb up these ladders to patch the balloons. If you tell anybody about what you did with these balloons, they look at you and say, "What were you doing that for?" But it was very important work.

After a year and a half, they decided that it was far too much work for girls, so we had to re-muster to another trade. We were being paid the same wages as the men—six pence a day (that's twelve cents by the way), plus room and board and our uniform. I re-mustered to the trade of radio operator transmitting by Morse code. I was sent to Blackpool, which is a holiday place now, but of course at this time they had barbed wire all along the shorelines. I did a year's course there for radio operating, and I was quite close to home so it was very nice. It felt like a bit of a holiday.

Then I was sent down, and we worked underground all the time. I didn't like that. I stayed with it for seven or eight months, and then I went to London to train as a telephone operator. I was still in the Air Force, and I was working in a tower when all these aircraft passed over on D-Day. We knew what was happening but we couldn't say anything.

You see I was on the station that had Spitfires, and they used to accompany the bombers out on every bombing raid. So it was a very busy place. At first I used to be frightened but eventually I just took it in my stride. I worked in a big old farmhouse with a square tower on the top which was camouflaged.

We rode bicycles, and I was very scared when they started the buzz bombs because they'd shoot them out from Germany, and you never knew where they'd land. I remember one night we were riding home from a dance, and this buzz bomb, we saw it coming, and then the lights went out. You didn't know where it was going to explode. So we all lay down in the ditch nearby. Unfortunately, the poor cows were hit. There were bits and pieces of cow everywhere.

They were very frightening, those buzz bombs, because you never knew where they were going to explode. They'd come in very low, and you could see the light above and hear the buzz. And then there was silence, and then there was an explosion. You got used to a lot, but it was very frightening when you saw that.

One of the good things about the times was that there were a lot of men. It seemed as if all the men from Canada and everywhere else were in England. I used to dance a lot. I loved dancing, so any time I could go, I danced. It was great. I had a lot of fun. And at eighteen-years-old, what else? I suppose my parents worried but I didn't think about it then.

I met my husband-to-be, Steve, at a dance in Manchester, at a tea dance actually. He was a good dancer. This was 1940, and we were married in 1942. We saw each other on and off for two years when we were able to. Leave to go home was restricted but we could always pop into London for half a day or something. So that's how we used to see one another. When we were apart, Steve and I used to send telegrams because that was the only communication. There were no phones so it was a telegram. Now there's no telegrams, I think. Faxes now.

I didn't fall in love right away. I thought I was in love with an Air Force fellow from New Zealand, actually. But that didn't work out and gradually, yes, I fell in love with Steve. I remember him proposing to me while we were dancing. We got married six months afterwards, and of course I couldn't get any clothes for the wedding. You see I was in the Air Force, and we had no coupons. Only civilians had coupons for clothing. So there was no wedding dress. I was married in my uniform, and no gold rings. The ones they had were called utility rings, and they turned your finger green. I got a new set when I came to Canada but utility rings were all you could obtain in 1942.

When my husband requested permission to marry me, we had to wait for six months while they looked into our backgrounds. Before they put in this permission requirement, there were a lot of men getting married that already had wives back in Canada. Not only Canadians, but Poles and Frenchmen too. Because you see, Poland fell and France fell so we had all these men in England. Men were a dime a dozen! You could have your choice.

My brother managed to get home for our wedding, and he was the best man. Steve brought a young pal of his to the wedding, and then my friends that I grew up with were all there. It was a church wedding. We had a very short honeymoon in a place called Southport, which is just a little holiday place, but very nice. It was only for a weekend though, because we both had to get back to our jobs.

In October, I'd applied for my discharge from the Air Force but they refused me because I didn't have any children. They said, "No, you just have to wait until the war is over." At that time, the Canadians opened up a women's division in England. Any married woman who was in the forces could transfer into this women's division but they only took forty at a time. If I could have transferred into that division, I would have received all my Department of Veteran's Affairs benefits like the men did when they came back. But I couldn't get into it because of the limited numbers that they let in.

Then I put in again for my discharge. I didn't have much hope, but all of a sudden one morning in October, the telephone rang, and I was told I had my discharge. I was so surprised. That was on a Monday, and I sailed for Canada the following Friday. I didn't have very much time with my family before I left. I had to send back every stitch of my uniform, right down to my underwear. So I had no clothes, and I had no coupons for clothes. But my father gave me his books of coupons, and between my sisters and his coupons, I got underwear, stockings, blouses and sweaters.

I had to be in Glasgow by eight o'clock on a Saturday morning so I got on a midnight train on Friday night going up to Glasgow from my town. My father took me down to the station. We said our goodbyes, cries and tears. Everything was blackout so you couldn't see. I got into this train and sat in a corner. All of a sudden, somebody struck a match, and here was a sailor sitting in the corner having a cigarette. He saw that I was crying and asked me what was the matter. I told him I was not allowed to say anything. But on the way up, we became talkative, and he asked, "Are you going to Canada?" And I said, "I can't tell you." Finally he got it out of me that I was going to Canada, and he told me that he was on a minesweeper that was going to escort us because of the mines in the waters.

So that was fine. The sailor helped me quite a bit when we got to Glasgow because it was all new country to me. I got on a bus with other war brides, and we went out to a school auditorium just north of Glasgow. All these women were there with their babies, and we had straw mattresses to lie on. We spent the night there. We weren't allowed out, and all of a sudden my name came over the microphone. So I went to the door and I said, "I'm Hilda Ross." Then I was told, "Oh, well your brother's here." And here was my brother, George. He had found out that I was there, and he was up in Glasgow too. His ship had just come in, you see. We went out on the town together.

We were put on the ship the next day, and we sailed that day. The ship was the *Ile de France*, and it was a beautiful ship that was also being used to bring home the wounded soldiers to Canada. There were two hundred war brides on this ship with me, and only twenty of us had no children. We were in a storm for three weeks. Oh, it was horrible. They couldn't go fast, knowing that there were mines in these waters. Of course the mine sweepers were sweeping for them. It was blackout, and you weren't allowed out on the decks, and every mother who had children was seasick.

So guess who had to do all the work? People that weren't sick, and it was all us girls that didn't have children. We used to have to go and feed the children, wash their diapers, and oh, it was horrible. It was horrible, horrible.

The best thing about it was that they fed the mothers and children first in the dining room. Then came the wounded soldiers who were able to walk. They were all on crutches or in wheelchairs. And the few of us that didn't have children, we were allowed to have the third sitting with the officers. We were treated like queens and saw food that we had not seen for a long time.

When we finally reached Halifax, we stayed on the ship a full day. I don't know why, but we did. Then we were hauled on to the trains. They came right into the ship. We were all put on one train, and then we started our journey. We had one Army officer in charge of us. He'd have the names of people and where they were going to get off at different stops. I was supposed to go to Winnipeg, and through telegrams going back and forth to my husband, I was sure he was going to be there to meet me.

Before we got to Winnipeg, we came to this place called Long Lac. It's where all the trains stop to take on water and goods. I thought, "Oh my goodness," because the land was so barren. All of a sudden, this Army officer came running through the train calling my name. I said, "I'm here." I had no shoes on, and was lying back, no makeup on, no nothing. The officer told me, "You're getting out here." I said, "Oh no, I'm not."

I explained that my husband was meeting me in Winnipeg, but the officer insisted that I had to get out here. I was absolutely petrified. The officer introduced me to a lady who must have been a member of the Women's Voluntary Service because she had a band on her arm. She took me to the waiting room where my mother-in-law was waiting with her husband and we were introduced.

Then it was a three-hour drive from Long Lac to Geraldton. And we went through the worst country. I have never seen such land. It was rocks and little stubs of trees. There were no roads. I thought, "Where am I going?" Anyway, we finally reached

Geraldton. Here it was wooden sidewalks and gravel streets. And I have never gotten over this yet—wooden sidewalks.

Now my mother-in-law was a lovely person, and so was her husband but I had thought I was going to meet my husband. The reason I ended up with my mother-in-law was because when my husband joined up, he left his mother's name and address as next-of-kin in case anything happened to him. So that was the reason I had to get off and go with her.

My mother-in-law's home was in a mining town with people of all nationalities. There were Swedes, Norwegians, Ukrainians, Poles, the French, all kinds of nationalities, and they were there to work in the mines. My mother-in-law had a lovely home but they used outside toilets. It wasn't my first experience with them because when we were in the balloon barrage, we just dug little holes for ourselves.

My mother-in-law made this beautiful meal and when we'd finished, all the neighbours wanted to come and see the war bride. And they all brought these great jugs of wine. I'd never seen them before. They had great jugs of wine just like you saw in the movies. And you didn't get a wine glass, you got a water glass. Chug-a-lug, chug-a-lug. They all came, and they all brought me wedding presents which was very very kind. I was more interested in seeing my husband but he wasn't arriving until three o'clock in the morning because that was when his train arrived.

I got a little inebriated because everybody was drinking to my health, and I was drinking to theirs. That's the way it was. So I was a little drunk when I went to bed. And I went to bed early. It must have been nine or ten o'clock when I decided that it was time for me to go to bed. When I woke up the next day, there was my husband waiting for me. That was wonderful. But I've never gotten over the wooden sidewalks, never. When he told me we were going to Fort Frances, that was the first thing I asked him, "Oh, do they have wooden sidewalks there?"

We stayed the winter in Fort Frances, and then in the spring we came out to Port Alberni on Vancouver Island. My father-in-law wanted us to go to Port Alberni with him, and we did. That's where my first son was born, and then my second son was born soon after, the same year. We now have a third son, too. In 1951, we moved to Comox. The airport was just opening and my husband got a job there as a carpenter. I worked at the base in the telephone office, so my trade came in handy. I was there thirty-four years, and I just retired seven years ago.

I'm really enjoying my retirement. I've seen a lot of change in Comox, much to my regret, because it was once a lovely, sleepy little town. In 1983, I went across Canada with a friend of mine. We drove across Canada, and on the way home we stopped in Fort Frances, and I would never have known the place. It's grown tremendously because it was once just a little sleepy town too.

The last time I visited England, I told my family and friends, "This is it. I'm not coming over here anymore. If you want to see me again, you'll have to come to Canada." But I've decided to go back to England with the war brides in May. We're all going to be in London for four days. And then a friend and I are going to take a side trip to Ireland because neither of us has ever been there. This trip commemorates the fiftieth anniversary of the end of World War II. I think I have to go.

*Lord and Lady Mayor of York visiting the war brides at the
White Rose Club for Canadian wives, 1945.*

Motor Transport Section, RAF, Colerne, 1944.

Sylvia Wilkes

"WE CAN'T WAIT UNTIL YOU FINISH MILKING THE COWS"

Sylvia Wilkes was born in Brighton, Sussex. She was an only child and she always wanted an older brother.

I was thirteen when war was declared, and to somebody of thirteen it was excitement, something different from the regular routine. I was at my Gran's and everybody was glued to the radio, wanting to know what the next step was going to be.

Because of the war I left school to go to work when I was fourteen. I went into service looking after a little boy and did other small jobs, and when I was seventeen I went into the Land Army. I was fortunate I could take my bike to work as the farm was only five to ten minutes away, and I could live at home. It was the kind of farm that had an overseer, a manager, and I was under him. We had cattle and pigs, and we grew grain and hay.

We were on the coast so we more or less got the brunt. We were right in line with London, and the German planes used to come over to bomb London. I remember one day there were nine or more bombs that dropped, because they tried to get the main road where the troops passed and the railroad was there. I think there were nine craters that we went to look at; they missed the road and they missed the railroad. There was a lot of troop action going on because they used to do manoeuvres and training in our area before they went over to the continent. Mother used to get cross with me, because the sirens would go and we had to get under the stairs. I would say, "I have to get up for work and if 'He' is going to get me 'He' will get me in bed! I don't want to be buried under the stairs."

We used to watch a lot of fights in the sky. The Spitfires would go after the German planes and we would watch them. One time we heard this "plane" go over; it was one of the first doodlebugs. The Spitfires used to try and get under their wings and tip them so they would go off course, because they were so mechanized. They would be aimed for London, so if our planes could tip them, it would upset the mechanism, and they would come down in the country area, before they reached London and did so much damage. It was one of those doodlebugs that hit my Gran's house, at five o'clock just before all the boarders were coming in for supper. Something gave her the sense to get under the table, so she got under this heavy oak table and it was the only thing that saved her because her house was demolished. I was coming home from the farm so I went to see if she was all right. If they had been all sitting around the table they probably wouldn't have heard anything. Gran found an empty building to live in for a time, then they found her a house trailer and she lived there for the rest of her life.

Living in the country as we did, it was three miles to the train station and we would ride our bikes or walk. I would go with my aunt Vi, who was only one year older than I was. Of course we had to ride in the dark because of the blackouts. I met my future husband, Jack, at a train station. My aunt and I had gone into town to a show and were waiting at the station to go home. You can imagine—there were troops everywhere, especially at the train station. We were standing there and my aunt said, "Lets go into the cafe for tea." I said, "I'm not going in because of all the troops in there." Jack—I didn't know him at the time—came out, and said, "If you don't want to go in there you don't have to." So my aunt and the Sergeant went in, and Jack and I stood outside. It was only for a few minutes, and I don't know how we got so attached in a few minutes. Our train came first and as we got on, he said, "Come back tomorrow night and come to the show with us." My mother was pretty strict and I didn't know if I could come back, but we said, "Yes, of course." Then he called out, wanting to know my name and I gave him my name. We went back the next night, and we thought we had been stood up because they weren't there. So we started to go to the show ourselves and as we went across the bridge, I said to Vi, "Oh, I like the tall one," and she said, "Oh, I like the little one." As we went over the bridge, Jack called my name, "Sylvia." Vi's wasn't the same one. The Sergeant was already engaged so he didn't come, and Jack had brought a blind date for Vi.

Jack was in the Army, in the Regina Rifles. I was sixteen when I met Jack and nineteen when we married in Arlington on September 15, 1945. Our reception was in the village hall. Mother knew people who, under the counter, were able to get the ingredients for the cake, and she borrowed a beautiful silver stand for it. I had my dress made, and different family members gave me coupons for the material. It was white, and I always wanted to design my own so I was able to do that. Jack wanted to stay in England after we were married. But I said, "We might as well go to Canada and let the government pay one way. We can always come back." But we never did.

I came to Canada in December 1946. They wouldn't arrange it so the husbands and wives could come together, but it just happened Jack was on the same ship as my aunt Vi. Even though they were on the same ship, they weren't allowed to talk to each other. In the First World War they arranged it so that husbands and wives could travel together, which was most helpful. My mother-in-law, a World War I war bride, and my father-in-law came back together with Jack.

We all collected together in London and it was an awful hostel. It was the last ship until spring, so it was come then or wait until spring. From London we went to Liverpool on the train. Then we boarded the ship. About an hour out, we hit a cattle ship. It was about five in the morning and I was up feeding my baby Keith when we felt this jolt. I went up on deck and saw all the cattle in the water. It was pathetic. The ship was damaged too much to go on so we had to go back to port again. Then we had to go home again for a week. So mother and I got busy, and we made up diapers with cotton wool and gauze. For me that was the beginning of disposables. We made up as many as we could put in a bulky case.

The name of the ship was the *Empire Brent*. Its name had just been changed for the voyage, as it was going back into civilian service. It had been the *Letitia*. Oh was I seasick for thirteen days, it was rough! This Scottish girl used to help me up on deck to get fresh air and cloak me to shelter me from the wind as it was so cold. Then she'd take me back down at night, and that's all I can remember of the trip. The last day I started to feel better. I said I would never go back to England again. We didn't think of planes in those days. No way would I ever go back on a ship!

When we reached Halifax, I was disappointed. I had imagined

it would be white with snow, and it wasn't. It was rainy and dirty just like Liverpool. We travelled quite a bit in-land before we saw snow. I was on the train three to four days. Jack met me in Regina. We stayed overnight and I got winter boots before we went by train to his parents' farm outside Abernethy. My father-in-law met us at the train station with his Model T. The snow was so deep we just drove the seven miles to the farm straight across the fields, instead of on the roads.

A month after I arrived, my son Keith went into the sanatorium at Fort Qu'Appelle. He had TB and he was just five months old. He was there for two years. We had taken Keith to the doctor for a check-up, and she said she wanted these tests done at the sanatorium. So we took him down, and they admitted him immediately. It was awfully hard on us when he was admitted. They said, "We don't want you to come back for two weeks, to give him time to get used to it and time for you to get used to it." When we got home we had this terrific storm, and we couldn't have gone down to see Keith if we had tried, as the railway was blocked. The first thing I did when I did get down was to pick him up, and the nurse was soon there saying, "You're not allowed to touch him." I think I would be different now; I would stand up for myself!

A month after that, my husband went into Regina hospital for an operation, and I was stuck on the farm, seven miles from town. It was coming up to Easter so I got my father-in-law to drive me to the train. I went and saw my son first. They were so short of help that they asked if I would be interested in working at the sanatorium. I thought that was just the answer, so I said, "I can't stop now because I am going up to the hospital in Regina to see my husband." I went and saw him and told him what I had done and went back and got the job.

When Jack came out of the hospital we rented a little house close to the sanatorium and he convalesced there. I stayed on and worked until Keith came out of the sanatorium. I think if Keith hadn't come to Canada he might not have lived, as one of his lungs was so bad. There is such good air for TB on the prairies. I worked in the kitchen at first, and then I got a job in the diet kitchen which was better. In the diet kitchen I delivered supplies to different floors and I was able to see Keith everyday. But he did not know me as his mother, just somebody who said "Hello" to him. The children were kept in their cots; they were strictly bed patients. Keith was kept in his cot for the whole two years and he had to learn to walk when he came home.

I had a miscarriage when we lived at Fort Qu'Appelle. The nearest doctor was quite a distance, but there was an Indian hospital and a doctor in Fort Qu'Appelle. I was having terrible stomach pains, so I went to see the doctor. He said I had kidney trouble, and I went back home. I collapsed, so Jack got hold of the doctor, and he said, "Bring her down to the hospital." The only person who could take me to the hospital—as there were no ambulances—was the undertaker, and his name was Mr. Stiff. When we reached the Indian hospital there happened to be a specialist from Ottawa visiting. If he had not been there at the time I would have died, as it was a tubal pregnancy.

When Keith came out of the sanatorium we rented a farm in Lorlie, and that's when my second son Robert was born. The first year we were there we were frozen out, the second year we were hailed out, and the third year the person who owned it wanted to sell. The VLA wouldn't put up the money for it, and we didn't have the money, so we move back to Abernethy.

When my baby was about to be born, I told Jack that I thought the baby was coming, and he said, "I will milk the cows and that will be done, then we will go." He was milking and I ran out and said, "We can't wait until you finish milking the cows." All of a sudden this rooster came at me and attacked me. Jack caught the rooster and wrung his neck and said, "You aren't going to attack anyone else." Finally he left the cows and we drove the four miles to the hospital. When he was registering me, he heard a baby cry, and he asked, "Is that my baby?" and the nurse said, "Yes." He was born that quick.

Next we went to work for another farmer and his wife in the Lorlie area. They had a big house so we were able to have rooms upstairs. I was the housekeeper and Jack worked the land. But the farmer was a drunk so that didn't last long. We moved back to Abernethy; I was expecting our third child, Colin, at this time. We rented a small house opposite the school where Keith went, and early one morning the school burnt down. Right after that Jack got a job rebuilding the school. After this we managed a farm in Abernethy, and then we moved again to a farm in Neudorf where our fourth son Peter was born. Then Jack put in for an Indian Agent's job, and a house went with the job. Jack was only in the job a short while when he had a nervous breakdown, because the job was much too stressful. He had to look after two reserves, which was too difficult for him to do. Of course, we couldn't stay there as it was a government house, a beautiful house, and we thought we were in luxury. We had running water, a TV and a deep freeze, all for the first time. We had some friends that lived in a little village, so we moved there to Kellaly. We found a little house and had to go on welfare for six months until Jack got better. Then we moved to Springside, and Jack worked at a radar base. After this we moved to Saskatoon, so Jack could train and work as a meat inspector, and there our daughter Joanne was born. Four years later we were moved to Humboldt, where Jack continued in meat inspection until he had to retire early, because of poor health, which was partly due to what he went through during the war.

Jack was on early retirement when he died from an accident. All four boys were living in Victoria at the time. Of course when their dad died they came out to Saskatchewan to be with me. They said to me, "Joanne is fourteen, and she won't be home too much longer. You will be left here to shovel snow in the winter time, so it is best you sell up and move to Victoria." So my oldest son and I built a house in Victoria with an in-law suite for Joanne and me. When my son was transferred I bought my own house in 1984. My mother came from England to live with Joanne and me until she passed away in 1991. Joanne is now married and a new mother, and I still enjoy living in my own home, with no regrets about having married a Canadian.

Isabella French

"I HAVE TO GO OR I WILL
FADE AWAY TO NOTHING"

---

*Isabella French was born in Glasgow, Scotland,
the eldest of three children. As a young woman
she loved to go dancing.*

My mother and father separated when I was nine. Mother said to my father one day, "Peter, either you go or I'll go and leave you with the three kids." He then packed his bag and away he went. Mother kept working. She worked at all kinds of jobs but mainly hotel work. She kept us all together. I went out to work before I was fourteen, to help support the family. I worked in a coffee house and tea room in the heart of Glasgow before the war.

The war broke out and they put me into war work in a big steel factory. They had four big levers, and I had to pull the levers for the molten steel. The old guy who was up in a crane would tell me what lever to pull, and because half the time I couldn't see him, I would pull the wrong lever. I stuck with that job for two weeks. I walked out on the evening shift one night, got on the bus and went home. I wasn't really allowed to quit war work, so I had to go down and sit in front of this board of men. I had to go back to the factory to work but I worked in the canteen.

I worked in the canteen for three years. Then I went to work in a distillery that made Johnny Walker whisky. It too was considered war work. My job was to make sure that the machine sealed the tops of the bottles. Some of the girls would get really drunk because they would drink the whisky if the bottles tipped as they were coming down the vat (the line). If anyone was caught drinking, they would be fired right away. On Christmas Eve we all received a bottle of whisky. After work some of the men would be waiting to buy our whisky. They gave us ten shillings for a bottle.

Sometimes I had to work in the empties room where all the empty bottles came in. We were supposed to be stacking all the empties up, but we used to drain them when the boss wasn't looking. We would have a lookout at the door for the hard hats (the bosses). We would pour all the drains into one bottle until we had enough for a full bottle of whisky. Then we would sell them to the men who worked in the factory. I have seen us getting a bottle a day. The men used to come in once a week and ask if we had any full bottles. We would get five pounds between us, which was a lot of money back then.

We got good money. We were paid weekly, something like five

pounds a week. It was cash in a sealed envelope, and when I was older I would sometimes open my pay pack and take a couple of pounds out of it. Mother never said anything, because as we got older we needed a bit of style. We would buy makeup and things. We always bought on the lay-away plan, so we could pay gradually for something we really wanted.

I have stood in a queue for two hours after work for five cigarettes. The cigarettes were small and thin. My sister smoked, too, and she would say to me when I got home, "Give me a cigarette." I would say, "No! You aren't getting one, you stand in the queue like I did." She didn't believe in queuing up, so I wouldn't give them to her.

If the air-raid siren went when I was in the middle of Glasgow, I always returned home. Being the oldest, I used to feel very responsible for the family, and mother would get really upset if I wasn't home. Whenever there was an air raid, she would run around trying to find her large woolen knickers. As the years went by, I would put her big knickers at the bottom of the bed, and as soon as the air raid sounded I would say, "Mother there are your knickers."

One night we all had to evacuate down to the air-raid shelter at the school. Once we were at the school they told us a land mine had dropped and we had to stay in the school. After freezing for four hours, the warden came and said, "It's okay ladies, it's only an old pram that had been dumped." My mother went up to him and said, "You stupid old fool, you have four blocks of people all in this school, for an old pram!" All the women in the shelter said, "Good for you, Maggie," and clapped.

I met my future husband, Gordon, when two girlfriends and I were going to catch the bus one night, and we were having a good time, joking and laughing. Then I heard this voice behind us: "See that tall one in the middle? I'm going to marry her." I said to my girlfriends, "They're drunk, don't bother with them." When we got to the bus stop, the soldiers stopped behind us. I noticed they were Canadian. We jumped on the bus, and I turned to wave good-bye to them. The next day I had to go to work, and I was running because I was late. I saw the two Canadians from the night before, Gordon and his friend, but I couldn't stop because I had to get to work. That night when I came out from work, Gordon was there, and who was there as well but the boy I was engaged to. So I said to one of my friends, "Go see the Canadian and take him around the corner for an ice cream or something, while I talk to my fiance." I knew right away I wanted to be with Gordon so I said to the Scotch boy, "The engagement is off," and gave him his ring back. I walked around the corner, and my friend and Gordon were sitting there. Gordon said, "You think you are pulling something on me—you have a boyfriend around the corner." I said, "Well I did, that was the boy I was engaged to." I went out with Gordon for three nights and then he went back overseas. He was in the Army, and he would go away and come back on leave every three months.

We knew each other six months and were engaged for three months. Gordon came back once and then the next time he came back, we were married on January 28, 1946. During my engagement I went to find my dad, because I wanted him to meet my future husband. His people had plumbing businesses in Glasgow so I found him through them, and he met my husband-to-be. For our wedding one neighbour played the accordion and another neighbour played the saxophone. We rented a little hall, and all my friends and mother's friends from the street came.

I never saved much, so I bought my wedding dress on lay-away and paid it up in three months. The neighbours all made sandwiches and the music was free. In Scotland when the bride and groom go away in the car, they throw out money. I didn't have any money on me, and I can hear my husband to this day when I asked, "Have you any change in your pockets?" He said, "What!" I told him, "You have to throw money out to the kids." He shook his head and said, "You sure have funny traditions over here." Then the taxi drew away and the kids were all running after the money we threw out.

The girl I worked with had a little place in Rothesay. It was a seaside resort that you reached by boat. She said we could use the flat for our honeymoon. It was a little hole-in-the-wall, with a small fireplace, but there was no heat, no food, no nothing. When we went to get coal, there wasn't any. We were starving, and there wasn't even a fish and chip shop open. Anyway we went to bed. We were so cold, we were freezing. When we got up the next morning, Gordon said, "We're going to fix this right now, we're going to get some food." "Well," I said, "I haven't got any stamps." By this time, he was getting kind of frustrated. I said, "Just follow me and we will go in the shops." In the shops, I said to the clerk, "We are on our honeymoon down here and we have no stamps." Luckily this guy took pity on us and gave us some tea, sugar, baked beans and a few other groceries. But we couldn't get coal. So that night we had fish and chips for supper and some baked beans. The next morning Gordon said, "To hell with this, we are going back home." So we turned up at mother's door and she said, "I thought you were on your honeymoon." Gordon said, "Honeymoon? We nearly froze to death. Anyone that goes to Rothesay in January needs their head examined!"

Gordon came back to Canada in March 1946, and I was to come in October. My mother said to me, "Isabelle, don't forget you're not going on a bus ride." I soon realized how far I was going. The trip itself was a nightmare. At the time I left the Glasgow station, there were a lot of Scotch girls changing their minds about going. So once the soldiers got us into the train they wouldn't let us out. As the train pulled away my mother collapsed, and they wouldn't let me out of the train. Through the window I saw my mother lying on the platform.

When I reached London, it was nighttime and very dark out; I couldn't tell you to this day where we were. We were taken to a hostel. They were herding us all in together, and I can remember the enormous door in this place. Two Canadian soldiers were standing at the door. I said to them, "I'm staying right here until I find out how my mother is, I'm not going anywhere. I want to talk to someone here, and you are not moving me until I talk to who-ever looks after this place." One of the Canadian soldiers told me to go and sit on the bench. He went into the next room, and then he came out and told me to go in. I heard one of the Red Cross women ask, "Is this the wild one we are taking to Canada?" I said, "I'm not going to Canada or anywhere until I find out how my mother is!" She asked who my mother was and I said, "I left her at the Glasgow station on the platform, and nobody will tell me anything." She asked if my mother had a phone nearby, and I told her to call the Springburn Police and they would go and see her. So I guess poor old mother was sitting breaking her heart when the police came. She said, "Tell her I love her, that I just fainted and I am all right now." When they told me, I said, "I will settle in now." They said I could teletype a note to mother and they would see that she got it, and I did.

I came on the *Lady Rodney*. It was just a little tub with only three hundred and fifty women on it. I was in a very small cabin with six women. I slept on the top bunk, and was very sick as it was so rough. There was a little steward that we called Samba and he was very good. By the fourth day of not eating, I was starving. I decided to go up the stairs. I guess I was weak—I could see the stewards fading away, and all of a sudden they came running down to me. They caught me as I fell back. I said, "Just take me up and I will try and have something to eat." I had a bun. Then as I was coming down, a young steward said, "Why don't you get some air?" So he called one of the Canadian Red Cross, and she strapped me onto a deck chair. She said, "There's the bucket." I nearly froze to death. Finally they came with a blanket. When I went back to the cabin, I told the girls that I felt a lot better. By the tenth day, I was just about normal again. One girl in the cabin, who became a friend, had her name called as soon as we docked, and they told her that her husband had been killed. She was crying and I asked her what she was going to do, but she didn't know.

We caught the train to Vancouver. The rules were that I had to have some place to go to. Since the in-laws had a home in North Vancouver, that was my destination. John, our steward, was getting tired of us asking him when we would get to Vancouver, so he told us to get all dressed up because the next station was Vancouver. We got all dressed up, and then he came along to tell us, "You didn't need to get dressed up as this is only Regina. You have two more days before you reach Vancouver."

I will always remember this young girl called Isabelle from the Highlands of Scotland. I smoked and she didn't so I gave her my candy rations and she gave me her cigarette rations. She asked me to see her off the train when we arrived at her station. I said to the Red Cross, "When we stop at Isabelle's station let me know, I want to say good-bye to her." When we stopped, there was one lantern and the snow was coming down in buckets. Isabelle and I got off the train with the Red Cross in the dark of the night, and we waited and waited for someone to come for her. I was getting kind of worried and so was the Red Cross. Finally a young man came out of the darkness with a torch. He was just a young boy. I asked, "Will you be okay, Isabelle?" and he said, "Oh, she will be fine." I did write to her for about four years. She was happy on the farm and had three children. She was from rural Scotland so she was used to the farm life.

The train trundled on towards Vancouver where Gordon, with his mother and father, met me. We immediately got on the ferry to North Vancouver to his folks' house, where I met his sister and brothers. Then he said that he had found a place in Vancouver by English Bay for us to live. So the next day we went down to the room he had rented. It was a tumble-down house, but it had a really gorgeous view. I walked in and said, "That's funny, the room slopes, the bed's down there and the table's up here. Is this it?" He said, "Yes, I was lucky I found a place."

The next day he said he was going out to look for work, and I said I would go with him. He told me to stay there and not to go out because I would get lost. So I remained sitting at the window until he came home. No work! The next day I was still sitting there when I saw some men go upstairs. I thought, "Gee, this is a busy place with men going upstairs." From this big bay window I saw a lady come in, and I went to speak to her. She said, "Come upstairs and have a cup of tea with me." I said, "Okay," and I locked the door and went upstairs. I thought, "Gee, it is a lovely room, but with all the pillows, it's kind of funny." When I went back downstairs, Gordon said, "Where were you?" "Oh, upstairs with that nice woman." "If I catch you up there again . . . don't you go up there again, Isabelle." I said, "There was nothing wrong with her; she was very friendly." "Don't you dare go up there again!"

After that, I thought I would get to know Vancouver, so I went out. That's when I met Margaret (my sister Nettie's friend from Scotland). I was out walking and I saw her and said, "Margaret Bell" and she said, " Isabelle Neilson" and neither one of us knew we had married Canadians. She was living in the old Vancouver Hotel.

One evening I was reading the *Sun* paper, and found an ad which said, "Caretakers wanted, wife to look after the house and man to do outside chores." So I said, "Let's go after that." It was away up in the Capilano Highlands, so we went on the streetcar until the end of the line and then we walked up. It was a beautiful big home with a little doll's house a short walk from the home. I really loved it there. I had to work from eight in the morning until twelve noon and babysit two nights a week.

Gordon found a job in a creosote plant in North Vancouver. It was where they made the telephone poles and dipped them in creosote. We lived on the estate for a year—we lived in the little house and every morning I would help the owner with the cleaning of her big home. Sometimes I would have to serve when they had a dinner party. I had a little white cap and a black dress to wear. Through the day I was the charwoman and at night I was the maid. The lady of the house was really good to me. I had a lot of episodes up there; it was a panic. Because we didn't have any rent to pay, we were able to buy our first car—a Model T. It was a whole one hundred and fifty dollars.

One time when the family was away in England, we were lying in bed on a Sunday morning. When I got up and looked out, I saw an enormous bear right outside the window. I jumped into bed and Gordon asked, "What's the matter?" I replied, "I told you the dogs were not barking for nothing." But when I jumped into bed, it tilted up and imprisoned us against the wall. "What in the dickens is the matter with you?" yelled Gordon. "Believe it or not, Gordon, there's a bear outside." "That's why you jumped in bed; you have been dreaming," "No," I replied, "I haven't been dreaming, you go out and look." Finally after pushing the bed out from the wall, he looked out and said, "Oh, my God, you run out and get the game warden." I said, "You run out yourself and get the game warden."

Gordon finally found the game warden and came back with him. We went and looked at the chickens, and the bear had killed them all. We then went to look for the pony. We didn't know where the pony was; it had run off. We finally found the pony in the bush. Gordon gave me a rope and told me to hold it across the path, and he would get the pony to come in my way. When the pony came in my direction, I let the rope go and away the pony went again. It took us two or three days to clean up the chicken coop and to find the pony again.

I was five months pregnant when we left there. I didn't tell my employer I was pregnant because I wanted to keep my job, and I knew I couldn't work there if I was pregnant. I was scrubbing the floor one day and I was really sick. She asked if I was pregnant, and I said, "Yes." She said there was no rush to leave but she could not keep me on as they didn't want a couple with a child.

We moved down to Lynn Valley to a little place. It had no running water. She was a terrible woman who rented the little shack to us. We had to go and get water from this woman who lived in the main house on the same property. After I gave birth to my son, the VON nurse came and said, "This house is condemned, you have no running water in it." She went next door and told them that the house could never be rented again. I kept it clean enough, with little curtains at the windows, and the floors didn't slope like the first place. But we had to get out of that place, so we went and stayed with Gordon's parents. Gordon and I and baby Bruce had a room upstairs. But I wasn't very happy there at all. The wartime houses were in North Vancouver so I went down and put our name in. Frequently I would go back to see where we were on the list. One time I went and a young boy behind the counter said, "You have to have two children, you know, before you can get in." "Well," I said, "I have that one and this one in the oven. How will that do, son?" He said, "You're still on the list." The next day they phoned me; that young boy was really a darling. We got a little wartime house and our baby daughter Doreen was born soon after we moved there.

Just before Christmas, and after Doreen was born, Gordon was laid off from the creosote plant. I said to Gordon one day, "We need milk for the kids but we have no money." So I got on the phone to my friend and told her that I had no money for milk. She told me to go to the Salvation Army for a food voucher. I had to go from North Vancouver to Vancouver on the street car, but I had no money. The conductor told me to go and sit down anyway. I was standing in the line at the Sally Ann in my muskrat coat, with all the down-and-out men, when the Salvation Army lady came and asked me what I needed. I told her I needed a food voucher, for food for my children, so she took me to the Captain. He gave me a twenty-five dollar voucher for groceries. I got some groceries, milk and Christmas pudding from Woodwards, and I had enough left to pay my streetcar fare home.

Gordon found a job in West Vancouver with the city, and he finally got on steady there. When Bruce my son started school, I got a part-time job at Woodwards working Friday night and all-day Saturday. I would give the next door neighbour a dollar for minding the children after school on Fridays and my husband looked after them on Saturdays. When both children were in school, I went to work full time at Woodwards.

The first time I went back to Scotland I took Doreen, who was five at the time. I didn't take my son Bruce because I think my husband thought I wouldn't come back if I took both children. I had only a one-way fare going over, that's all the money I had. But I was so homesick, I had to see my mother. My husband said, "Wait until you save enough to come back." But I said, "I'm going now, Gordon. I have to go or I will fade away to nothing." I was there two months and he sent some money. Then he borrowed the money for me to come back. In Halifax on my way back with my daughter, I was sitting on my suitcase in the train station. I had only a coach fare to Vancouver and no extra money for a sleeper on the train. I didn't look forward to sitting up on a coach seat, for six nights with a five-year-old. Then a lady from the Salvation Army approached me; she must have thought I was a sorry looking soul. She asked me if I was alright, and I told her I wasn't looking forward to the train trip, sitting up all the way. She told me to sit there and she would be right back. She returned with a ticket for one sleeper. I felt that she had saved my life. When I got off the train in Vancouver and saw Gordon and my son standing there, I thought, "If only I had been able to take Bruce to Scotland with me!"

It was always on my mind how good the Salvation Army was to us. So four years later when I was able to, I went right down to the Sun Building in Vancouver, and stood in line again with the down-and-outers. When the Salvation Army lady came along again, I asked for the Captain and she took me to him. I thanked him very much for the help the Salvation Army had given my family, and I paid him back the money that the Salvation Army had given me.

I have been very fortunate. When I was working at Woodwards, I would get three week's holiday a year. So I would fly over to see my mother, and I was able to bring my mother out four times to Canada from Scotland. The last time she came out, I thought she would stay, but she was homesick and wanted to go back to Scotland.

We were married thirty-two years when Gordon passed away. All my life, half my heart has been there in Scotland, and half of it here in Canada. All my life it has been like that. But now that the years have passed and my family has grown up, I look at my children and my three grandchildren and I know that Canada is my home.

Audrey Anderson

"TAKE COVER—THAT'S A CLOSE ONE!"

Audrey Anderson was born in Hurstpierpoint, Sussex, into a close happy family. When war broke out she was working as a Health Visitor for an Assurance Company.

I was living at Woking, Surrey, when I first met my husband Ralph. I didn't see much of him until six months later when, on a blind date, he turned up. From then on we were a couple. He had come to England in December of 1939, as a member of the 49th Edmonton Regiment, the First Division. He later transferred to the 4th Princess Louise Dragon Guards, Reconnaissance Regiment.

We were married in 1941, on the 6th of December, in a beautiful church in Bearsted, Kent. Our wedding was small as most of my family were away fighting in the war in various parts of the world. I didn't have enough ration coupons for a wedding dress and I didn't want to wear my sister's, so I wore a suit instead of a white gown.

The first time I went into a shelter was in London, and I said I would never go in one again. Children were crying, and it was stuffy and smelly. However, after I married and had a baby, I had what they called a Morrison table shelter, which looked like a big steel table with wire meshing on the sides.

When I lived in Woking, the planes would come in over us to drop their load on London, and if they were turned back before they reached their target, they would drop it on us on the way back. After my husband went overseas for the Sicilian Invasion, I moved to Fareham near my family (close to Portsmouth which was under constant attack). We had a close escape one morning walking over to see my parents. I had to cross a bridge over a railway line. The Germans started to drop a stick of bombs trying to hit the line. A bomb dropped in front of us, another behind us. Rather scary! I think I set a running record. The baby loved it, bouncing up and down in her pram.

The raids were continual, and to add to the discomfort there was an ack-ack battery at the end of my road. When the raids became really bad, my parents would come over and pick up my baby Gale and me, and we would go to a summer home we had in Wales to have a bit of a rest from the air raids.

We got used to the raids, but those awful little buzz bombs were rotten. We would hear the tick, tick, tick, just like a motor bike engine. Then when the engine stopped, and we couldn't hear anything, we'd count to thirty and it was either coming towards us or going away from us. The other big bombs were the V-2s. They of course were dreadful: because we couldn't hear anything, and they would just bang down and that was that.

There was a wonderful feeling of camaraderie in England at that time. It was no use complaining, as there was always someone worse off than you. I lost my windows but someone else was bombed out. A window was nothing—that was the way we looked at it.

Rationing was very tight: we had two ounces of corned beef and maybe one egg a week but mothers and babies received extra. Babies and children were a priority during the war, and everything that could be done to keep our children healthy was done. Every time we went to town we joined a queue to see what was selling; it might be bread, it might be bacon, or apples, oranges or anything. If we saw a queue, we would more likely join it than ask what it was for. The government registered everybody for rationing coupons for food and clothing. My number was DMW 124-6; I still remember it. We could also buy from the black market, but I didn't see too much of that.

My daughter was born in 1942, with collapsed lungs, and after several worrying weeks I had to take her up to Great Ormond Street Children's Hospital in London. They put her on special food that had been made for babies during the war. Ten weeks later, she was on a placard as one of "Britain's Bonniest Babies."

When I applied to come to Canada, my husband had been wounded a second time in North Africa and was due to be sent home. Britain was blockaded for six months due to the invasion of Europe, so I had to wait. When I finally sailed, my husband was sent to England for six months!

On October 13th, 1944, I caught the train from Fareham, Hampshire, to London, on the first leg of my journey to Canada. Unfortunately, the train was bombed on the way up to London and we had to finish the journey by bus. Consequently, I missed all of the war brides that were meeting in London. However, the

RTO soon sent Gale and me after them. After a short rest, we were all sent by train to Greenock, Scotland, to join our ship, the *Isle de France*. Since in peacetime it had won a blue ribbon for speed, we did not have to go in a convoy. We sailed on Friday the 13th, which turned out to be a bad omen.

Off the coast of Ireland, we had to dodge a U-boat, and when we were two days out of Halifax, we had a fire on board that further delayed our crossing. The crowning story was that—being the first boatload of war brides, returning soldiers and prisoners of war—we were met by a Royal Canadian Air Force plane that came out to welcome us and buzz the ship. We had not been warned and, thinking we were being attacked, we all took cover.

My luggage had been left behind in London, because of my delay in arriving to board the ship, so Gale and I were taken off the ship early to buy suitable clothes for travelling to northern Alberta. I eventually received my luggage some three months later.

It was a rather nice trip across Canada on the train, watching the girls get off to be met by their new relatives. One of the things that amused us most was all the different things to eat. We had been living on soya flour bread for such a long time that when we saw the white bread it looked lovely. However, it didn't taste as good as it looked and didn't have the same body to it as our wartime soya flour bread.

Gale unfortunately got enteritis so when we reached Edmonton she had to go straight into the Royal Alexandra Hospital. She was there for ten days. This was very upsetting for both Gale and me as we had never been parted and she was only twenty-three months old.

I finally left Edmonton for Beaverlodge, Alberta, in November 1944. I was lucky I came ahead of my husband; it gave me a chance to settle down. My father didn't want me to come before Ralph and said I wouldn't like it. So I was determined to enjoy it, and I think that's what saved me from being homesick.

We travelled in the winter on a snow road. Then, as spring came on, the snow went and the mud came. I said to my mother-in-law, "I shall be glad when the weather improves and we get down to the real road." She replied, "My dear, that is the real road." It was a gravel road and I had been waiting for the pavement to come through.

At first I didn't think the war had affected me, but during a terrible storm while I was in Edmonton, my host and hostess found me crouching under the bed with my daughter, taking cover. Later, when I got to Beaverlodge, they were shifting snow off the kitchen roof and it came down with a bang. I instinctively shot under the table with Gale, and called to my mother-in-law, "Take cover—that's a close one!"

When I first arrived at my relatives' home and they showed me the bedroom downstairs, I looked all around to see which was the safest place to put the crib. My mother-in-law couldn't understand why I wanted the crib pushed under the stairs. I said I thought it was the safest place if the roof went. Those were the only times when I realized that five years of war had had an effect on me.

My husband had been in college when he joined up, and when he returned to Canada he didn't want to go back to school, as he had been overseas for five years. So we bought a farm. My knowledge of farm life was zero, but I'll always try anything once. After we bought the farm, Ralph built us a house, and we had the first wind charger in the district, so I had electricity long before others.

When we were on the farm we got together with other war brides and their families. There were a lot of returned men in the district, so the wives and families would get together in the spring and summer, when we could. We didn't organize officially, but we called ourselves "The War Brides."

I was one of the first war brides to go to the Peace River District. As a result, I was often asked to represent the others. Through representing the war brides, I took part in many special events. I had a meal with the Governor General and breakfast with the Prime Minister. I have been lucky. After fifty-three years of marriage, four children, eight grandchildren and three great grandchildren, I am glad I came to Canada.

Joan Corney

"WE HAD TO PITCH IN JUST LIKE THE MEN DID"

---

*Joan Corney was born in
London and grew up in Wimbledon.
She was fifteen years old and just out of school
when World War II began.*

At the beginning of the war, I worked at an education office—what would be called a school board office in Canada. Actually this office was in the process of evacuating all the younger kids from London. I was just a junior right out of school myself, and I was running around from school to school with messages and instructions as to where the children were to go.

Then I quit and got a job at a place that had been an engineering firm in peacetime, but during the war was doing aircraft work. I started there as a junior, the second female employee in the office. The factory originally employed all men, but as they were called up, they were replaced with females.

This firm was a good place to work. Everybody pitched in during those days. More and more women were called in to replace the men that went to war. Only the older men who were too old to be called up were left there in the factory. I began working there in late 1940, and I was there until late 1945, I guess. During this time I remained at home with my parents.

I started out packing parcels and answering the phone. I was still young but one day I was called up to the boss's office, and when I came down I was the buyer for the firm. I had to do all the ordering of materials and tools. I nearly had a fit because I'd never had a good head for figures, and I had to cost all the jobs. I also had to phone around London to buy the tools and materials.

There were two brothers, with the older brother running the place, and the younger brother in charge of all kinds of things. I was called up a second time to the boss's office—when I came down, the younger brother and I were the "aircraft inspection department." I always say I don't know how we won the war! So I was given my own office, and we had to inspect every piece that was made in the factory. We stamped our approval. I was about seventeen at the time.

The factory had an all-glass roof that had been painted black for the blackout. The sirens were going constantly during the blitz. We had heavy old typewriters and many ledgers, especially at the time I was doing the buying, and every time the siren went, we were told we had to put everything under our desks. We were constantly lifting these heavy typewriters and all these books. Then one day, I had just got into the shelter, and there was a terrific crash. The whole glass roof of the factory crashed in but luckily everyone had got out in time.

It took quite awhile to clean up. It was difficult but we all pitched in. You always did what you could to help. Around this time my mum and I became auxiliary fire fighters, much to my dad's disgust. He didn't want us involved but we went and took our training. For training, they had a huge shed made of corrugated iron, and they had filled it with anything that would burn. Then they set fire to it and closed the doors until it really got going. We were trained to put it out. Auxiliary Air-raid Patrol people taught us what to do. My dad was not very happy with us doing this work.

I can remember one day at work, my mum phoned me and said, "Well, that's it. The last ceiling came down. We don't have to worry anymore." We'd moved all our furniture into the one room that still had a ceiling. Everything went. We had no roof and no windows. We couldn't get the front door open half the time because the floor had buckled up. One day we couldn't get home at all because there was an unexploded bomb in a church directly behind our house. I also remember that where we lived there was a road that circled around our houses, and often during the night, trucks with anti-aircraft guns would drive around and around on this road firing at the enemy aircraft. One night we saw a parachute coming down, and we thought there would be a pilot on it but it turned out to be a land mine. So it didn't really pay to run towards them!

I was on the bus heading to a place called Tooting Broadway when V-2 rockets started coming down. Those things landed and exploded before you heard them. Our bus had come to a stop when it suddenly went right up into the air and came down again. There was no warning. Later we heard that those V-2's had wiped out a whole row of houses. It got to the point where I was riding my bike to work because it was easier to jump off the bike and flatten yourself on the ground than to try and get off a bus quickly.

Another time, I had just got to work on my bike when a V-1 buzz bomb came over. I jumped off my bike, letting it go flying while I dived through our office into the shelter. I just made it before this buzz bomb landed. Some of these bombs, when the engine cut, would drop like a stone, while some would glide on for a block or two. You never knew just what they were going to do, so you ran for shelter as fast as you could. Once I had just freshly sharpened a pencil, and it went into me and broke off when I stumbled against the side of the door of an air-raid shelter. It's still in there. That's my war wound.

The bombing was scary but I did get used to it. I know, because I would still go to the theatre all the time. I think I never missed a week going to a theatre. And I don't mean the movies, I mean the stage shows. Once when three of us were returning home from the Balham Hippodrome, which was a stage show, a double-decker bus came along. Normally, nobody would ride on the top deck because of the shrapnel flying. But this bus was full, and the bus conductor said, "Well, if you get on this bus, you have to go upstairs." So we thought, "Well what the heck, we'll go." To take our minds off what was going on, the three of us sat up there singing all the war songs we knew.

My cousin in Wales would often write and say, "There's a big dance on Saturday night. Come on down." So I would take the train down. I went down to Wales in October of 1944. Since my family lived in Barry in Glamorgan, I would have to get a train from Barry to Cardiff, and when I returned I would take the London train from Cardiff. Usually the trains to London would start in Cardiff, but on this particular day the train started from somewhere else. I got on the platform at Cardiff station, and it was packed with troops. When the train came in, it was also packed with troops.

I was standing there surrounded by all these soldiers, and I was thinking, "Oh, I'm never going to get on this train!" Then somebody grabbed my suitcase and just shoved me through the crowd and onto the train. This helpful stranger was Bob Corney, the man I would marry three months later. We stood up in the corridor all the way to London. I found out that Bob's mother was Welsh and he'd been in Cardiff visiting his cousins.

We stood talking all the way to London, and we made a date for a few evenings later. It turned out Bob was stationed with his friend not too far from where I was living. He was able to come up to Wimbledon about once a week.

I don't remember Bob asking me to marry him, but we got married three months after we met. Bob had met my parents, and they quite liked him. His father was from Kent and his mother was from South Wales. My relatives said they weren't coming to the wedding in London with all the bombing going on. But all of Bob's relatives thought: "Oh, poor chap! All that distance away from home. We've got to go to the wedding." So the church was full of his relatives. Some of my workmates came, including a girl who was a refugee from Belgium.

Bob and I were married in Holy Trinity Church, Wimbledon. That's where I was christened. It was in January, snowing, and no heat in the church, because of the war. It was bitterly cold. My wedding dress was my eldest cousin's. You couldn't buy one at that time. All the bridesmaid dresses were borrowed, too.

When I tried to order flowers for the wedding, I went to every florist, but nobody would take an order because there weren't many flowers during the war. Finally this one florist said, "Well, I'll take your order but it'll probably have to be artificial flowers, being January." I had to go and pick them up on the morning of the wedding; they were pink carnations—real ones.

One of the local firemen was a baker, and he made the wedding cake. Of course we couldn't rent a hall for the reception, so we had it at our house, no roof, no windows! Our wedding was at two o'clock in the afternoon. Because Bob's friend couldn't make it at the last minute, a fellow I worked closely with in the office was our best man. I still keep in touch with him.

After our honeymoon, I continued to live with my parents. I was going to say that we were lucky to have a roof over our heads, but we didn't even have that. We married in 1945, and I was twenty years old. Canadian soldiers were being shipped over to the continent, and Bob was next on the list to go but then the war ended.

Bob put my name down right away to come to Canada, so I was one of the early ones to come. Once you were on the list, there was nothing to do but wait until your name came up. You had no idea how long you would wait. I came in May of 1946. My mum was very, very upset at the time. I was their only child but my parents never tried to stop me. Bob left for Canada shortly before I did.

Before leaving England, I had joined the Canadian Wives Club in London. We used to meet, and they would talk to us about Canada. But at the same time, at that age, you'd never been out of England, and you really didn't know where you were going. When I told one of my school chum's mothers that I was going to live in Canada, she asked where, and I said, "On Vancouver Island. It's on the Pacific Coast." She kind of looked at me and asked me, "Hmmmm. Well how do you get your food?" And I, being a devil, told her, "Well, I *think* they come over and drop it by parachute." I don't know whether she ever believed me or not.

When I was notified that I was going to Canada, I went to a big old house in London that had been taken over for the war brides. We stayed overnight there, and the next day we were taken by train to Southampton. My mum and dad took me to London. I didn't know until later that after we'd parted, my mum developed such a serious nose bleed that she had to be taken to the hospital. It was the stress of the situation.

When we arrived at Southampton, the *Queen Mary* was docked there, and we all thought, "Oh, we're going on the *Queen Mary!*" But there was a little inky-dinky banana boat parked behind it, the *Lady Rodney*. We were lined up alphabetically, and because my last name began with "C," I was one of the first in the line. So I was thinking, "Oh great! I'll have the pick of places." But they started loading us into the *Lady Rodney* from the hold up. They had put bunks in the hold, and that's where I slept for ten days.

It was quite an experience on that little banana boat. In the hold, they had put two- or three-tier bunks, and so I guess they squeezed in a couple of hundred of us. The food was wonderful because we hadn't seen white bread all during the war. And lemon pie, that was first time I had lemon pie. The food was great.

The trip took ten days, because apparently we had to sail south to avoid icebergs. When we reached Halifax it was nice to see land again. We docked on May 24th which was Victoria Day. Because it was a holiday, they told us we would have to stay on board until the next day. The longshoremen were on holiday.

On the boat we were all sitting around, and I was down in the hold sitting on my bunk bed talking to some of the other girls. From the hold, there were two sets of stairs, one at each end. Suddenly, we heard a movement and we looked around. There was a man standing at the top of the stairs. He came down two or three steps and stood there looking at us. Then he proceeded to expose himself. There was one long scream, and then we took off up the other stairs. Welcome to Canada! I think he was one of the dock workers who thought, "Oh, those poor girls—ten days at sea."

The Red Cross was there to help us to our train. At Montreal, they took us by bus into downtown Montreal, and we were able to go around and see the sights. In fact, I think I bought my first camera; we hadn't been able to buy cameras in England for years.

We had Red Cross nurses travelling with us across Canada. Just before we reached Saskatoon, one of the nurses came to me and said, "Pack up all your gear." I asked why and she said, "You've got to get off the train at Saskatoon." Again I asked why, because I didn't know anybody in Saskatoon. But she insisted that I had to get off because she had a telegram with those instructions. She showed it to me and it said, "Please arrange for Joan Corney to de-train at Saskatoon." It was signed "George Corney." I told the nurse I didn't know a George Corney. The only George Corney in my husband's family was dead and buried in England. She still wanted me to get off, but I was so upset and protested so much that she said, "Well, I'll tell you what. I'll get off the train with you, and we'll see what it's all about."

We didn't get into Saskatoon until eleven o'clock that night.

When we arrived, the nurse came with me. The station was totally deserted except for an older couple standing there. We walked over to them, and of course I was scared stiff. These two looked at me, and then the woman rushed over to me and threw her arms around me. I was quite frantic: "Who are you? Who are you?" I asked. Then she asked me, "Where's the baby? Where's the baby?" Finally I shouted, "I don't have a baby. I don't have any children."

Only then would they listen to me. And there *was* another Joan Corney. They'd been informed that their daughter-in-law was on the train. But the other Joan Corney wasn't on my train. We had no war brides with children. It turned out their son was in Vancouver. So all the way from Saskatoon to Vancouver, I was wondering, "Which husband is going to meet me?"

That trip across Canada was exciting in a way, but you know, six days on a train is unheard of in England. You begin to wonder where you're going. It was a long long way. It had taken me sixteen days to travel from England to Vancouver. There were a lot of people at the station when we arrived, but my husband was there on his own. It was a relief to see him and know that he was the right husband. We stayed overnight in Vancouver. I can still remember that first morning. We went to a restaurant for breakfast, and seeing what some of the people were having for breakfast—great stacks of pancakes, sausages, bacon—I couldn't believe it. I don't know what I had, I was so overwhelmed.

We caught the CPR ferry to Nanaimo and then drove to Duncan. In those days the city of Duncan was very small. Having come right from London, it was quite an adjustment. At first we lived with my husband's parents. Bob's one brother was married and living in Victoria. My husband had bought some property, and the first Sunday I was there, he said, "Come on. We'll walk down just a few blocks, and I'll show you where we're going to live." Looking back, I can say I was a pioneer in Duncan, because at this time the area was just stacks of tree stumps and bush. And I helped to clear it.

We cleared enough land that we could build a little two-room house, and then we moved in just before Thanksgiving. We bought what furniture we needed. In those days, you couldn't buy bathtubs in Duncan, and we had just built the little two-room house. One corner of the bedroom was going to be the bathroom and one corner of the living room was going to be the kitchen. The bathroom area was to include a shower, toilet and wash basin. While Bob's parents were in Vancouver for a few days, they were in the Hudson's Bay Department Store which had bathtubs for sale, so they bought one and had it shipped over. We had to take the wall out to get the bathtub in.

Bob's dad had been acting postmaster throughout the war, and Bob had worked in the post office before he was in the war. After the war, Bob's dad wanted to go back to his old job of being the senior man rather than postmaster. They had a competition for the position of postmaster, and Bob got it. This was quite soon after we were settled in Duncan.

Around this time, my husband and I were at a store shopping with my in-laws. The woman who ran the store had recently been to England to visit a sick relative. She stood there and said that she couldn't understand what everybody in England was complaining about. Everything seemed alright to her. She just couldn't understand why the English people were complaining.

I was standing there and trying to contain myself, but it just got too much, and I let her have it with both barrels. Later when we were outside, my mother-in-law said, "How could you! How could you talk to her like that?" I said, "Well, I've been all through the war. I've been bombed to bits. We've been short of food. And she stands there, and says, 'How can people complain?'" So I wasn't very popular at that time. You are in a new country with new people, and you try not to hurt them, but there comes a point when you have to say something. Still, I think most of them knew. And look at all the families that had sons and daughters over there. There wouldn't be all these war brides if the Canadians hadn't been there. So I think that most Canadians knew what it was like in England.

The people that bought the house next door were not very nice, so we decided we would look around for another place. And that's when we bought our big old house. We had quite a bit of property there. My son was born on February 13, 1950, which was also my dad's birthday. My daughter was born five years later. I had three miscarriages in between.

Our daughter was three months old when my husband had to go into the hospital. They told him, "You're in for at least a year." We were in Duncan and he was to be in Victoria. Bob was actually in the Victoria hospital for eight months. He had tuberculosis which was common in the community in those days; our doctor always said that Bob got it from working at the post office.

It was through my husband being ill that I got a job in the Health Unit in Duncan, and I worked there for fourteen years. I was in the office, and ended up in charge of all the tuberculosis work, making all the appointments. I had learned a lot about tuberculosis, having it in the family and everything. It would have been the late 50's, I guess, when I started there. I still keep in touch. Every Christmas I hear from most of the people I worked with. Those were good years in the Health Unit. It was 1975, when I left. I lived in Duncan from 1946 to 1975 when Bob and I moved to Victoria.

Bob died in 1984 so I've been on my own for ten years, but I'm over at my daughter's place nearly every day. We are close, and my son is very dear to me, too. I found out about the Vancouver Island War Brides through a friend when it first started. Their first reunion was in Parksville that year. Bob was ill, so I went with my friend and her husband. It was fantastic to be with the other war brides.

Looking back at women's experience of World War II, I'd say that we had to pitch in just like the men did. From that, I think we learned that we could cope with anything. I think women's equality is a good thing. So many women now are doing things that they could never do before.

Violet Giroux

"SHE WAS ALIVE WHEN SHE
WAS PUT INTO MY
AMBULANCE"

*Violet Giroux was born in London.
Because of a hip injury she spent most of her
childhood in hospital.*

When war was declared I was working in a London hotel in my aunt's bar. From the beginning I was in the Civil Defense part-time, and went full time in 1940 about six months after. I was an ambulance attendant, and would go out with the ambulance and bring the injured people to the hospital. We had training with the St. John Ambulance.

I was in the air raids most nights. We got it full force since we were in the East End of London. We would stay at our depot because as soon as the siren went we had to be standing by with our ambulances. I didn't mind when we had to go out. I preferred going out to staying at the depot. But the only thing was you couldn't show any light. You would hear the shrapnel from the shells coming down, going plomp, plomp, plomp on the roof of the ambulance.

The first ambulances we had weren't proper ambulances; they were big cars, made over into ambulances. We had those for two years, then we were given the proper ambulances. At the depot there were the heavy rescue squad, the light rescue squad, and then the ambulances. The heavy rescue squad went to the scene first, then the light rescue squad, and they would be followed by the ambulances. I remember once, this lady died on the way to the hospital. I didn't know because she was alive when she was put in the ambulance. They said, "You have to take her to the morgue." I said, "She was alive when she was put into my ambulance or else I wouldn't have her in there."

We used to try and cheer up the people. They would be smothered in soot and bricks, and we would try and cheer them up with the promise of a nice clean bed. There was one hospital they hated; they use to call it the butcher shop. "I'm not going there, am I?" they would ask and we would reply, "No, you're going to so and so." The hospital was situated in a nice setting though, on a common, a big open space with trees.

I got used to the bombing. When I was with a group it was not too bad, and when I was alone I would go to bed and try to sleep and I didn't care. When I heard the siren going sometimes I would get up, especially when I heard the doodlebugs, the flying bombs. I would look to see where it was going and if it was coming towards me, I would hurry up and get dressed and get out, but usually I would go back to bed. In those days you didn't get a lot of sleep because you were gadding around.

At the depot it was twenty-four hours on duty and twenty-four hours off. Afterwards I found a second job in the city at Trunks Telephone Exchange, and of course the city got merry hell from the bombs as well. We didn't receive much money in the Civil Defense. We were paid the same as the Army, three pounds a week. So I would work at the telephone exchange on my days off. I used to have to be at the telephone exchange at six at night and stay overnight. They gave us a bed and breakfast. I then had to be on duty at the depot at eight o'clock the next morning.

The city burned like mad from all the bombing. I especially remember one Christmas trying to walk across the road with all the hose pipes and flooded streets. The city was where all the businesses were so it was a target for bombing. Leytonstone where I lived was about a half hour bus ride, so I used to come up to the city on the bus. We were supposed to stop while the raids were on. We did at the beginning, but not after. They would say, "Everybody off," but we used to sit there and we wouldn't budge.

We would discuss who got it last night, at such and such road. At the depot where I was stationed, a Canadian plane was shot up and came smack down on part of the depot. Six of our personnel were killed while they were practising for a concert. All the crew of the plane were killed; it was hit by a German plane.

I was always buying clothing coupons, a half crown a coupon. It was a lot because we weren't getting much money. We never had nylon stockings, but the girls used to paint their legs with a seam up the back—usually wiggley.

I met my husband in 1941. We had had a very bad winter, raids every night and in the day. So the government gave all the London Civil Defense a free pass to get out of London and go where they wanted on a free holiday for a week. My friend and I went right up to the Highlands, Inverness, and it was on that train that I met my husband; he was going to Aberdeen. When he got to Perth, he and his friend were supposed to change for Aberdeen. But when the ticket inspector came around they pretended to be asleep so they came on to Inverness with us.

They went to the YMCA; we had booked a bed and breakfast place but it was two miles out of Inverness. There were only two buses a day, so we had to walk. When we got to the little bungalow, one clock chimed, then another chimed and another. Since it was nine o'clock in the morning you can imagine the noise that was going on. We went to meet the fellows downtown in the afternoon. My friend and the other fellow were married, so my future husband, Gerry, and I paired off. Gerry was a private in the Army and he used to waterproof the trucks that were going to the continent, for places like Dieppe.

We were supposed to get married a year later, but Gerry was sent up to Scotland. Then he had a row with the CO (Commanding Officer), so we decided to wait until the end of the war. There was a time when I didn't hear from him very often, and I thought, "Oh he is playing around." I decided to play around, too, and I met an American who wanted to get married. I said, "No, I'm already engaged." He asked, "How long have you been going with him?" and I said "Two years." "Oh, I'll write to him and if he doesn't want you, I do." I said, "No, I will tell him," so I wrote and told him.

Gerry came to the house that weekend and my friend said, "Oh, Violet has gone out." He asked, "What time will she be back?" Anyway, I got back at ten that evening, and he had just left. He said, "Tell her if she wants to see me to meet me tomorrow at ten-thirty at the underground." I thought, "Oh my gosh," so I rushed out at ten-thirty next morning and met him. In the meantime Peter the American had given me a smashing ring; Gerry had just given me one made from an old airplane part. I said, "I can only stay until eleven. I have to meet Peter." So Gerry said, "Oh alright, where are you meeting him?" I was really meeting him there actually, so I said, "Oh I am meeting him at Queen's Gate a few stations up." So he went and bought my ticket and one for himself. He saw me on the train, and he got on the next coach and followed me. When I reached Queen's Gate, I hopped out, crossed over and went back to where I had come from, and he did the same. Anyhow once I had seen Gerry, I didn't want the American. I met Peter and he knew I was miserable, so I said, "Why don't you go to the West End and have a nice time, because I'm going to be miserable all day." He said, "Oh you still love him do you?" I said, "I guess I do." I didn't see Gerry again that day so I wrote to him right away saying I was sorry, and he wrote back, and then we started seeing each other regularly again. He said, "The next time I come on leave I don't want to see your hand smothered in Gypsy rings." It was a smashing ring. Pure jealousy, I guess. Of course I gave it back to Peter.

Gerry was overseas in Holland when he received seventy-two hours leave in which to do everything to get married. I didn't even have a wedding ring. They used to say you must listen to the radio because if the men's numbers came over the air it meant that they were getting some extra leave. We were married in Lewisham, London, April 14, 1945, in the registry office for myself, and in the Catholic church for Gerry. I had bought my dress two years before. We had quite a nice wedding breakfast with our two friends at Cheesemans, a big department store. Altogether we had nearly a week together before he was sent back to Holland until July.

Then Gerry was in Aldershot until September, when he was sent home to Canada. But they wouldn't let me go because he couldn't find a house. For one year at the end of the war, while I was waiting to go to Canada, I went to work at the E.N.S.A. headquarters (Entertainment National Service Association) as a telephone operator. Finally, when I came over we had to live with his mother. They wouldn't let you go unless there was somewhere for you to go.

I went from Southampton, on the *Aquitania*. We were supposed to come in March of 1946, but the Canadians had a riot down in Aldershot; they were fed up with waiting to go home. So my trip was cancelled and they sent the troops home instead. I finally came in June and arrived in Canada on July lst. I wasn't sick until I

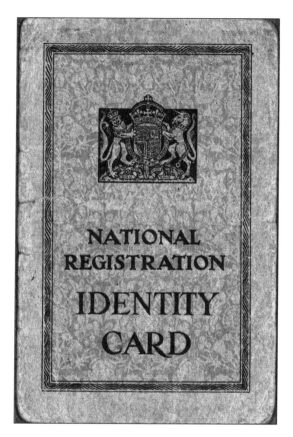

Violet Giroux's Identity Card for official entry to Canada.

got on the train in Halifax, and then I was sick as a dog. The nurse asked, "You sure you're not pregnant?" And I replied, "I'm not pregnant. I haven't seen my husband for nearly a year." The food on the ship was delicious but I think that's what made me sick on the train. I had never had baked onions and I ate some—they were sweet and they were delicious. We also had white bread, which seemed lovely after the whole wheat stuff we had eaten in England.

When Gerry met me in Canada, he was in his civvies, and I thought he looked like a bookmaker. He had a tweed check jacket on. I used to smoke in England. So he said to me, "You know it's not considered nice for girls to smoke." He had a sister who was nineteen, and when we got home, there she was smoking like a chimney. I said "What did you tell me?" I had quit smoking for him. He said, "Well she didn't smoke before I went to England." Of course she was only about fourteen when he went to war.

We finally found this house out in the country across the St. Lawrence River, for thirteen hundred and some dollars. We took my mother-in-law with us to see it. I asked, "Do you think it will be alright?" It wasn't the sort of house we were wanting. It had a pump for water. We didn't even look for water when we bought the place. After, I said to Gerry, "You didn't see how the water works, did you?" It had no inside toilet, nothing. It needed pulling down and rebuilding. But I didn't care as long as we were on our own. When we wanted to go to the toilet, which was outside, we used to have to bundle up because it was so cold. Even though it was thirty or forty below outside, it was often beautiful and sunny, so I thought to myself I'm going to clean that toilet and paint it. I got up at eight o'clock one morning and went down to the village and bought a gallon of white enamel. I worked at it all day until three-thirty, the ceiling, the seat, the walls everything, shiny white. When my husband came home I said, "Come see what I've done." "Oh, no," he said, "that's not going to dry for weeks." I was so disappointed. We had to put newspaper over everything and that spoiled it all.

We had a cat that came with the house. The first day we didn't see it. The next day I was scrubbing the kitchen floor, and when I put my hand down by the stove, I felt this fur. I let out such a yell, and out came this great big tabby cat. We called it Sour Puss. The house also had a great big Quebec heater, and it used to get so hot we had to open all the doors and windows. We lived there for two or three years.

Gerry worked at the CNR and had to go into Montreal to work every day. We were married thirty-two years before Gerry passed away in 1977. We didn't have our own children, but we were foster parents for twenty years in Quebec. For my work with the Civil Defence I received the "Defence of Britain" war medal. I came to Victoria in 1984, but I'm still sorry I left Montreal.

Margaret Mitchell

"HAVE YOU ANYTHING ELSE
TO WEAR BUT THOSE
JODHPURS?"

*Margaret Mitchell was born in Gourock,
Scotland. When she was ten, her family moved
to Bedfordshire, England, and then to the
Isle of Wight. At the age of sixteen,
she went to work as a nanny.*

In 1939, I finally decided to leave my position as a nanny because I didn't particularly enjoy the lady of the house, shall we say. I took off for London and joined what was called the London Auxiliary Ambulance Service. We had to study first-aid and a map of London, of course. If we were sent out to help another ambulance station, we had to know where to go. I didn't have my driver's license when I joined. I started to learn once I was in London. In fact, I learned how to drive a bus all around London, which was rather adventurous of me.

I rented a room for awhile, but then I met up with a woman at the ambulance station. She was a very nice person but rather depressed. I don't know quite how it came about, but she said that if I would like to come and stay with her, there was a spare room where she was renting. She was renting an upper floor apartment. She was about fourteen years older than me but we had a good time together. I was a really naive young miss.

At work, we had to go out whenever there was a bad air raid in our vicinity. In the meantime, we had to practise first-aid and mock-up different kinds of accidents. The worst time we ever had was when a bomb hit a telephone station. In those days, the telephones were run on batteries. Some medical people were called in to give hypodermic needles to the people in there. Bones had been crushed but we couldn't move the people because the acid from the batteries was dripping all over the place. Bombers were passing overhead, and there was glass all over the pavement. It was horrifying but we just didn't think about it. We had to do our work.

The blitz over London was terrific, and sometimes when an enemy bomber was trying to escape the fighters, it would drop its load and run. So every night you'd hear of someone's place having been hit or someone knew someone who had been hit. When you're younger, you sort of take things in your stride. I remember saying to my dad, "It's all so exciting, isn't it?" And he said, "You'll find out differently."

One of the reasons it seemed so exciting was that we had all the Allies in London: the Polish Army and Polish Air Force, and soldiers from New Zealand and Australia. I had a little bit of time for a social life in London. Thank goodness I was able to go to the ballet and plays once in awhile. They did close the theatres for awhile until they could see how things were going. I went to the Old Vic and saw *Macbeth* which thrilled me to bits.

After I became ill and returned to the Isle of Wight, I met my husband-to-be, Bert. One night my youngest sister Eleanor decided she was going to the community dance. The dance hall was a new hall that was kitty-corner away from us. Eleanor came home about nine-thirty that night and insisted, "Oh Margaret, you've got to come to the dance!" "Well, alright," I said, "but I'm not fit to come to a dance. My hair isn't done." Then she told me, "Oh come on. We have some Canadians over there." I thought, "So what?" But anyway, just to please her, I went over.

There were at least three Canadians. Bert stood with his friends on the other side of the room and decided he was going to ask me to have a dance. But I think it was the man who turned out to be the best man at our wedding who came up first, and that was alright. I just loved to dance. As a young woman I hadn't really gone to many dances but I have a natural sense of rhythm.

Finally Bert came up to dance with me. Towards the end of the dance, he asked if he could walk me home. I said, "Yes." And then he asked me if I'd like to go out on another occasion. I agreed and then I really floored him, because when he asked where to meet me, I said, "Well you come to my house, of course." Most of the young ladies had said, "Meet me at the corner of such and such a place." But not Miss Gardner. I'm not going to be a stood-up fool! Sure enough, he did show up.

We went to this film. It was a story by Somerset Maugham called *The Letter*, I think, with Bette Davis in it. Well, Bert was bored stiff, but I just thought it was great. I insisted on staying until the end of the movie. When we came out, we looked for a place to have coffee, but this being wartime you know, places were closed up fairly early. I guess Bert was too shy to suggest that we go home for a coffee. But we kept making our little appointments to see each other.

Bert was in the Engineer's division, and they had a dance at the camp. I guess it was put on by the Army people for recreation, and I was invited along. All the village people could go too. Bert was trying to clump around in his Army boots, and after awhile, he said, "I think I'll go and put my gym shoes on. I can't get around in these." So he took off and when he came back, I was dancing with another man, much to Bert's chagrin. And the other man was a really good dancer. However Bert won in the end.

We were married six weeks after we met. And it wasn't a shot-gun wedding either. I didn't feel as if I were head over heels in love with Bert, but I liked the way he respected me. He didn't try to push himself on me or try any fancy tricks. And that got my respect. This reminds me of an old Canadian expression about finding a person who is good to live with: "We ride the river."

We were married in London November 5th, 1941, on Guy Fawkes Day, at a registrar's office called Marlowes Road off Kensington. It was a small, quiet wedding, naturally. You see, even if we had wanted to marry in a church, you had to call the bans, and neither one of us belonged to any church. My father treated us to a luncheon with a few of my friends and my two sisters. For our honeymoon, we went to Ripley, a small place outside of Guildford, and we stayed at a small country inn. I think we were the only guests there. It was quite pleasant.

Our first-born arrived on August 13, 1942. All the old ladies in our neighbourhood were busy adding up the numbers of days until his birth, but our son Stephen was conceived within wedlock. He was born at St. Mary's Hospital in London where Sir Alexander Fleming did his lab work for penicillin. I was still living with my friend, but after awhile I moved out of London because there were buzz bombs by this time.

I moved to somewhere outside of Slough, and stayed there for awhile. Then we went to another place, which was outside of Reading. I think Basildon was the name, and we lived in a three-hundred-year-old cottage that had been modernized inside. I was sharing it with another woman, and it was quite comfortable. By this time, of course, D-Day was approaching. Soldiers were allowed to go home but not too often because they were sending all the men to a gathering place.

But in the meantime we knew that number two son was going to arrive. This would be in 1944, and Bert wrote to his parents who lived in Alberta. Mr. Mitchell, Bert's father, wrote back and said that he would sponsor us. So he set the wheels rolling, and

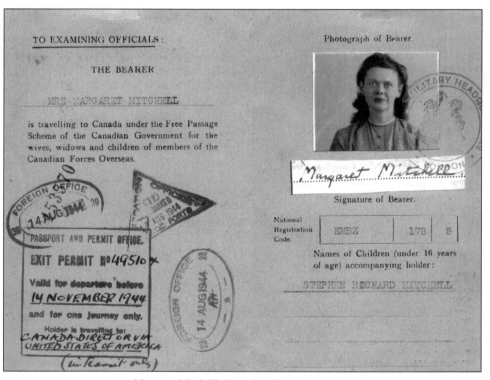

Margaret Mitchell's Canadian Travel Certificate.

about a week or so after my eldest son had turned two, we set forth on the *Aquitania,* and we sailed from my home town, Gourock, where I was born.

At this time, it was hard to make communications because of the war. You had to be careful to whom you spoke and that sort of thing. I asked a young man if he knew the Gardner family, because I still had cousins in Gourock. He said, "Well as a matter of fact, I do." I said, "Would you ask them to pass along a message to my father that we are on route." Of course, we didn't know the name of the vessel then. We were taken out to the ship by tender which is a little tow boat.

Our ship was mainly taking troops home this time, but there were also a few war brides. We were in the upper decks. One bad thing did happen during our voyage. We had a lice infestation on board because the ship had previously carried refugees either from Gibraltar to Malta or vice versa. And some of these refugees had been living in caves with no facilities for proper toileting during that time, so you can imagine.

It took four and a half days to reach Halifax, and then we were held off Halifax harbour because it was rumoured that there were some German submarines nearby. When we finally got off the ship, there was a train waiting for us. Somewhat snooty Red Cross nurses were there to help us. I think they looked down on us for taking their men. They really were quite haughty but we ignored them.

I got on the train and was headed for Edmonton. I can recall that we war brides kept looking out of the train and saying, "I wonder what kind of house we'll have? Oh look at those houses. They don't look very nice!" At this time, Bert was still over in France, and he hadn't really tried to prepare me for Canada, the rat. His parents had a farm about forty miles west of Edmonton.

I was not apprehensive but I was wondering what my in-laws would be like. They met me in Edmonton but for some strange reason, they hadn't arrived on the platform when I got there. Someone came up to us from the YWCA, and they asked, "Isn't there anyone here?" And I said, "There was supposed to be." So they flipped us off to the YWCA, much to Mrs. Mitchell's disgust, because they had to come looking for us. In the meantime, Stephen was suffering from summer diarrhoea. That was a problem. I met my in-laws when I was trying to clean Stephen up. And I still had the lice problem! And I was not very gainly being close to six months pregnant.

My in-laws bundled us into their old 1929 car. When we got off the pavement and on to a dirt road, I didn't realize at first that it was a dirt road, and that it had rained recently. So the way the car was sliding around, I just wondered, "Can't this man drive?" but I kept those thoughts to myself. When Mrs. Mitchell by instinct realized I wouldn't know what was happening, she said, "Oh it's been raining, and the roads are slick and it makes it difficult." And of course, they didn't have good tires in those days.

My sister-in-law, Jean, waited at home wondering why we were so late. It was a very peculiar supper, but by that time, I didn't really care. I just wanted something to eat. Everyone was quite friendly. Mr. Mitchell's people had come out during the nineteenth century to Ontario. I think it was Grey County. Then they eventually moved out to Alberta. They were members of the pioneer families. They had a mixed farm: some grain, a few cows, a team of horses. They also kept a bull which Stephen promptly climbed up on, much to Mrs. Mitchell's horror. But I think animals know when it's little children and don't get upset. Stephen thought it was great. The Mitchells also had chickens and that sort of thing.

I sort of helped indoors mostly—I didn't do any of the farmwork. For one thing, there was another son who had his own farm but he had come down to help his father. And there was a younger son at home who was a pain in the neck. My sister-in-law Jean was training at a nearby hospital so she advised me to see an obstetrician. When I went into the hospital on December 18th to have Robert, they had arranged for Jean to be on the maternity floor. So that was rather nice. Although just imagine spending your first Christmas in Canada in the hospital. But actually it was quite pleasant because it was a fairly modern hospital.

If I do say so myself, I am quite an adaptable person. I felt pretty well accepted by the family. The neighbours all around invited me to spend a day or two with them to get to know them. Mr. Mitchell was quite upset about this but I thought it was great getting to know the community. Then one day this particular lady who had lost her son in the war, asked me, "Have you anything else to wear but those jodhpurs?" I said that, well, they were comfortable, but yes, I had other clothes to wear. Then she asked, "Well, do you think you could manage to get into a dress? We're having some ladies for tea." I said okay. What she didn't tell me was that they had arranged a kitchen shower. So that was quite a surprise.

Bert had been overseas for four and half years. Now all his men were getting leave. Finally he arrived home in April 1945. We went to meet him, and we did get on the platform that time. There was a really weird Edmonton *Journal* reporter who asked us about Stephen. Later when she wrote up the arrival of the servicemen, she made it look as if we had Stephen two years before we were married. Anyway, we didn't care. It was a great reunion because Bert hadn't even met his second son.

Soldiers had the option of getting out of the service or returning. Bert opted out. Later Bert thought he'd like to farm, and I thought that was a great idea at the time. But unfortunately we were too close to the parents. I thought we should move away and farm somewhere else. Bert applied to the VLA (Veteran's Land Act), and he acquired a quarter-section about four miles north of where his parents lived. It was still too close to his parents for me but we only had to see them once in awhile.

We decided to build a house, but in the meantime we lived in two rooms that were actually granaries while we were building our house. Before they brought in steel granaries, they would build these twelve foot by ten foot little wooden sheds, and they would have a hole at the top so they could pour the grain in. The sheds were storage places until the grain could be taken to the elevator. So we had two granaries. One had the kitchen and living room area, and the other one was the dormitory. There was a little platform between the two so that the children wouldn't have to walk in the mud when it rained.

We lived there until we got our house built in 1946. Unfortunately it was never completely finished. The kitchen ran full-length and then the living room. There would have been bedrooms upstairs eventually, but we never did get around to it. It was my husband and his brother who worked on the house. They used something like a big scoop shovel that would have a horse hitched to it, and they'd guide this into the shovelled out basement. Bert was working on the farm and at the same time picking roots. We had grain, a couple of cows, chickens, a couple of pigs. It was no wonder he eventually got sick.

All of a sudden, Bert could hardly walk. His knees were swollen and once his eyes turned pink I said, "It's time you went to see a doctor." It was 1950 and he had rheumatic fever. He was in the hospital for a week or so, and I didn't know how to milk. I never learned because I was too busy looking after the house and children. By this time, we had four sons, Stephen, Robert, Christopher and Rodney.

The doctor told Bert he shouldn't try to do a lot of hard work, so that ended our dream of a farm. I had liked farm life. I wasn't new to farm living because my father's sister married a farmer, and he was quite a well-to-do man. People in Canada often talk about their big farms, but this uncle of mine had a good-sized farm, and it was quite well-established. In any case, I really enjoyed the farm life, the smell of it, the smell of hay. And I thought it was a great atmosphere and environment in which to raise the children.

With the help of friends and neighbours and relatives, we sort of staggered along until Bert was released from the hospital. He decided to go to McBride, BC, one hundred and thirty two miles west of Jasper and totally surrounded by mountains. But there was not the kind of social activities or intellectual considerations that I would have appreciated. Don't ask me why Bert wanted to go there. We got a homesteading grant. You can travel by train with your livestock and all that sort of thing at a special rate. So we got our cows and our horses and our very small amount of furniture, and moved to McBride.

It was quite interesting living in the bush. We stayed in a place on the Fraser River outside of McBride. Moose would wander into the fields on our farm. They looked to me like horses with horns on them. We lived there from 1950 to 1954. Our son Michael was born in August of 1951. Our son David came along in February of 1953. Then we packed everything up and came all the way down by train to Vancouver Island.

It's just a mystery why we came to Vancouver Island. It was in August. The first night after we came off the ferry, we stayed in a boarding house just on the outskirts of Nanaimo, quite near a park, I think. We needed somewhere just to put our heads down. We were all exhausted. But then the landlady didn't like the idea of housing so many children, so we went all the way up to Qualicum.

In the meantime, Bert was hunting for a place where we could stay, and he finally found this place that had cabins. He had rented a cabin that would more or less hold all the Mitchells. Then Bert decided it was time the holiday was over, and he got on a bus to the south. He liked the look of Duncan so he got off the bus there.

I couldn't figure out why we hadn't come to Vancouver Island in the first place. To me, it was more like the UK. It was interesting to me that I came eventually to another island. If I had my druthers, I'd have a house right near the ocean. But it's hard to find nice beaches, because they're so polluted.

We didn't buy a house right away. We rented a place first. Duncan was a small country town but now it's grown. Bert took any jobs that were available just for us to survive. He went and got some work out on the West Coast. They were building a road to Tofino. He had the contract between Tofino and the lighthouse, and that kept us afloat. In the meantime, I took in children and babysat them for awhile. We managed to survive that way, by subsidizing Bert's cheque with my earnings.

In 1959, my good friend Kath Watson decided that my house

would make an excellent place to have a nursery school. So the nursery school began in 1959. I have a copy of a video about our nursery school which was produced by Shaw Cable last year. I insisted that they have Kath, who started it, with us in the interview they held. Several years ago I was also interviewed by Stan Peters of CBC Radio, and I have a tape of that too.

When Kath eventually had to bow out, I was obliged to take over the nursery school, but I wasn't at that time fully qualified. I had the natural instincts and experience with children. But the powers-that-be figure you should have a license. So I did hire a woman who was a primary teacher, and that worked out for awhile. Eventually, I guess in 1962 or '63, I went to university and took the required courses. I got the qualifications and the license. You see, that was the thing.

I put quite a number of people on the road to success because they came to us to start their training, and often would say, "I think I would like to go and get qualified." Our nursery school grew to the point that people were calling and trying to have their children's names put down a few years ahead. We have a total enrolment of thirty-two children. But we take sixteen children per sitting. We like to keep the numbers as low as possible. We christened the school "St. Christopher's." I didn't mind, because I have a son named Christopher. But then people would say nervously, "Does this have any religious connotations?" I would say, "No, not at all. We don't teach religion. We just try to teach children to be polite, listen, and be obedient."

The school is still in our house and it takes up more than two-thirds of it. I have a third woman supervising the classroom, and we have an aide who helps. Our six sons, Stephen, Robert, Christopher, Rodney, Michael and David all still live on Vancouver Island.

Joan Charters

"JUST IMAGINE IF YOU HAD
STAYED IN ENGLAND"

---

*Joan Charters was born in Exeter.
As a young girl, she and her brother loved
to row boats along the canal that
runs through Exeter.*

T he last Christmas that my father was alive, I was given a big doll. In those days we used to put our pillow cases at the head of the bed and I remember waking up and seeing this beautiful doll. After my father's death, my mother went back to work as an assistant manager of a hotel. Then she bought a big house and she rented rooms. That was the way she was able to raise us.

I was working in the bookkeeping department for a large motor firm in Exeter when war broke out. We heard on the wireless that war had been declared. Of course, the blackouts were immediately started. When we were walking with our flashlights along the streets in the blackouts, the warden would come along and shout, "Put out that light—an air raid is coming," and then you would hear the sirens.

Shortly after, I left Exeter to work in Bournemouth. I just wanted to get away on my own for awhile. I worked in the office of a large dairy firm which did their own vehicle repairs. When I went there to work, they had three men in the office, and of course they were all called into the service. So I took over the office. My job was to keep records of all the repairs and time sheets. At times I had one or two girls to help me.

We had to do the warden's job at night, and we each had to take our turn. They put a shed up and we had our bunks there to sleep. In the garage they did sub-contract work to keep the men, so they didn't have to go into the service. They had to have women on the sub-contract job also, so we would take our turn to be air-raid wardens one night, and on the other night it would be the men who would take their turn. We tried to sleep, but our boss was awfully nervous, and would come in and keep us up talking. He could sleep the next morning, but we would have to get up and go to work.

I remember well the first warning raid we had in Bournemouth. We had underground pits for the men to work underneath the cars. I was the only woman there at that time, and all the men dived down into the pit before I could even think to get down with them. After awhile somebody decided that we ought to have a cup of tea. Well, nobody would volunteer to go up and make the tea, we were all so scared.

I remember the first real bad bombing in Bournemouth. A friend of mine and I had been out to a hotel, just sitting around with friends, and we heard this bombing. When we dashed back to the house, there were holes that we had to walk around. You could see and hear the glass shattering. They had dropped bombs right in the street. It was frightening with all the buildings damaged, and all the glass in the streets. The wardens were out directing us, and everyone was in a panic. The next day when we saw the scene in daylight, we could not believe our eyes. It was really scary.

Bournemouth is on the water. It was a beautiful place back then. I remember one Sunday morning I went to the corner shop to get the paper, and the planes came over. As they passed, you could almost feel the glass vibrate—they came so low. Then I heard this terrible explosion, and I thought it was quite close to where we lived. They used to billet the Canadian Air Force in the hotels on the cliffs, and the Germans were after the hotel that the Canadians were in. They didn't hit the large one. They hit another one but they did kill about two hundred Canadians. They dropped several more bombs, and other people were killed as well.

I went a couple of times to the bomb shelter. After awhile we didn't panic. We became used to the air raids. We got to know that these raids that went on all night weren't affecting us but were up in the north of England. Otherwise we could have been up all night for nothing.

I lodged with a friend until mother came to live with me when our home in Exeter was destroyed during a heavy blitz. Then I had to find a place for the two of us. It was very difficult to get a place in those days, but we discovered a little apartment. Not long afterwards, one of the women who worked in the workshop lost her husband, and she had a fair size apartment that she offered to share with us. So we moved in with her and stayed through the war.

Rationing was something else. I remember the time when we

all had one egg and a quarter-pound of bacon a week. We used to make a big evening meal with that. Where I worked at the dairy firm, we had an old fellow there, and his job was to go around to the farms collecting the eggs. This man learned that we liked duck eggs, and he would bring us some to help us out. We got to know how to ration our food. This is how I gave up sugar in tea: we decided that if we wanted cakes, we would have to give up our sugar in tea in order to make some. People had to queue up for everything. I didn't have to because I had mother with me, and she did all that. One thing that wasn't rationed was meat pies, and mother would go and queue up for those.

I was in a hotel with friends when my future husband was introduced to me. At that time I had no idea of ever meeting up with a Canadian. I did have one or two boyfriends and was supposed to meet up with this Scotch fellow. You see the Canadians and Americans had so much more money than our guys did that they were not too popular with the English fellows. When my friends introduced Al and his friend to me, for some reason I couldn't get shift of him—he just hung around. I don't know what happened, but the Scotch fellow didn't turn up so I ended up with Al walking me home.

At that time Al was with the Army Service Corps, in the cooking trade. We didn't go out very long before we were married. We met in November and married in May 1944 because D-day was coming up. Al was to go to Germany, and he went at what they called D-plus-10, ten days after the invasion.

We were supposed to wait three months to get married so that our backgrounds could be checked out. The army authorities came around. I have never heard anyone else say this, and I don't think I dreamed it, but when they interviewed me they said they had contacted Al's parents as well and had the marriage approved. I always had the impression that they did this to know what the girls were going to.

As we didn't have any relatives in Bournemouth, we had a very small wedding. I didn't have a white gown or anything like that. We couldn't afford it, and we couldn't get the ration coupons to buy one. My mother was a marvellous dressmaker, and just before the war I used to go to dances in long gowns that mother made for me. So I had a long blue velvet skirt which she cut off to street length, with a plum-coloured top and a little hat.

Al wore a civilian pinstripe suit. One of Al's friends gave me away. After the ceremony we went back to the apartment and had a little lunch and of course the wedding cake. Al's sister had baked a square dark fruit cake which she sent over from Canada for Christmas. We had decided that we were going to save it for the wedding cake, and my mother made almond and white icing for it. We were married in a lovely little stone church called Pokesdown. We didn't have any splashy wedding pictures, but somebody came along to take pictures.

After our daughter Lorraine was born I had to go back to work. In those days we had to work at something because they needed the women in the work force. Of course Lorraine had mother to look after her. And the woman who owned the house was very fond of children. Her mother was, too, so Lorraine had three nannies to spoil her.

Al's family would send small packages over from Canada. One time they sent a pound of shortening. We used to love round potato chips in batter so we took the shortening and used the whole pound to make the potato chips, instead of saving it for something proper. We really, really enjoyed them. Oh, that was a treat.

In wartime England, there was an organization for the war brides which was set up by the Salvation Army, and I belonged to the one in Bournemouth. It was called the Maple Leaf Club, and I became the secretary. We learned a lot about Canada, about the money, the clothing and what to expect. Just as the war ended, the club had a convention in London. The girls came from Scotland, Wales and England, and two of us went from Bournemouth. We had a wonderful three-day trip with all expenses paid.

I had been let go from my bookkeeping job at the end of the war because the men were coming back. I had to go on unemployment. They tried to send me to all sorts of jobs. I had to go and search for work, and I was required to report a couple of times a week to the unemployment office. I also had to go there to queue up for my cheque.

The man who did the subcontracting at my former job eventually took me to work at his company. They were making wooden tops for children—the kind with string around that could make them spin. So to keep me employed and out of the hands of the unemployment people, he gave me a job until I left England.

Most of the Canadian servicemen came back to Canada in 1945, but Al stayed on with the Army in Holland. They were told that if the men stayed on with the army in occupation, they might have a chance to travel back to Canada with their wives. But it didn't happen that way. Al came back in May of 1946 and I followed in August of the same year, with our daughter Lorraine.

I came to Canada on the *Queen Mary* sailing from Southampton. I had a very good friend, and she brought mother down to see me off. It was pretty hard on mother as Lorraine was her girl. She had practically brought her up while I worked. Mother did follow, and came on the *Queen Elizabeth* the following December.

I had seen the *Queen Mary* a few years before the war, just after she was built—never dreaming that I would come to Canada on her. That was in her heyday, and she was beautiful. Then she was converted to a troop ship for the war. The first night out we struck a storm. It was terrible as she rolled with the waves. I managed to get up on deck the next day, with my little girl. I covered both of us with a blanket and after that I felt fine. The food on the ship was fantastic—beautiful white bread and rolls. We also had plenty of fresh fruit, which had been so scarce during the war.

When we had received our sailing orders, we were told to wear trousers, and I wore grey flannel ones. We were also told to pack some luggage for the cabin. I had clothes for Lorraine and a small steamer trunk for myself. The rest of my luggage was in the hold of the ship. Well, the small trunk for the cabin never did get to the cabin, and all that I had was what I was wearing. The night before we were to disembark they were supposed to announce where our luggage was. I waited a long time for my name to be called to bring the trunks to the cabin. It turned out it was two or three weeks before I received my luggage.

My first impression of Canada when we docked—one I will never forget—was the white buildings. I thought they looked marvellous. When we were in the train looking out, the things that impressed us most were the coloured roofs of the houses, because in England they were all the same colour. They looked so pretty.

Al's parents lived on a farm thirty miles outside of Moncton, New Brunswick, at Mackee's Mill. Al was working in Moncton at that time, and we stayed at the farm until our apartment in Moncton was ready. He commuted back and forth to the farm. Thirty miles in those days on the road was not like it is today. We had an old car and the tires would go. You couldn't get good tires in those days.

Al worked for a food company as a shipper, and he was there for five years. Then one day Al came home and asked me, "What would you say if I went back into the forces?" The Air Force was advertising for cooks. So I said, "Fine." He had to go ahead, and I packed up the apartment and went back to the farm to stay until I could join him. He was posted to Ottawa, and that's where we were for four years. We were moved around quite often until Al retired from the Air Force.

We had our hard times here in Canada. Most of us did, I think. After the war things were pretty bad, but we came through the tough times. We lost Lorraine when she was three from croup. We have one other daughter, Patricia. Al has been a wonderful husband and we get along great. In May of 1994 we celebrated our fiftieth wedding anniversary. Al often teases me and says, "Just imagine if you had stayed in England!" Yes, I love it here in Canada!

Eve Mitchell

"I'M SORRY, BUT I JUST CAN'T GET ON ANOTHER BOAT!"

Eve Mitchell was born and raised in Hove on the south coast of England. She was thirteen years old when the war started.

My granny and I were listening to the radio when Chamberlain came on to announce that we were at war. It was only a little while after the radio announcement that the air-raid siren went off, and we all hurried outside to see what was happening. I remember that the lady next door rushed down her stairs and shouted, "My God, the buggers are here already!" And that was my introduction to the war.

In our area, our school days changed because we had evacuees sent down from London to attend our schools. The children of our area went to school in the mornings, and then the evacuees came to our school in the afternoons. Those of us who went to school in the mornings would end up at a church hall or any other hall that might be available to us. I can't say I liked school. You had to go until you were fourteen but there seemed no point to it after that. So I went out one Friday and got a job. I had gone as far as I could go by this time anyway, unless I were to go to a trade school.

I went to work at a factory called Dubarrys which used to make face powder and other cosmetics. But during the war they also made aspirins, and they had a box department that made all the packages. At first, our employer used to have air-raid spotters up on the roof, and every time a plane or something was heading towards us, we'd have to rush down to the basement. But the amount of time that we were away from our work proved to be too costly so our employer decided to wait until the planes were right overhead before we were instructed to go downstairs. This kept us working as long as possible. Soon we became used to the air-raid threats which occurred on a regular basis; they just became a way of life.

My workplace was in Hove yet it was still a half-hour bus ride from home. I was happy to be working, but it was tiring at first. We worked from eight o'clock in the morning to six o'clock in the evening, and we also worked Saturday mornings until twelve-thirty.

At home our family had what was called a Morrison shelter. We didn't have a bomb shelter that was outside the house. This was probably to avoid digging up all the gardens. Instead, we were given a great big metal table called a Morrison shelter and it was placed in the living room. If anything had come down, it would come down on top of the Morrison shelter which was totally made of steel. Because the Morrison shelter was so big and the room was so small, it became our table for eating as well as a kind of activity centre. It was where we worked on puzzles and where we wrote. We had no choice—it dominated the room.

Mum worried all the time because of the babies and the children. My aunt was staying with us; her husband was in the Army. My mother and my aunt used to bundle the children up and sleep with them in the shelter. Can you imagine my mother expecting me to sleep with her and my aunt and all the kids in the small space of the Morrison shelter? And then I would have to get up in the morning to go to work!

Every night something was going on. The guns were firing or the air-raid siren was going off. After sleeping in the Morrison shelter, I just couldn't get up in the mornings, and I finally said to mum, "If I'm going to die, I'll die in bed, mum." So I stayed in my bed and said "Don't bother."

The bombing and air-raid sirens were scary at first, but it would have been even more scary if we'd had bombs dropping every night around us. As it was, we went to dances and to the movies. At the movies, they would flash a notice on the screen when the siren sounded and then show the all-clear signal, but usually nobody had moved at all. Of course if you were nervous, you could leave. On the streets, we had air-raid shelters made of concrete so that if you were caught outside and you found that things were getting bad, you could duck into one of these shelters. There was always somewhere to turn into if you couldn't make it home in time.

During the war I was always working, and I enjoyed having my own money. I had a lot of fun because there were so many men around. As soon as one division moved out of Hove, another one came in. They could each only stay a certain length of time before they had to pull out. I'd go down to a dance hall and find a new set of faces. I know it sounds cruel but I was young. The dance hall was just a bus ride into Brighton. Our favourite dance hall was Sherry's on West Street. The Regent, with its spring floor and famous dome, and the Royal Pavilion were very lively places.

Yet there was hardship of course. The worst part I found was the winter. We had double daylight savings time to save more daylight but we had to travel on these very dimly lit buses. Eventually your eyes did get used to it. The streets were always dim as well. We had to put blackout curtains on every window so no light showed through. Otherwise, some irate air-raid warden would knock at your door and tell you to put that light out. You had to put a blanket across your door so that as you opened the door, no light would show. You made black cloths to cover your windows so that nothing would show. A light would be a dead giveaway to an enemy plane that was flying overhead and looking for a target.

We had six years of this daily routine throughout the war, so we did get accustomed to blackouts and lack of light. However, early on when my dad was still working at his night job, he set off for work one evening and then returned a short time later. He had a great big gash on his head. My mum asked him, "Whatever have you done?" He replied, "I walked into a lamp post." Then he added, "And I stood there apologizing." That's how dark it was at night.

How I met my husband-to-be, Ray, is very interesting. I was actually going out with a friend of his, and one night my boyfriend brought Ray with him. They actually had gone AWOL to go out. My boyfriend met another girl at a bus stop and picked her up for Ray. I didn't think much about Ray at the time. After all, I already had a boyfriend.

At the end of the evening, Ray had to walk the other girl a long distance to where she lived because the buses had already stopped running for the night. Then he walked all the way back to where I lived. It was about two o'clock in the morning by this time. The boys then walked to the railway station, but the trains weren't running either so they picked apples off a tree and ate them for breakfast while they waited for a morning train. Ray told me later that he was already taken with me that first night we met, but I don't recall thinking anything about him. I was eighteen years old at this time. Before I met Ray, I'd had a number of boyfriends but our relationships never lasted more than a few months. This was because many of the young men who were in the armed forces would be based in England for only two or three months before shipping out to the war. Anyway when you're young, you're not that serious about anything.

After our double date, my boyfriend and Ray went overseas. I never heard from my boyfriend but I heard from Ray. He wrote a number of long letters to me. Then Ray was wounded in Holland and transferred to a hospital in England. One day I stepped off the bus that brought me home from work, and there he was on the doorstep. He had just been released from the hospital and got leave to come and see me, but he was in rough shape from a shrapnel wound. My mum loved Ray, and it's funny because she used to loathe the other young men that I had been seeing. But Ray could do no wrong. She thought he was just marvellous.

Eventually Ray asked me to marry him, and I said yes. Of course, my mum was very happy because she liked Ray so much, and my dad was okay about it, too. Then Ray had to get permission from his Commanding Officer to marry me. I had to meet one of his officers as part of the process. After our marriage was approved, we planned our wedding and were married in 1944.

Ray was in the infantry, and he was based at Petworth in Sussex for the rest of his time in England. Then he was sent home in January of 1946. Like all the other war brides, I had to wait until I was assigned to a ship that would bring me to Canada. I was getting a bit nervous because I was pregnant, and if you were six months along or more, you had to wait until after your baby was born. I even went up to Canada House in London but they said they couldn't do anything to help. I had just been back from London for a week when I finally got the papers that said I could go. I was to go across on the *Letitia* from Liverpool. But first I had to go to London and leave from there. At the appointed time, my mum and I left for Brighton Station. It was packed with these girls and screaming kids. I knew a lot of them because they had lived in my town. We all travelled to London and went to the hostel for the war brides which was near Hyde Park. That was where we were to stay until we caught our train to Liverpool. At the hostel there were all these crying ladies and the kids were crying too. Mum and I had to say goodbye to each other, and I kept saying, "Don't you dare cry! Don't you dare cry!" So she didn't cry and that kept me going.

I did have mixed emotions. You're eager to get to your husband and you're eager to start a new life, but you're also leaving everything you've ever known. Still you have to take into account how young most of us were, and we just didn't have the fear that older people would have. You don't actually realize that you're not going to come back.

The next day we caught the train to Liverpool. I'd never been there before, and I'd never seen such a scruffy place in my life. Then we went aboard the *Letitia*, and I was downstairs in the hold of the ship. There were about ninety bunks and there were no windows of course. The toilets had canvas in front of them instead of doors and there were some sinks, too. It was hardly a cruise ship. In fact, it was a former hospital ship. The transporting of war brides was a big operation. We were all told where to go but there was a lot of confusion and a lot of unhappiness.

I was horribly seasick for a long time, and finally the other girls came to get me and propelled me upstairs about three flights up where they sat me on the deck in a deck chair. I just said, "I know I'll be fine with a cup of tea." They got me my cup of tea, and after that I started to feel a bit better but the first few days were terrible. It was really quite rough coming across the Irish Sea, and this was my first experience on a boat of any kind. Then we finally arrived at Halifax. It was delightful coming up the channel into Halifax. We could see these roofs that were all different colours. We were so used to brick row houses all exactly alike.

When we got off the ship we had to go through Immigration. After that, a soldier took our suitcase for us and put us on the train. Each war bride was assigned a berth, and then our trip across Canada began. It felt good to get off the ship, and it was nice to walk on land again. There were some girls that I knew on the train but we were all getting off at different stops. That was what was so hard. When we first came to Canada, we really didn't know anyone, even to say hello to.

Those of us going all the way to Vancouver had another week of travel ahead of us. It was a big train and we were used to the smaller electric trains that travelled throughout England. During the trip, I kept thinking, "Gee, they must be really religious in this country," because I kept hearing church bells ringing. During the six years of war, we did not hear any church bells because that was to be the signal of an invasion.

If there had been an invasion, then all the church bells would have been rung. But of course that never happened so the church bells stayed silent. So when I kept hearing this bell, I thought that there must be a lot of churches in Canada. But I couldn't see any. I didn't realize that it was the bell at the front of the train that I was hearing all the time.

By the time I reached Vancouver I was very grateful that the long, long trip from England was almost over. When I got off the train, it was early morning and there were all these people on the platform. With so many people there, I thought, "I'm never going to find him." Then all of a sudden this man grabbed me and I yelled, "What are you doing to me?" It was my husband. You see, I'd never seen him in civvies before so I didn't know who he was. It took me some time to get used to his new look and then I thought, "Well, he doesn't look too bad." The next thing I knew, Ray was saying, "Come on, we've got to catch a boat." I replied, "I'm sorry but I just can't get on another boat. We'll have to live here."

I didn't realize how close we were to Victoria. We only had to catch the CPR ferry from Vancouver to Victoria, which is on Vancouver Island. It was actually quite a nice trip but in those days it took all day to get to Victoria. You had to leave at seven o'clock in the morning and did not arrive in Victoria until five o'clock the same day. It was a day-long trip but it was an enjoyable voyage because of the beautiful Gulf Islands that dot the water of Georgia Strait between Vancouver and Victoria. So Ray and I had our first day together with just the two of us, and we were able to catch up on all the news about each other. The ferry ride also gave me time to calm down before I met Ray's family.

I was six month's pregnant when I arrived in Victoria. Ray's mother was very good; she was actually from Eastbourne in England herself. After we met, she said, "I guess you'd like a nice bath," and I said, "Oh, would I ever!" It was just what I needed after that long train ride. We stayed with Ray's parents for the first while.

After our son Paul was born, we moved into a little room just to be on our own. Ray and I slept on a single bed (good job we were both thin) and the baby slept on a six-year-size cot which dominated the room. We cooked on a hotplate in the closet. While we lived in our little room, Ray began building our first house. At this time, he was working as a freight truck driver.

At the same time, Ray was also interested in building and making things. After we'd lived in our first house a little while, we sold it and bought another house that was only partially constructed. We lived in the basement while Ray built the top. We kept on going in this way—buying and fixing up houses to sell. Some time later, Ray became a logging truck driver and continued his building on a part-time basis. In 1955, my mother came over to visit us and my daughter Shelley was born while she was here.

One day when Ray was about forty, he came home and asked me, "Would you mind if I quit my job?" He was a logging truck driver at the time. So he spent the rest of his working years as a self-employed builder. When Ray began doing building work full time, our son was working at the parliament buildings and asked if he could come in with his dad. He loved building, too, so they went into business together. Eventually I also worked with Ray. It was my job to choose the paint, cabinets, carpets, etc. I enjoyed this work very much; I liked to see the finished products. Ray always says that I'm too impatient. I like to have the front door on before the roof is on. When we drew up the plans for each house, we always tried to design the house as though we were going to be living in it. I participated in this process, and my son is carrying on the same tradition. He's built about nineteen houses in the Dean Park area. It has been very satisfying over the years to be responsible for the construction of good family homes.

About ten years ago Ray decided to retire, and our son Paul now runs the business by himself. After years of living in different houses, we are now residing in a condominium in Sidney which is close to Victoria. For some time now we have been interested in boating (how, I'll never know), and have had several boats over the years. Our daughter Shelley also has a boat but our son's interest lies in antique cars. Paul married a Dutch woman whose parents came to Canada after the war. Ray and I have two grandchildren, Kevin and Leanne, who are now teenagers.

It's been quite an adjustment for me to live in a condominium after always living in houses for so many years. But our condominium is right beside the ocean, and *Kismet,* our cabin cruiser, is parked right outside—she is thirteen years old and has given us many happy memories. The name "Kismet" stands for the patterns we've always observed in the way our lives have evolved. Aboard our *Kismet,* Ray and I often go on trips along the coast to explore all the beautiful islands and inlets. With the horrors of World War II (and my aversion to boats) long behind us, we feel like we're living in paradise now.

Ann Picard

"WHEN WE WOKE THE NEXT
MORNING WE WERE IN
CONVOY"

Ann Picard was born in Lancashire.
Her parents died when she was very young.
She was raised by her father's family in
Newcastle upon Tyne.

When you reach the marvellous age of sixteen you have to go and see what is happening in London. After I did the usual family fighting about leaving home, I decided I wanted to stay with a cousin in London. I was too young to drink, but I managed to get a job by lying. If you could add two and two you got the job. I told them I was eighteen. A lot of barmaids lived in, and I did, too. It was cheaper and if you were fairly young, they kind of supervised you.

I remember the day when war was declared. I was in London and had a hell of a toothache. I was cleaning my teeth and was so excited that I didn't rinse my mouth and tooth paste got up behind a damaged tooth. It swelled up, and they took it out even with the swelling.

I was in London all during the bombing. In fact the night that I actually left London was the first night they didn't have a bombing raid. By that time, I was a little tired of being up all night. They wouldn't let you stay in your room because you had to be at ground level. We usually went down to the billet room, a part of the hotel where I was working.

I then went to Guildford. I was offered a job in Guildford at the Red Lion, not knowing that this was the centre for the Canadian troops. All during this time I had been dating, and at the time I was engaged, but my fiance lost his life at sea. In 1940, on New Year's Eve, I met my future husband, Rene Picard. We were having a big dance that night at the Red Lion, for which we were flogging tickets, and I sold him a ticket. He asked, "Will you be there?" and I said, "Oh sure, later." I promptly forgot about it, but I did show up later and he was still there. It was very funny because he said, "You and I are going to get married." I said, "I don't think that your mother knows that you are out. Go home!" I told him I already had a boyfriend, and he said, "That doesn't matter, we are going to get married." That was New Year's Eve 1940, and we were married at Easter, three months later. The funny thing was, we didn't have many dates because when you're in the war, you don't get out whenever you feel like it. When he did ask me, I began to think about it and actually went home to Newcastle to put it in perspective. I met with a lot of opposition. They didn't want me to marry a Frenchman. My uncle felt sorry for anyone who wasn't English. I argued, and the family argued back. Possibly if they hadn't argued so much, I might have thought more about it. But when you are that age and someone says you can't do something, you do it, just to prove a point. I remember my uncle saying Montreal was the dragnet for all the riff-raff of Europe and no place for me. I couldn't figure out how it could be so because Rene was such a gentleman. They came around in the end, and my uncle paid for my wedding when he figured he couldn't change my mind.

When Rene arrived he had a suitcase full of cigarettes. Heavens, you could have bought the whole family for that. We were married April 14, 1941. It wasn't a big wedding. All our clothes were bought with coupons, and they didn't give you extra coupons because you were a bride. Anything you bought you had to make darn sure you could use it afterwards. I didn't have a white dress; I had a two-piece blue outfit that I wore for a long time afterwards. It was very nice but also practical. Rene just wore his dress uniform.

We went back to Guildford after the wedding. He was a Sergeant in the Army. I was a city girl, and now I lived on a farm. I had never really lived in the country so it was quite a new experience for me. The day that we were married was the first time that women conscripts were called up. I would have been one of them if I had not married a Canadian. I didn't know it then but once we were settled, I went and reported. It was then I found that as the wife of a Canadian I couldn't enroll. My husband told me that he didn't know if he was the lesser of two evils, and I said, "You never will."

If you weren't eligible for conscription, it was actually easier to find employment. People did not like to employ women who were eligible to be conscripted. I went to work in a steel plant where we made shells and casings for the bombs. Basically what I was doing was making valves. I had my own machine. I was in the machine shop and we did the grinding. I was the eighth woman in there. It was kind of intimidating to walk into the plant with all these men, and they are waiting for you to fall down—especially as I stood five feet one and weighed about ninety-five pounds. They look at you, as much as to say, "I wonder what's going to happen to this one?" It kind of surprises them when you do figure it out!

There was a couple working at the plant, and she came to me one day and asked, "Do you always work the night shift from seven in the evening to seven in the morning?" And I said, "Yes." Her son had been called up and they had an empty room. She said, "If I have an empty room they are going to put evacuees into it, and you may not understand, but lots of times you don't want to leave someone in your house when you are not there." So we moved into their room. Christmas 1942, Rene came home with a bottle of scotch and said, "We will open it at New Year's." Either it was stolen from the bar, or he bought it very cheap, but we couldn't have bought it on the open market. New Year's came and New Year's went, and he did not show up. Of course the stories came back, you know what these Canadians are. . . . Two weeks went by, and no sign, no phone call, nothing! Then a friend of his came to our house and said, "I think I can tell you now, if you are looking for your husband, he is possibly in Canada by now." He said, "I can't give you all the details," but he gave me the name and address of another camp, and he gave me the sergeant's name. He suggested that I go there to find out. So I took a day and went down there and the Sergeant said, "Just hold your horns in and you will hear from him as soon as he makes home, and he is on his way home." He told me later he tried to get off the damn train when they took them up to Scotland to board the ship. He said, "I did everything I could to get in touch with you. When I left England I couldn't tell anybody, either. They didn't know I was gone until I arrived here, in Canada."

So he wrote me a letter from Quebec and he said, "I would suggest you start trying now: see what you can do about getting over here, it is going to take a long time!" So I went up to Canada House in London and talked to them, and they put my name on the list. They can't say that they have a ship coming in on

Thursday. They tell you nothing; it's war time! Time after time I would go up, and I would say, "How are you doing?" Well Mr. and Mrs. Grace, the couple that I moved in with, asked me, "Did you ever suggest that you would pay some money for this?" You see, I was working twelve-hour shifts, and I never had anything to spend my money on. So it was piling up. I never took my Army allowance because I learned early on that I didn't have to take it out of Canada. I had a bank account in Canada, and the government was putting my Army allowance in there. So the next time I went up to Canada House, I suggested it and by the time I got home there was a telegram saying come back, they thought they had a ship I could travel on. They asked me to go to the American Embassy. I had to get my visa to travel through the States. Anyway, that idea went down the hole because the ship I was to travel on didn't even make it to England.

I went once more and I hadn't got home again before I was called back. When I went up they told me how to pay the money. I paid for everything in England; it cost me two hundred pounds and I was only allowed to bring twenty pounds. I am not saying that's all I brought. I had a nice little jewel case, but it was very hard to change pounds into dollars. I couldn't let them know at home when I was going. I was told to be in Liverpool at such and such a time, and such and such a place. Mr. Grace wired ahead and got me a hotel room, but I had no idea how long I would be in the hotel room. They can't say you are sailing tomorrow. That's why I had all my money with me.

We were only there overnight, then we had to report to the docks. It was kind of funny because nobody could say where you were going. We kind of just stood there looking at each other. Then they took us into these big halls, and we had to surrender our gas masks and so many other things. They even went through my photo albums. I had taken some pictures on the base and written captions on them. I could have the pictures but I had to send the albums back. It was there that I first saw Mounties who were not in red uniforms, because now they were dealing with Canadians. The finance man was sitting there and he said to me,

"I am sorry, it is only ten pounds that you can take. You only have ten pounds, haven't you?" and I nodded. We never went back to the hotel. We were taken out to the ship by a small boat. Our ship was named the *S.S. Bayano*. It was a big yacht, with about ninety people on board. There were about fifty ships in the convoy, and we all met up at the mouth of the Mersey River. Actually we saw only our ship that first night, but when we woke the next morning we were in convoy, with ships all around us. Away on the horizon we could see a couple of destroyers at the head of the convoy. They took us about half way, then the Canadians took us the rest, so we were escorted the whole way across the Atlantic.

We ate very well. Of course after eating rations it was kind of nice. But it was a long trip and we had many submarine alerts. There were two of us in the cabin and we shared a bathroom; there was nothing glamorous about the accommodation. There was no entertainment. You made your own entertainment if you wanted to. We also did fire watch; anybody that could, did. In March in the northern Atlantic it was rough at times. I saw my first iceberg. I heard there was an iceberg in sight early one morning, so I rushed up without shoes. It was such an impressive sight, the sun shining on it. It looked like sparkling pink icing. Someone said, "You're standing in your bare feet," but it was something to see and I didn't notice my cold blue feet. You never went anywhere without a life jacket hanging on you, and you couldn't close your door because if there was a hit, the doors could warp and you wouldn't get out of your cabin. They were on a short chain and you could not shut them.

This was basically before the war bride program started. I was very fortunate to get aboard and I think it was because I was persistent. The Scottish lady who shared the cabin with me was returning from visiting her mother. She had lived in Vancouver for years, but had been caught in Britain at the beginning of the war in 1939, and this was 1943. They just picked the cabin mates out of the hat, so this is how I came to share with the Scottish lady. It was seventeen days by the time we arrived in Montreal. When we landed in Halifax, I was terribly excited to be back on land. But when I saw those big freight trains. . . . (Do you know how huge Canadian trains are compared to the ones in England?) Of course the train going from Halifax to Montreal seemed to stop at every lamp post. At least I thought it did. But I don't think I will ever forget the sight of Quebec City; as we came up along the St. Lawrence, we could see the citadel from the train, and I thought, "Boy, would I love to get off this train."

We got into Montreal quite late at night. Rene was there at the station with his family. Their home is in St. Jeans, Quebec, about twenty-six miles from Montreal. I stayed with his sister for awhile, and then I went to work. Rene was still in the forces but he knew he was getting out, so I stayed with her. It was marvellous staying with her, she tried to teach me French. They didn't really want me to work but I knew I couldn't sit around and do nothing.

My husband's friend suggested I look for work at the Air Observer School. The English, Dutch and Polish boys would come over, and they were given a quick series of lessons, approximately ten weeks in length, on how to become pilots, navigators, and bombers. These schools were all connected to airports. St. Jeans had an airport and a school which was number nine. When I first started, I was working in the hanger and I was doing everything on a plane except dismantling engines.

When a training plane such as the Avro Anson came in for a check, it had to be stripped down. At that time the gas tanks were on the wings. You couldn't see it, but they were taped and glued down, and the tape and glue had to be pulled off. I learned to use a screwdriver. The pieces underneath were removed and it was made ready for its check-up. I also painted them inside, I did that for a little while. Then a job came up in the parachute room and I packed parachutes. There is a series of checks and counter checks and if a chute failed they could trace it to you, because at every stage there is a signature. These parachutes were in the plane and after so long they had to be brought into a big airing room, where they were run up to the ceiling to dry, because dampness is an enemy. Also you never knew if a little acid had spilled on the cover and seeped into the silk, so we really had to check them out to make sure there was no damage to the silk. Then there were always two of you to pack them, and you spent a lot of time simonizing the tables that they were done on, so that nothing could snag them.

My husband was a customs officer. After he was discharged from the Air Force, he got a posting with customs on the Vermont border. They told us there was a house there, and that we could have the house for about thirty dollars a month. By this time I was expecting my son, and we had to pump the water into the house. I had never seen big wood ranges, so I wasn't sure how ours operated. The house had been wired for electricity, but the war had interrupted things and it wasn't hooked up. So I learned how to light an Aladdin lamp. They have mantles in them. I would light the mantle and run, because it would go poof. I would be out of the room until the light took. It was an entirely different life. My son Michael was born in July 1944, and my daughter Lynn was born in 1948. We had a nice place. We were right on Lake Champlain which, in the summer, is a beautiful resort. I really adapted very well.

When we came out west in 1962, I had no trouble adapting. We had built a home and were only in it three to four years when my husband had a heart attack. He seemed to get over that one, but then he had two others and the last one he had while driving the car. I said to him, "I don't know why you don't consider taking early retirement." Our son was finishing high school and our daughter was just going into junior high school. I thought what better time to move; we are not pulling them out of school at a crucial time. I didn't want to go back to England because I knew he wouldn't settle there and I didn't think my children would.

He came home one day and said, "How would you like to go to Victoria?" I thought he was talking about South Africa. "No, I am not going!" Then he explained that it was Victoria, British Columbia, on the west coast. He said that he had been there as a young fellow and loved it. "Well," I said, "that sounds reasonable." He took that for yes, and the first thing I knew, everything was on the market. He said, "We'll make the trip out on the train and we will rent a place." But when we got out here we discovered we like space and renting wasn't an option. We arrived on Saturday, bought a house on Sunday, and moved in on Monday. I kept the house until two years ago, when I sold it.

I returned to England in 1991 for the first time. I went with a young friend. She called me up and said, "I am going to England with the band and I need a roommate, don't you think it is time you went?" So we went with the Legion Band and we stayed at the universities. One day I said to her, "I'm going to take the day and go up to Newcastle to do a little relative tracing." Over the years we had lost touch. Well I got there and I couldn't find anyone, and I only had the day. But when I was there I picked up the local newspaper and brought it home to Canada with me. When I come off a trip, I usually throw everything into a drawer and forget it. I had done this, and about six months later I pulled the paper out of the desk, and I thought I would do something about it. So I typed a letter right then to the newspaper. I told my story, asking for any information about my family. About four weeks later I received a phone call: my cousins had read my letter in the paper. So I went back again in 1992, and the ones that met me at the station hadn't been born when I left. I'm the only one left in Victoria now; my husband died and my son and daughter live in Fort Nelson. I love Victoria and I won't go anywhere else.

Margaret Presley

"EVERYTHING THAT'S DIFFERENT SORT OF HITS YOU"

Margaret Presley was born in Scarborough, Yorkshire. At the age of fifteen, she began a four-year apprenticeship to become a hairdresser.

I was eighteen when the war started. At the age of twenty-one, I went into the Air Force. I wanted to be a wireless operator but they said, "You're a hairdresser. That's it." Looking back, I could kick myself because I wanted to do something different.

So I was a hairdresser in the Air Force, and I did the hair of the women in the force. I became well-known and had a good time. I had my own little shop, and that was kind of nice. I got to know all the girls anyway, and I got a few favours that way, especially from the cooks. They'd give me extra food. I was at three different stations while in the forces but compared to some, I didn't have to travel an awful lot. I was at Dishford, Topcliff in Dalton, and one other station in Leicestershire which I didn't like particularly.

I met my husband-to-be, Irvin, when we were on the same station. I'd been down in Leicestershire, and I came back up to Yorkshire. I met him in the spring of 1944. We fell in love pretty well right away. I was going with someone else at the time. You know, during the war we always had boyfriends. But this attraction was almost like love at first sight, I guess. My family liked Irvin too. The only thing they didn't like was that he was a Canadian. I was their only daughter, so my mother was very upset. But at the same time, she never stopped anything. My parents were very kind.

Irvin and I were married in the fall of that year. We had met in April, and we were married in November. We had a lovely wedding in St. Mary's Church on the hill in Scarborough, and we had a nice reception. The thing was I didn't have a long dress because I was in the forces and couldn't get coupons to get clothes. A short dress cost so many coupons; it was much more for a long dress. For me, it wasn't all that big a thing. It never bothered me. I was married in a nice blue dress, actually. We went to Edinburgh for our honeymoon. It was just for a few days because that was all the leave we could get. We came back, and we were stationed at different places but they were only about seven miles apart. We found rooms at this little house between our two stations, and we used to cycle back and forth to the house to have our time together.

We did that until I became pregnant in March, and I got out of the forces in June. You had to apply to leave when you were pregnant. It didn't take long to go through. Some girls were just dying to get pregnant after they got married. When anybody went on leave to meet their husband, we'd ask, "Well what happened?" I'd done three years of service, and that was enough anyway. So I was quite glad to get out but I loved my time in the forces. I really did.

My husband went over to Canada ahead of me. And he kept saying, "Well, you should come with the other war brides. How come you're not coming?" I don't know how some war brides got to go before other war brides—whether it was the time from when you were married or what. But some seemed to get over faster than others. The thing was that my mother was hoping that I would get over to Canada before I had my child. In the end, it was actually better that I gave birth before I left, because my parents were able to see our child. Still, it was very hard for them when I left. Mother was heartbroken. When you've had children of your own, you can understand.

My son Murray was born in 1945, and then we had to wait until the following year to come to Canada. I think one of the sad points I found was when my mum and dad came as far as London with me to give me a hand on my way to the ship. When we got to London on the train at King's Cross, there were all these double-decker buses filling up with brides. Of course my mother would have liked to know where we were going because she would have come to see me that evening. But that was it. It was all closed. I don't know why, because the war was over by then. But they wouldn't allow any information. So we had no idea and that was pretty sad. Oh God, I remember one girl who got so fed up, she just said, "Well that's it! I'm going back home."

Then the next morning, we still weren't told anything. We didn't know when the ship was going or anything. We were scared to go too far to get breakfast, but we had to buy meals. We were all worried in case we missed our departure. So we just had to wait. We didn't know what was happening. And there wasn't any baby food for Murray. But once we got on the ship, it was fine. I came over on the *Queen Mary*. The *Queen Mary* was a fine ship but it was so big. And it's hard when you have a small child because you can't get around. You have to carry him everywhere. And you know with some of the children so big, it's pretty heavy at times. We didn't have nurseries or strollers to push them around in. We just kept them with us. Of course they had high chairs when we went to eat. Luckily we were only on the boat four or five days, so that was pretty good. No complaints there. Red Cross workers used to open the cabin doors and ask, "Everything all right in here?"

I arrived in Halifax on the fourth of July, 1946. You feel some apprehension because you know you are going to meet your new in-laws whom you've never seen before. And you don't know what kind of people they are, although you have a feeling they are going to be alright. I did feel rather comfortable about that, but it's just that you are strangers at first. And everything that's different sort of hits you. It really does.

I got on a train in Halifax, and then when we reached Montreal, the Red Cross came on and said, "Now you people can go and get a meal," because we had two or three hours to wait. They told us, "We'll look after the children." That was a bit of a break for us. We were all sort of tired and upset. I remember this was the first time that we used tea bags. I had never seen them before, and I thought, "Heavens, what's this?" Of course, we were starting to pour the tea right away and you have to wait (we found out later you have to let it steep). We thought it would come out too strong.

My destination was Ottawa, and we arrived there eventually at one o'clock in the morning—a great time to meet your in-laws. My husband's family lived in Cumberland just outside Ottawa. My father-in-law was quite well known around there for farming. It was really a French-Canadian community on the main Montreal highway. People were kind to me. I was one of the lucky ones, I guess. Some of the war brides weren't that lucky; some of them had some pretty rough experiences. But my husband's family really welcomed me.

My husband was from a large family and he was the youngest of eight children. But even before I got married, my father wrote my husband's father because he said that, "If I had a daughter getting married in another country, I'd want to know a bit about her." My father was quite a good letter writer, and so he did that. And I think my husband's family appreciated that. It was a very nice way of introducing me to my husband's family. We lived with Irvin's family for two or three months, and then we found a little place in Cumberland. That was nice. My husband went to work in the civil service in Ottawa. He went on the bus every morning. So I had my first long winter in Canada. But I think having a child stops you from being lonely—I was too busy to worry. And my mother wrote a fair amount to me, which really helped. Then my husband re-enlisted into the Air Force when I had another child in 1950. Irvin went back in the forces because he never really found a job that he liked. After his civil service job, he was selling appliances, and that didn't work out. It was difficult for these service fellows. But I was really happy because I liked the Air Force life.

In 1952, we were sent to England for three years. Actually the children and I went ahead of my husband. I went by boat again, and I loved the boat trip going over. I had a great time. We went back on the *Empress of France*. That was a lovely ship. Our two sons were so good. The elder one could go to movies on the boat, and there was a good nursery there for the other one who was just toddling. My brother met me in Liverpool. I had written a letter to him while I was on the boat and it arrived ahead of me so that's how he came to be waiting for me.

We lived in Rutland. I don't think it's a county anymore. I think it's been encompassed by another one. It's between Leicestershire and Nottinghamshire. It's actually very pleasant there, and I made quite a few friends. There were two or three other ladies—some were Canadian and some were English—but they were married to Canadians of course. There was quite a group of us that met together in the village, and we used to have our little knitting and sewing parties with our children. My husband bought a car over there, and we could drive to my family's home. My parents were happy to have us back in England, of course, and so was I. They had a chance to meet my younger son, David.

We came back to Canada in 1955 because my husband wanted to get out of the forces. It was hard to give up living in England. But he had to come back to Canada to get discharged, and besides jobs weren't that good in Britain. So it was just as well that we came back. We had a lovely voyage across the ocean from England.

Irvin put in to come to the West Coast because I wanted to be near the sea. I'd never been to the Canadian West Coast but I wanted to see it. So we came to BC, and lived on Sea Island near Vancouver. We brought back the car we'd bought in England, and it was a long drive from Halifax to the West Coast. We came mostly through the States because the Rogers Pass wasn't finished then. It was a wonderful trip.

In 1957 my daughter was born so we bought a house on Sea Island and lived there for awhile. Then my husband was posted to Comox on Vancouver Island. First we lived on Marsden Road in Courtenay, then in the village of Comox and finally we lived on the base. After that, my husband was posted to Prince Edward Island—all the way back to the east coast of Canada. We were there for four years.

I actually didn't mind it, although I wouldn't have liked to live there permanently. I didn't like the winters but the people were very friendly. After living there for four years, we drove back to the Comox Valley. We lived in an apartment for a month, and then we bought the house I'm living in now.

My husband was a flight engineer in the Air Force but he ended up being medically released after he had an accident when he was flying. After that, he found one or two jobs doing different things. And then just when he was happy working with the cadets down at the Spit in Comox, he found out he had cancer. He died in 1975 when he was only fifty-one years old. It was sad, very hard on everybody really, something you don't expect. So that's the way it's been.

And you sort of pick your pieces up. I've been busy. Well, I worked at different things at different times, but I never really worked all the time because when you have children, you can't do that. Since 1971, I have lived in this house that we bought when we returned to the Comox Valley. I had never lived in a house this long before. Even in England, I think the longest we lived in one house was ten years.

When I was having some work done on this house, my older son asked me, "Mother, why don't you think about getting another house somewhere?" I simply said, "I like this area." And I don't think I'll ever want to go. I know my neighbours here. I can walk to town if I need to. At home I love to listen to music, and I have my garden. I just feel that I am away from everyone, and that's what I like.

Marjorie Stephenson

"HE SEEMED TO BE ALL HAT AND TIE"

Marjorie Stephenson was born in Germany. When World War I broke out, her father was interned in Germany as a prisoner of war. Her mother took her three children back to England to await his return.

When war was declared I was walking down the driveway, and I felt my stomach drop. For several months before the war started, my parents and I were boarding at Linfold Farm, as my parents were looking for a house or land to buy. Since I liked the farmer and his wife, Ron and Elsie, I immediately joined up with the Land Army. We had no electricity, and we had to pump our water from the well. We had twenty cows to milk by hand. I was the only one who could get near the bull. He didn't like the farmer at all. I worked seven days a week—looking after the cows and chickens, and in the fields haying and harvesting. It was hard work but I enjoyed the variety of jobs. Being on a farm we were able to augment our food rations, which was helpful. We also received extra rations for manual labour.

We had quite a few dogfights (involving fighter planes) over us, and three bombs dropped in a field quite close to the house, but no major damage was done. The leaded windows of the four-hundred-year-old farmhouse bulged out, but were not broken. The last two years of the war we had doodlebugs come over. They were unmanned missiles. You were told to lie flat anytime you heard the engine cut off, because they were coming down right away. We got caught one morning in the barnyard when it was foggy, but it came down about a mile away so we felt rather foolish.

There were two army camps each side of the farm, and we received a lot of help from them in the haying and harvesting season. When our tractor became stuck in the mud (which was quite often) they would send over a Bren Gun carrier to pull us out. Archie, my future husband, was stationed at one of the camps. I met him in the pub in the village. He was a Quarter-master, with the South Saskatchewan Regiment.

I remember one day the farmer's wife and I were on top of the wagon laying the sheaves, with about six people pitching them up (some were experts and some not). Archie was very critical of our having two people on the load. He complained, "They could load it without anybody up there." They had their chance when the farmer's wife, Elsie, and I left to do the milking. It was the only load that tipped before it got to the barn. We reared a gaggle of geese one year, and Archie bought them for the troops' Christmas dinner. They took them up on the Sussex Downs to kill and pluck them. If you have ever plucked a goose you will realize what a job that was.

I taught Archie to play squash, and he couldn't beat me, so he asked me to marry him. He had asked me several times, but I didn't want to leave England. When the war came to an end, I didn't want him to go, so finally I said yes, I would marry him. We were married March 8, 1946 in Kirdford church. I didn't wear white, because it was too difficult to get clothing rations. We had a week's honeymoon in Bournemouth. I had a baby Austin which I called Polly. I drove my father to the wedding but left Polly at the garage, so no one would tamper with her. I then took a taxi to the church. We had a great reception in the vicarage, then we drove down to Bournemouth and parked Polly in front of the hotel. The next morning we went outside and found some old shoes tied onto the back of Polly. So everyone knew we were newly-weds.

It was very difficult to leave to come to Canada. I had to leave my dog behind. I also had a very nice little Welsh pony that I considered mine, and I had to leave him as well. My sister went to Brazil to live, just before I left, so it was hard to leave my mother and father. Archie was a schoolteacher before the war, and he looked into teaching jobs in England, but he didn't think it would work out. I didn't think I would like to live on the flat prairies of Saskatchewan, where my husband was from. A friend of mine in Kirdford had a cousin who was the principal of Brentwood College in Victoria, so Archie was able to get a job as teacher and housemaster at the College.

Archie came out ahead of me on the *Aquitania* in May, and then I came out on the same ship in August 1946. It was nearly all war brides, and those of us who didn't have children were put on D-deck in hammocks. Some of the war brides were from Holland and Belgium, so all the announcements were given in three languages, which made it very difficult to hear what was being said. Everybody kept talking when their language was not on. But it was quite chummy.

It was an awful train trip across Canada; I am not a good traveller and was quite sick. It was very hot in the daytime, and if you opened a window you were blackened with soot. The train had trouble getting up a hill the night before we got to Winnipeg. I thought all my bones would be disconnected, the way it kept starting and stopping. Archie met me in Winnipeg. He had booked a private drawing room on a Pullman train and it pulled out just before ours pulled in, as we were three hours late. I got off the train in Winnipeg, not knowing if he would be there. I ran along the platform and found him flying up to meet me. He seemed to be all hat and tie. He was able to get on the war brides' train, and we chased the other train across the prairie. We caught up with it in Moose Jaw, where we transferred to it, and were able to use Archie's reserved drawing room—very deluxe.

Archie's friends met us in Vancouver, and then we boarded the ferry and came over to Victoria. We went straight out to Brentwood College. It had a wonderful view, overlooking the Saanich Inlet, and we lived right in the College. Most of the staff were new and from England, too, so I never really felt homesick. I didn't find it very different here from England, as it seemed so English here.

My parents came out to visit me in 1947. They were at the College when it burnt to the ground. We lost almost everything but fortunately had a little insurance. The staff tried to keep Brentwood going, and that fall we opened up in the Shawnigan Lake School. They lent us Copeman House. In 1948 we moved to Pat Bay High School (which was empty) and the staff rented the White House (three families and extras). It was a lot of fun. We had our first daughter Wendy in 1948, and then unexpected twins in 1952—a son and daughter, Penny and Ronald. What a surprise. Archie later became principal of Belmont Junior-Senior High School and stayed there until he retired. I love to go back to England and have been back several times, but I do love to come back to Canada and my home in Victoria.

Vi Pearn

"GOODBYE LONDON, I
HOPE I'LL SEE YOU AGAIN"

*Vi Pearn was born in Wimbledon, Surrey.
At the age of fifteen, Vi began work at a bake
shop. Two years later she got a job
as a telephone operator at the
London Telephone Service.*

W hen I heard that war was declared, I had this sort of sinking feeling and said to myself, "Oh, no." But after awhile, we found that nothing much was happening; bombs were not dropping in our area. We had to get up and go to work every day. Everything was normal in that respect, except for rationing of things like food and clothing. And that's why we went dancing when we could. We lived. We didn't just bury ourselves under the air-raid shelters. I was still working as a telephone operator. Because our work was essential service, we couldn't get out unless we were under twenty-one. Many of the girls managed to leave by going into the Land Army or joining the forces, but I couldn't because I was twenty-one that year.

Keeping things going in communications was vital. If bombs fell on certain telephone lines, they would rupture, and then the engineers had to get in there and fix them as soon as they could. It was a lot of work, important work, and that is why you could not get out. Telephone operators used to receive signals from France, messages to somebody on the south coast when they knew planes were leaving France and coming over. Then in London we would get a call from Brighton or wherever it was. A telephone operator would plug right into a certain exchange on our switchboard, and would say, "An air raid in progress heading for London."

So then you were prepared when an air raid was imminent and was coming over in the daytime. Willesdon exchange in Moresdon was a place with a lot of factories that had been turned into munitions factories, and certain telephone operators were given a list of all the factories. They quickly phoned these people because with the din in those factories, the people couldn't hear the sirens too well, so we'd have to phone them and tell them that an air raid was in progress. I was one of the people chosen to do this. But most of us had a turn at it. Heinz factory was on our switchboard and so was Rotax where my brother worked. The factories were always glad to know because they also had their safeguards to put into place.

We also had to take part in the fire watch for our telephone office. It was rotated so that there'd be an engineer and a few of the girls. We would stay down in the basement of the telephone exchange. This was the safest area, and they put up bunks there so you could sleep. You were trained how to use these stirrup pumps and how to extinguish the little incendiary bombs that might come on a track which many of the telephone exchanges had.

We used to play cards and make the most of those times on fire watch, which would come up about once a month. These fire watches were in addition to our regular shifts. We'd stay overnight, then go home the next day and sleep. About half the time you could sleep while on fire watch, but sometimes you couldn't, because if the raids were on, you had to be ready to go quickly and extinguish any fires. I never did have to put a fire out.

Sometimes the bombing was only at night but it could also happen during the day. When the Battle of Britain was on, I was out at a telephone exchange near Epping Forest, and there were air raids going on in the daytime. Bombs were dropping, and the chestnuts were falling off the trees because of the gunfire. The artillery guns were trying to shoot down the German planes.

Often bombers passed over while we were working, sometimes quite a few. I saw a Messerschmitt go right past the telephone exchange, with our little fighters catching up to it. It was exciting to see this during our lunch hour. But I don't think it penetrated how serious it really was. You didn't really feel scared. Sometimes you did, but not usually.

Only once did I sleep in an air-raid shelter. Eventually my parents got one of those Morrison shelters, something like a dining room table, only metal. I hated to sleep under it, but my mother made me sleep there sometimes. We always had our suitcases packed in case we had to get out in a hurry. Some people say it was the best time of their life. Looking back on it, it wasn't all bad. But it was grim, very grim. We were a bit fatalistic, and being so young, we would think: if one of those bombs has our name on it—so what? You lived from day to day.

We didn't have it as bad as some people, but nevertheless there was everything from the unexploded types of bombs to those that came down by parachute and devastated wide areas. But I didn't pay too much attention to land mines. I just prayed that we wouldn't get hit by one. You might not get to sleep right away but eventually you went to sleep and didn't think anymore about it. And you woke up the next morning.

Once in the cinema, my friend and I were watching a Carmen Miranda film. The air-raid sirens went off and we didn't know whether we'd stay or not. We decided, "Oh well, we'll just see what happens." But all of a sudden the whole cinema shook really badly, almost like an earthquake. So we got down behind the seats. Then I remember getting up, and the first thing we did was light up a cigarette! That was one time we were a little bit scared. The bomb seemed to have gone off not far away. We came out to see the devastation, but it was further away than we thought, although the explosion had shattered everything all around us.

I remember reading about one old lady in London. She was bombed out, and they got the husband out. But when the warden wanted to get her out, she said, "I can't go now, I've gotta get me 'at on!" She was in her nineties but she couldn't go out without her hat on.

My family never had an incident where we had to evacuate, except once when I wasn't home. When I did come home, the road was barred, but I went under the barrier because there was nobody there to tell you that you weren't supposed to. My family was gone because of an unexploded bomb that had come down in the daytime, but I didn't know this. So I stayed and slept there all night. Nobody knew I was there.

I put lights on but you couldn't see lights from the outside because we had total blackout. After awhile, I started phoning around to try and find out where my parents were, but in the end one of them phoned the house to see if I was home. That's how I found out. I was alright but I was severely reprimanded by the air-raid warden for coming through the barrier. It was my fault. I wouldn't call this a comical incident. It was a stupid thing to do. But of course all those things stick in your mind.

Whenever there was any problem during the war, people helped each other. One night when there was an air raid, a bomb went right through our neighbour's house. The young man of the house was just walking between the kitchen and the living room, and some shrapnel coming through the roof hit him. His mother phoned my mother, and we went over there like a shot to help. He was severely injured. We didn't realize it at the time because he was conscious and talking, but a piece of shrapnel had entered his brain. He eventually died. Throughout the war we were all in the same boat, and there was camaraderie with your friends and neighbours. When the war ended, the camaraderie stopped too.

I also joined the Red Cross and trained to work as a volunteer nurse. Then I was able to go to a nearby hospital in my spare time and look after patients, children sometimes. After my regular shift at work, I'd go home quickly and change into my uniform. Then I transformed into a nurse. But when a patient called out, "Nurse!" I never answered. They'd have to call out, "Hey, you there!" That was funny. For me, nursing was a nice break, and I enjoyed it very much.

In 1941 I met my husband-to-be, Harry, while I was on a two-week vacation at a holiday camp. He was stationed quite nearby at Boxgrove which was near Arundel Castle. It was about six months before we became serious about each other. He had a previous girlfriend whom he was getting over so it took awhile.

I kept in touch with Harry by letter. He got along with my family, although they were never that close. But I was over twenty-one, and they never said, "Oh you shouldn't" or "You can't" or "We don't like the idea of you going out with a Canadian." The Americans they didn't like so much, but the Canadians were alright, funnily enough.

We were married on January 9, 1944. I borrowed my best friend's gown but it looked different on her than it did on me! She had a nicer figure than I had. Lots of girls got married in a little suit or a pretty dress but my friend wanted me to have her wedding gown, and we were basically about the same size. I really wasn't keen on a big white wedding. I thought it was a bit showy during wartime, but my parents wanted me to have a white wedding. There weren't too many people, maybe fifty at the most. We were married in St. John's Anglican Church in Wembley. I had two bridesmaids who were friends of mine and still are. We had our reception in a tea room, the Tudor Tea Room, I think it was called. It was just a lunch, not an evening reception.

We went to Bournemouth for our honeymoon. Bournemouth is a lovely seaside resort, really a rather quiet place, but with a lovely dance pavilion. They had afternoon tea dances. But everything closed down at nine o'clock at night. We stayed at a house that had been converted into a hotel. It was a nice little place, the sort of hotel where retired people would go when there was no war. We had a week there.

Once you married a Canadian, you knew you were going to Canada. It was in your mind, but you didn't plan much, although any time somebody would give you a gift, you hoped it was something for your home. I didn't worry about it much, but when the war ended, I thought, "Well this is it. We're going." I really didn't have butterflies in my stomach until I received the letter from Canada House with the date I would be sailing on the *Queen Mary*. My mother took me out that day. I really felt kind of bad. I had very mixed emotions about leaving England and going to Canada, but it was just that one day when it really hit me that I was going. I had two week's notice before leaving. Not much time, and I had kept on working. But in the end I thought, "I'm going to have to quit work while I have time to pack!"

My mother came up to London and said good-bye there. I was able to leave the hostel for a few hours and make a few phone calls. I phoned an aunt of mine up in Scotland and kissed a few lamp posts goodbye. It was a "Good-bye London, I hope I'll see you again" type of thing in my mind. My mother came only for the one day because nobody knew when we would be leaving. The war was over but they still kept everything hush-hush.

We left on May 22nd, 1946 and arrived in Halifax on the 27th. It was lovely on the *Queen Mary*. I was seasick only on the first day. After that, I thoroughly enjoyed myself. I had lovely walks every day and bought souvenirs. I had cookies which we hadn't much of in England. And there was other sweet stuff like chocolate bars. It was also lovely to have some fresh fruit. I quite enjoyed the meals, and the weather was good. Coming in May, it was really lovely.

Vincent Massey, the Canadian High Commissioner to Britain, was on our ship. When we arrived in Halifax around suppertime, they had the red carpet out and a military band to greet Mr. Massey. But as soon as the ceremony was over, they rolled up the red carpet and put it away. Only the girls who were going to be living in the Nova Scotia area disembarked that night. The following day the rest of us got off the ship. The wonderful thing was that every woman was escorted by military personnel. If there were two children, there'd be a soldier with the children and one with the mother, carrying a bag for her. It was very well arranged. I thought that was wonderful. They had to take you to where they had your luggage, and then you went to where they had large signs with your initials in great big letters.

When you were on the train, you met a different set of girls. I started making friends with other girls who were going to Winnipeg, which was my destination, too. I couldn't believe it when we'd go to sleep at night passing this vast body of water. A great big lake it was. We asked the porter, and he said, "Oh it's Lake Superior." Wake up in the morning, still Lake Superior! I said, "This train is going the wrong way. It's going alongside the ocean." It was such a phenomenon because we'd never travelled farther than from London to Scotland, which was about five hundred miles, to visit relatives. Oh the vastness of this new country!

The morning we arrived in Winnipeg, we'd already had our breakfast on the train. Then it was all utter confusion, utter confusion. This was because they allowed the husbands on the platforms. We'd never seen them out of uniform. That was really a confusing few minutes, but when Harry and I spotted each other it was fine. Then I met the rest of the family who had come to meet us.

After that, we all piled into a taxi, and to heck with the luggage. We would be getting that later. My mother-in-law had a huge meal ready. But I couldn't eat. I just had a cup of tea. They must have thought I was awful but I couldn't eat. I'd just had a real good breakfast on the train. This would be about ten o'clock maybe, and the family was starving because they hadn't had their breakfast. I always remember that.

I hadn't seen Harry for nearly a year. He had gone home in July of 1945, and I came over in May the next year. My husband stayed on in the Army for awhile, in the pay office. In the meantime he was looking for a civilian job, which he found with the Grain Exchange in Winnipeg. Harry really wanted to be a certified accountant. He was good with accounting but he didn't take the course. He could have done it through the Army but he didn't. So he worked at the Grain Exchange, and then eventually got into the Royal Bank in Winnipeg. It was quite a good job, actually.

Houses were scarce when I arrived, so we lived in an apartment. Actually, we had two rooms in a rooming house. I had never seen or heard of a rooming house in my life. We had quite a nice big room with a kitchenette. My husband had found it and got it all ready for us before I arrived. We went there that first day after breakfast. Oh yes, the family was looking forward to showing me the place. It was located in quite a nice part of Winnipeg near Red River.

I liked Canada and enjoyed going shopping in Winnipeg. It was a lovely time of the year. I remember that some of the girls didn't like Winnipeg, but I didn't expect it to be like England. My father said to me before I left, "Remember. When in Rome, do what the Romans do." I said, "Oh, and the same in Canada? Okay." I got along very well with Harry's mother and father.

I had no intention of working over here. I thought I'd worked enough. I did work eventually but not when I first came. I wanted to have children and settle down, get into a house eventually. We had four sons. A year after I arrived, our first son was born. When our second son came along, we were living in one of those "peace-time" homes they had built for the servicemen. We were on the list, and we got a nice bungalow with two bedrooms and a full basement. It was brand new.

I was quite happy and busy with my children. I had joined the war brides club right away. It was called the "British Wives Club" in

Winnipeg. We did a lot of entertaining at old folks' homes and other charity work, too. We had lots of drives to raise money for children's funds and Christmas funds, including the Christmas Cheer Board of Winnipeg.

With my small children, I didn't have too much time but it was nice to go to these meetings and laugh at all the mistakes we made when we came to Canada—the names of things that were different and meant different things. We had a real good giggle. We were all in the same boat; we used to enjoy that. I belonged to the Winnipeg War Brides Club for thirty-eight years, and now I'm enjoying my membership with the Vancouver Island War Brides after moving to Victoria ten years ago.

Doris Johnson

"BANANAS AND WHITE
BREAD WERE WONDERFUL
TO HAVE AGAIN"

Doris Johnson was born in Dover.
She had one older sister and brother. She was a
young adult when the war was declared.

I volunteered to go into the Air Force, just before girls were conscripted for the war effort. My parents were very much against my joining up. I used part of the Air Force travel warrant to go to London and visit my sister north of London, not far from Wembley. When I got there, she said, "Dot, why on earth do you want to join the Air Force?" By then I was starting to get cold feet. I stayed there for the day and when my brother-in-law came home for lunch, he asked me to go see his boss that afternoon. I asked why, and he said there was a job waiting for me.

I thought there was nothing to lose in going, so I went to see him, and I immediately got the job. I had used part of the warrant on the railway, so I wrote the Air Force and told them unforeseen things had happened since I left home, and that I was unable to join. I said I would reimburse them for the warrant, but I never heard from them again.

I was then trained as a mechanical engineering inspector. The job dealt with a lot of fine measurements. I was one of the first people to work on radar when it was still in the secret room, although I never actually saw it together. I enjoyed my work, and I guess it must have shown because I was asked to work on radar. It was very exacting work with micrometers and gauges and I enjoyed it.

I lived with my sister while I worked, and I intended it to be temporary but she and her husband wanted me there so I stayed. We were bombed out in 1940. We had a bomb land right in the front garden. It was a wonder that we were not hurt, as it was a bomb that was full of shrapnel. They had told us that time-bombs were being dropped and to make sure to keep a suitcase and some food in the hallway, ready to run. So my sister and I did that, and when this bomb dropped it went right through everything, even all our clothes that were in the hallway. My sister had a tin trunk with canned food which she had gradually saved, and the shrapnel went right through the tin trunk and right through the tins. She had two little children who were in bed at the time of the bombing. The older one, who was two years old, was sleeping under the bed with a mattress on top and a mattress underneath;

the younger one was in a crib. When the blast came, the child underneath the bed was fine but the younger one, John, in the crib was just smothered in glass. I remember that I climbed over the door and grabbed John before he could roll in the splinters of glass. We were sure that he had glass in his eyes because he couldn't open them. It wasn't long before a doctor arrived on the scene. He said, "Of course he can't see you; you have the flashlight shining in his eyes."

We spent the rest of the night in a shelter with some neighbours but it was very cramped and hot. The next morning we went over to the church hall and had some toast and tea. Then we stayed in a self-contained flat which was commandeered by the councils. We stayed there for about two years, until the house was put together again.

I didn't feel the effect of the bomb at the time but I did afterwards. I remember the next day my sister and her husband both went out, and I was alone with the children. Her husband went over to the house to get his tools, and he found that somebody had already taken his tools. In the bedrooms, somebody had already unscrewed the electric fireplaces, waiting for night-time to take them. When my sister went to get her sheets and things out of the cupboards, they were all filled with holes. When I had to go back to work a couple of days later I was feeling shaky. I guess I started to realize what had happened, especially going to work with my coat peppered with holes, and the same dress I had on the Saturday night. Everything was rationed, so you couldn't just go out and buy a new dress and coat.

The rationing was very tight. If we put all our coupons together, we would have a tiny roast on the weekend. I remember my sister sometimes bought what you call sausage rolls. They were like dried up old beef in pastry, but she would heat them through and put some oxo on them for dinner with potatoes. Potatoes were readily available, but meat and sugar were harder to come by. We got used to living with less and didn't expect otherwise. If there were oranges or anything scarce available, we lined up for them, then we gave them to the children. Once in awhile there would be an egg or so for sale and there were powdered eggs we could eat if we were hungry.

Most of the men had gone to war. My brother-in-law was home because he was on a reserved occupation. The women were not only conscripted to work, we were also conscripted for fire watch at night. I was working from seven in the morning to seven at night everyday, except Sunday when I got off at four. After awhile they managed to give us one day off every eight days, but the employees became mixed up and would turn up for work when it was the day they were supposed to be off. We didn't get any time to do anything for a long time. Being on fire watch was pretty hard. We'd come home from work and it was getting cold at night, and we would have to go out again in the cold.

My parents in Dover were in a dangerous spot because it was just twenty miles across the strait to the continent. They were shelling Dover from the French coast. When I did get a weekend off and wanted to go home, I had to get permission from the police to visit my parents. They would check my mum's house on Sunday to see if I had left to go back, so I had Friday night and Saturday, at the most, to visit. When I got on a bus they would want to see my identification. When I got off at the station, they had to see my identification again. They made a note of where I said I had been, and they would go and check to make sure I had been there.

I met my future husband, Albert, in Dover in 1943, on a weekend I had off. I was walking down the street on Saturday and had stopped to look in the music store. Suddenly a voice behind me asked if I liked music. I looked up thinking it was a stupid question, otherwise why would I be looking in a music store. Anyway, I said yes, and we started to talk about music and the next thing I knew he was asking me to go to the show. So we went to see *Madame Curie,* then we had dinner and went out dancing in the evening. He was looking for company and I was, too, in a way, although I didn't realize it at the time. He was stationed at Hythe, not many miles from Dover. The funny part was I couldn't take him home, because I had just met him. If I had known him all my life I would have been inclined to take him home, but I didn't dare go home and say to mum, "This is so and so."

He was going to spend the night at the Salvation Army, which most of the men did when not on duty. The buses had stopped early so we had to walk home. By the time we reached the Salvation Army it was about ten o'clock, and they had put the lights out and closed up. So that night he had to sleep in the shelters on the seafront. There were gun emplacements there. When the men changed shifts, they put a coat over him to keep him warm. During the night, a shell hit the Salvation Army, and Al always said that I saved his life by keeping him out till after ten o'clock.

We went out for about a year, but I didn't see much of him during that time. We saw each other when we could and we wrote a lot. When D-day came he was overseas. Then he was injured, although not badly, and came back to the hospital when the war was fairly close to being over.

We were married in 1945 after the war had ended, in a little old Anglican church called St. Andrew's in Dover. We had a fairly big wedding. I really didn't want a large one, but I knew I was going away and that it was mum and dad's wish. Everything was catered for. That was the easiest way to go, because restaurants were allowed a certain amount of food. It took months to get enough raisins for the cake with everybody putting their issues together. Then a friend made the cake and iced it. I bought a second-hand dress made of white cream satin, and it fitted as though I had it made for me. The head-dress was all soft feathers. I wanted to bring it over to Canada but mum wouldn't part with it.

My parents didn't like the idea of my going to Canada. My husband had said that he would stay in England if I wanted, but I couldn't imagine doing that. I thought I could adapt more easily than Al could. It hit mum and dad hard since I was the youngest child. I lost my mum a year after I came to Canada. I went back for the first time in 1969. My dad remarried but he died before I got back.

My husband was from Gull Lake, Saskatchewan, but he had left home before the war. I came alone to Canada, as he was on leave and already in Gull Lake. At the end of February, a few months after our wedding, I travelled to London where there was a large house for the war brides who were going overseas. Once we got there we were under military rule, and had to do whatever the authorities at the house said. It was supposed to have been a short stay of up to two days, but there was some delay so it was a bit longer. From there they took us by bus to Liverpool where we boarded the ship. Bands were playing. That was the worst part, I think. I had an awful feeling; I felt like running back down. I thought, well I am here now and this is it!

It was a war bride ship called the *Letitia,* and I shared a cabin with four other girls. I met some women on board but we never kept up a correspondence. Coming to a strange country, it was enough just trying to adapt to the new ways and keeping in touch with family back home. I had promised my mum and dad that I would keep my fare to go back, because I had been earning good money during the war. But you know when we got over here and were starting from scratch, we needed to use the money.

The trip took ten days altogether, coming right across to Halifax then to Saskatchewan on the train. I lost my luggage when I got on board ship. I had a little bag with me with a few odds and ends in it, but my luggage was down in the hold somewhere. Then one day a steward came and said, "Mrs. Johnson, I think I have found your case." He brought me a black bag, like the old-style doctor's medicine bag. He was so happy when he brought it up. I looked in and found my husband's long underwear. So I still didn't have much in the way of a change of clothes.

When we arrived at Halifax, we were supposed to stay put and wait for our escort to carry our suitcases to the train. But I didn't stay. I hurried right up the nearest street from the train depot. I had some money that looked to me like buttons, which I didn't know the value of. I went into a store and picked out a skirt and blouse to change into, and told them to help themselves to the money. I hurried back and got back to the platform just in time. It was a good job I moved quickly. We weren't supposed to do that but I was desperate. I had to meet all my new relatives and I had no change of clothes.

The trip across Canada seemed to take forever. There was one station we stopped at for quite awhile, and they had bananas for sale. I hadn't seen a banana for years so I stocked up on them and they tasted so good. When I was settled into Gull Lake I kept going to the store to buy bananas. I hadn't realized how much I needed a banana. I put them out for the family as I wanted to share them, but it seemed I would turn around and they would be all gone again. Bananas and white bread were wonderful to have again; the bread in England was grey. We had white bread on the ship, but not being too hungry at that time—between homesickness and seasickness—I didn't feel like eating.

It was difficult meeting my new in-laws for the first time, because they all arrived at once. It was overwhelming. My husband met my train at two in the morning and about eight o'clock the next morning, my mother-in-law was knocking on the door saying the company had arrived. All I could see was a sea of faces and I didn't know who was who. My husband was from a family of eleven, with their spouses and their children. I have often wondered what I said. I could have said or done anything because it was so overwhelming.

We stayed two weeks with my husband's relatives, then got on the train for BC. My husband's leave was up, and he had to get to BC to be discharged from the Royal Army Service Corps. He was a truck driver most of the time in the war. I was sure glad that my husband had firmly made up his mind to come to BC, because there were relatives offering him some land in Saskatchewan to stay there. He had been working on Vancouver Island before he left for the war, so that was lucky for me. I don't know if I could have stuck it out living in Saskatchewan, with there being so many relatives around, not that I have anything against the relatives. They were all very nice, but when we were on our own, neither of us had anyone to take sides with, and we had a lot of laughs together. I remember that I told the baker not to call anymore because I would bake the bread. Then it turned out so heavy, my husband said he would put it under the bridge to hold the bridge up. Things like that were funny to us, but I would have been embarrassed if relatives had been around.

When I got to Parksville, people were really kind. When we first arrived, we rented a cabin at Parksands near the beach in Parksville. The cabin had a little wood cook stove, sort of like a little camp stove, and every time I turned around, the fire would go out. I would be thumbing through the cookbook trying to decide what to have for supper, and then it would be too late as the fire would be out. Still, I loved Parksville and the beach.

We bought a piece of property, which seemed to be in the sticks, but really wasn't far up the road. Then we couldn't get nails to build with, and there was nothing to rent so we had to buy a house. That meant we had to go pretty short of things since we were starting from scratch. People at home knowing I was travelling, gave us cash, and I only had a few pillow cases that I brought with me. I didn't have anything like a bridal shower so we needed a lot. But we learned to get by, cleaning our teeth with baking soda and things like that.

I found using different currency in Canada difficult. My husband asked me to go and see the bank manager to arrange financing for our first property. The bank manager seemed to understand my difficulty with the Canadian currency. He had been in the forces in the First World War so he was really kind and quite helpful. Still, it was quite an experience. The lady who worked in the funny little post office told me that two bits was twenty-five cents and a dime was ten cents. She was always anxious to see what was in my parcels from England. She was so curious that I used to open my parcels right in the post office and show her. By that time I had a girl and boy, Judy and Brian, and I would show her the little dresses and outfits that had arrived. Ten years later, we were blessed with another daughter, Heather.

When the girls were in Girl Guides, I knew they needed leaders so I became a leader and enjoyed it. I had always been interested in Guiding. If I was going to a Guide meeting, I would always put a rice pudding and a stew in the oven. Over time I became a bit wiser about the stove, and I would put some coal in the fire to keep it going. I liked Guiding and over the years was a Brown Owl, a Girl Guide Captain and a District Commissioner.

We bought a corner store after Al my husband got out of logging. We called it Al's Corner Store. Of course there were long hours in that and little money, but we stayed with the store for five years. Later we developed a mobile home park and campsite in Parksville which we called Golden Dawn. Al and I had been married forty-three years when Al passed away in 1988. Being without Al and on my own is something I don't think I will get used to. It is very difficult at times. I now live nearer to my two daughters and their children in Victoria, and I enjoy their company. I also enjoy the company of fellow war brides who all shared similar experiences. A wonderful bond of friendship has developed over the years.

Audrey Waddy

"IT'S ONE OF THOSE
CANADIANS, HE'S COME
FOR WATER"

Audrey Waddy was born into a large family of six children in Tinsely Green, not far from London. She remembers her mother sewing beautiful clothes for the children.

W ar broke out when I was thirteen, and I remember that day very clearly. We had been at church and we were coming home from the service. Mother had gone ahead and we were dawdling along behind when a man pulled up in his car and asked us if we knew war had broken out. We quickly ran home and told our mother that war had been declared but mother already knew; the wireless was on when we ran into the house.

Actually, we knew that war was imminent, since we had recently made blackout curtains for our windows. As well, we had been issued identification cards, ration books and gas masks. The masks were horrible things and we had to carry them wherever we went, even to school. If we went out without our identification card and gas masks, and a warden stopped us, we would be sent home. At nighttime we hung the gas masks on our bedpost. We made cloth covers for the gas masks and carried the bags over our shoulders. At school during sewing classes, morning and lunch breaks, we knitted gloves, scarfs and balaclavas for the troops. We were constantly knitting.

To reach my senior school it was necessary to walk through the airport to board the train. It is now the London-Gatwick airport; during the war the airport was a Royal Air Force Station. The airport was officially opened in 1936, and the vast number of planes were German. So the Germans knew all about the airport and we knew that we would be attacked once war broke out. When I went through the airport on my way to school the guards would demand that I stop and identify myself. They would say: "Halt, who goes there?" and they would show their rifles. If we did not have our pass we would not be allowed to enter. The large barrage balloons, like the Good Year Blimp, were up surrounding the airport. It was a fighter station and the Spitfire aircraft took off from there. It was quite frightening actually, especially when you were walking in the dark and someone barked: "Halt, who goes there?" and a rifle and bayonet were pointed at you.

I remember very clearly the first bombing, as it was in the middle of the night, December 1939. I shared a room with my sister and suddenly the room came alive with the banging and crashing sounds of anti-aircraft guns firing at bombers. We sat up in bed and put the sheets over our heads. I can recall my mother rushing into the bedroom as we cried out to her and asked her what was going on. Our mother told us to calm down, that the Germans were trying to bomb the airport.

I remember our mother ordering us to get up, grab our pillows and run for the dining room table. Sometimes we would stay under the table all night. One night two bombs collided in mid-air, and the light and flames of the exploding bombs could be seen through our bedroom window. Those experiences were really frightening, and our mother did her best to calm us down, because she had experienced some of the horror during the First World War.

Several of our neighbours had built bomb shelters and had died in their shelters. So you really didn't know where you were going to be safe. However, we chose to stay under the table rather than in the garden in a shelter. The bombing usually started about five o'clock in the evening and didn't quit until six in the morning. We called those the night raids. Constantly, night after night! Of course there were bombing raids during the day, even when we were at school, so we had to hide under our desks during the day.

I think my mother was quite relieved when I finished school, as she was concerned about me being at school when the bombs were being dropped. Every time I said goodbye and left for school, I could see the worry on her face that I might not return home from school. I also worried that our house might not be there when I got home. It was a terrible feeling, and each time when we said goodbye, I did not know if it would be the last time we would be a family.

The Germans did bomb the airport but they never really damaged the landing field. They bombed all around the field. I was riding my bicycle over to my father's farm one Saturday morning to ride the horses. On the way a plane came down at me. He came straight towards me and I could see his face in the cockpit of the plane. That's how low he was. I flung myself into the nearest ditch and the next thing I knew he had fired his guns right over my head. The bullets hit one of the homes a few miles away. You would have thought that when he saw a young person on a bicycle that he wouldn't fire; but no, he came right at me. Actually he was so low that the guns at the airport began firing, but the guns could not swivel low enough to hit the plane. The soldiers had to rip off the sandbags protecting the turrets. He came in low on the road and then zoomed up and away.

I remember saying our prayers in assembly at school every morning. We prayed for friends and schoolmates that had been lost in the war. I remember the pain at losing a dear schoolfriend. She and her entire family had been killed the night before. Her house had not been too far from ours. It was very sad and we never got over the feeling that we could be next.

Our rations were meagre and I just don't know how our mother managed. There were times when we craved certain foods. Although we had a dairy farm, everything that we produced, including the milk from the cows, had to go to the British Marketing Board. We could not keep anything for ourselves since every product was itemized: how much milk came from the cows, vegetables and so on. It was a real headache for my father because everything had to be catalogued and was collected daily. We had only our rations to live on and the few extra vegetables that my father grew. I think we practically lived on vegetables and powdered eggs, because we had so very little meat. We craved chocolate; our monthly ration was two ounces per person. Each month we would go into the sweet store for our chocolate ration. That was a real treat. We had one fresh egg a month, and I remember that once my egg was bad. I boiled it, found it to be rotten—and cried. We did not see any citrus fruit during the entire war; however, we had some apples in addition to the vegetables that we grew in our garden.

We used to buy clothing coupons from families with a lot of children, if they did not use them all. As teenagers we would buy the coupons to get extra clothes. We had to mend our own stockings with a hook and we would do this night after night, mending, so that we could wear them the next day to work.

In the early years we thought we were losing the war. However, Sir Winston Churchill was wonderful. We listened to his speeches on the wireless and most nights he would come on and say: "We will fight in the ditches, we will fight in the streets, we will fight in the trenches. We will not give in." As young people we knew that to be the truth. As a matter of fact, a German plane crashed near our backyard, and my sister and I kept the pilot up a tree with a pitchfork until the wardens came and got him down. We could see he was in pain, but no way would we let him down until the authorities came.

One day in 1941, while I was crossing the airport, I met my future husband. The Royal Canadian Artillery were stationed around the airport, and the Canadians were in the farm fields behind our house. They had erected a Bofors gun tower there. My sister and I had many friends at the airport, and my sister would go to dances there on Friday and Saturday nights. She often went by herself as I remember saying no to her on many occasions. On Christmas 1941, my mother encouraged me to go to the dance with my sister. I agreed to go, and that was the night that I met my husband-to-be. I had seen him once before as he was stationed in the gun tower behind our house.

I remember that he had come to the house to get some water for the crew in the gun tower. He had been doing this for several months while I was at school. My mother liked him and welcomed him in our home. As well, he often used our electric iron to press uniforms. He would make two shillings sixpence on every uniform he ironed. He was always wanting to make a bit of extra money for leave, so he pressed his buddies' uniforms.

One Sunday morning just prior to Christmas, there was a knock on the door. I said to my mother, "I will get it, mum." When I opened the door he was standing there. The first thing he said was: "Hi babe, I have come for some water." I replied that he should help himself. My mother asked, "Who is that Audrey?" and I replied, "It's one of those Canadians and he has come for some water." She then asked: "Is it Bobby by any chance?" and I asked,

"Who is Bobby?" Again my mother said, "If it is Bobby, tell him I said hello." He was standing there with his water pails and said, "Yes, I'm Bobby." I then left and he went and got his water, and I did not speak to him until the dance at the airport.

Ten days later when I went to the Christmas dance, and while I was sitting with my circle of friends, I saw a Canadian soldier coming towards me. I hoped he was not coming to talk to me. Sure enough, he came over to me and picked up my hand and said, "Hi babe, I remember you very well, you and the long red hair." I recall thinking that he was very brash. Several seconds later he asked me to dance, so I got up and shyly went to the ladies' room and stayed there. Later I told my sister that I did not want to stay at the dance and that I was going home. She said, "Oh Audrey, stay a little longer." I told her, "No, I don't want to." So she took me home. Once we got home my mother told me that Bobby was actually quite nice and he was just a lonely young man. He was always talking about his family in Canada.

My mother played the piano and used to invite some of the servicemen to come and sing around the piano, especially at Christmastime. One night we had about half-a-dozen young Canadians from the tower behind our field, singing in our home and that's how I really got to know him. He was only in the tower behind our house until March. Then he was transferred to the South Coast for commando training, as the Dieppe raid was being planned at that time. So I actually only knew him from December 1941 until March 1942. He was twenty-one and I was sixteen, and I was not romantically interested in him.

Just before my sixteenth birthday I received a letter from the war office, saying that I was needed for war work. I discussed this with my parents and my mother asked, "What would you like to do?" I told her that I would like to be a nurse, the same as she had been in the First World War. Mother told me I had to be seventeen before I could go into nursing, and that I should decide on another type of work. I had to have some kind of war work, so I went to the airport and applied for a job at the RAF station. I wrote a small exam, and they said that I could start in the office typing pool. I didn't like it, but I also knew that it was war work and everyone was needed. Besides typing, I was a messenger girl and took all the memos to the various departments throughout the airport.

On my travels through the airport I went to two field hospitals. I became friendly with the Irish nursing Sister who was in charge of one of the hospitals. I told her that I was interested in nursing and that I would love to be a nurse. We really clicked, and one day she told me that she needed a student nurse in the hospital. I was excited but told her that I was not quite seventeen. She said not to worry, that she would arrange a transfer for me and that I could work under her as a trainee nurse. I immediately went into the hospital and I just loved it. I was a field nurse with the Department of National Defence, and worked in emergency nursing for accidents at the airport. We wore a blue and white striped uniform, white apron, white collar and cuffs, black stockings, black shoes, a white cap and a red and black cape. My wages started at two pounds a week, and when the war ended I was earning four pounds a week. I remained with the hospital until I left for Canada in 1946.

There were two hospitals, and I had to go from one to the other, as needed, which was quite often. I worked twelve hours a day, and I did not get a day off in the first seven weeks. We would go to work, go home, go to bed, get up and go back to work. It was constant work as there were many accidents at the airport.

Sunday evening was my session for writing letters. I wrote to my school chums who had joined the service, and also to my brother who was serving in India. I wrote about eight letters a week. Bobby knew that I wrote letters as he was at our house on Sunday evenings. He would ask me what I was doing, and I would tell him that I was writing to all my school friends. He told me that I was not like his little sister, as she never wrote to him.

Not long after Bobby went to the South Coast, the Dieppe raid took place (August 1942). I was absolutely surprised when I got a letter from the Red Cross. I had already started my nursing career and wondered why they had written. However, the letter said that

Bobby was missing in action and was presumed killed, and that he had given my name to be notified in the event of his death. The Red Cross said that he had requested I correspond with his father and mother.

I asked my mother why he had asked me to do that. My mother said that she did not know why, but that Bobby was like family. I thought that it was rather strange. About six months later I received another letter from the Red Cross. It said that Bob had survived the Dieppe raid, that he was a prisoner of war, and wanted to correspond with me. So I started writing to him, and with each letter he got a little more serious. I sent him a photograph of myself, and he wrote back and said that he wanted to marry me. I wrote a letter back to him and said, "Absolutely not, I'm just writing to you because you are a prisoner of war, I have no intention of getting married." Actually I hadn't, because I loved my nursing work, and when the war was over I was going to London to finish my training. I was taking courses but they did not qualify me to be an RN and that's what I wanted. However, I corresponded with Bob for three years until 1945.

D-Day was the most magnificent day of our lives in Britain. There were thousands of airplanes in the sky; it was black with aircraft. Our aircraft, not German aircraft. There were thousands of troops going to the English coast to board ships to go over to France. We could see all that, and we knew that things were on the move. That was a great day for Britain and it was wonderful for us.

Finally the war ended. Britain had survived six long years of defence and the fight was finally over. One day I received a message through a telephone call from the local Grey Hound Inn. We did not have a telephone so the message came to the local pub. The message said Bob Waddy was coming down to see the family, and that he had been in the hospital for a month, on his release from the POW camp.

Bob arrived and we started going out. He was extremely quiet, very thin, not the same brash person he had been before he was taken prisoner of war. I was nineteen and he was twenty-four. We

Kriegsgefangenenpost *(prisoner-of-war post card)* to Audrey
from her husband-to-be, Bob, in Germany, 1943.

went out in May, were engaged in June, and married in July 1945. He wanted to marry quickly as he said that he was going home to Canada and wanted me to come home with him. This was shocking, because I had not thought about going to Canada. He came down every weekend from Farnborough, north of London. I thought, "What am I going to do, here I am being rushed into all of this, getting engaged and married all within six weeks?" I didn't have time to think about it, as he was the first man I had gone out with seriously. I recall Bob saying, "If we don't marry now, I'll be sent back to Canada and never see you again!" One night when we were out walking in the garden, Bob said, "Please marry me or I'll phone you every day and keep writing letters until you say yes." So I said yes, and we made plans for the wedding on July 21st, 1945.

My sister's fiance came home from Malta three weeks prior to our wedding, and my mother suggested that we plan for a double wedding. So we rushed around to get organized for the double wedding. Several people said they knew where to buy a wedding dress without coupons but that it would cost more. So my sister and I went to London and bought our dresses in the black market shops. We ordered extra flowers and made the extra arrangements with the hotel for the reception. We had a garden reception in the afternoon, then went to the hotel for dinner. We each had a huge bouquet of beautiful flowers. My aunt made the wedding cake, and my elder sister scrounged some extra sugar to decorate the cake. After a wonderful reception we left on our honeymoon.

My husband ordered a taxi for London, and my sister and her husband left for Devon. Before we left, the manager of the hotel gave us a beautiful big bottle of champagne. I put the bottle in my suitcase, but as we were leaving in the taxi, the driver threw my suitcase down and the bottle broke all over my honeymoon clothes. Everything was covered with champagne. I left all my clothes in the suitcase until we got to Scotland, with the exception of a nightgown which I took out to dry. We never did get our bottle of champagne.

It was when Bob told me that he was going home to Canada in

October that I realized that he was leaving and that I was still working in England. He told me on the last day before he left that he had made all the arrangements for my travel to Canada. I recall him saying, "Everything has gone through and you should be receiving your papers shortly. I want you with me when the baby's born." I had just discovered that I was six weeks pregnant, and if I had the baby in England I would have to wait three to six months before I could travel.

Three weeks before I was to leave for Canada (February 1946), I had not yet received travel papers. When I finally heard that I was leaving England, I was told to transfer my money to the nearest bank where I would be going. I knew that I had married a Canadian and that Canada was six thousand miles away, but I had not really thought about leaving. When my final papers arrived from the Canadian government, I had to travel to London and stay in a hostel for a day and a night. There were about five or six hundred war brides at the hostel. The other war brides seemed to be happy, but I felt sad, because this was my first realization that I was leaving my family behind.

We boarded the steamship *Letitia*, and were assigned our cabins. There were twenty-one of us in a huge cabin; some of us had beds while the other girls slept in hammocks. We had a breakdown, and it took eleven days to cross the Atlantic. We were also sailing in convoy and had to go around the mine fields. Most of the trip was rough and foggy. It was wonderful when we sighted land. All the girls scanned the shore and screamed: "There's land, we're in Halifax."

Once in Canada we boarded our train, and met the Red Cross nurses. They were wonderful. I was told I was very quiet, compared to all the other girls. I remember saying, "Well, I'm leaving behind my family and I've been quite seasick." I was really feeling very sad and homesick, although excited that I would be seeing my husband after almost six months of separation. We crossed the Rockies and arrived in Vancouver, and there was a band to meet us. I couldn't find my husband so I decided to stand where I was and wait for someone to rescue me. Soon my husband and his father found me on the station platform. I loved his father from the first minute I met him.

I stayed with my in-laws until we had the baby. Bob had joined the army in 1939, right out of high school, and did not have a job. His father told him that he had to do something soon, since he had a wife and a baby on the way. The only job he could find was as a baker so he did that for four months. I arrived in March, and our baby girl Roberta was born in June 1946. We were able to move into wartime housing in September. After the baby was born, we all sat around the dining room table and we decided that Bob should go back to school, as he needed to finish his education. He needed a trade; his father was adamant about that.

Those were very hard times. We had one baby, and eleven months later we had a baby son, Allen. Bob went to university and spent two years articling with various companies to be an accountant. We lived on one hundred dollars a month, and we had to pay thirty dollars a month rent.

After Bob finished his course in 1947, he went to work for the Income Tax Department in Vancouver. He made one hundred and sixty dollars, which was sixty dollars a month more than before. The extra money was marvellous.

We decided to move to Vancouver Island in 1950, and Bob found a job at a saw mill in Honeymoon Bay. He studied and took his lumber-grading exams and got a position as a Lumber Grader. We lived in a float house on the lake with only a cold water tap, a wood stove and a biffy outside in the trees. One cold winter night in 1951, I was alone with the children when Bob was at work. It was a very, very cold winter and the water pipes were frozen solid under the house. I was putting the children to bed when I heard a terrible noise around and beneath the house. I took a blanket and went into the children's room. I thought there were animals outside because we had a lot of cougars and bears in the area. I thought, "If I have to jump out, I'll jump out of the window and take the kids with me." The noise went on until three o'clock in the morning, and when Bob came home from work I had all the doors and windows locked. I was absolutely terrified, and yet I had not been that terrified during the war. I asked Bob what the terrible noise was. He replied that the sounds were the ice breaking up. It was the spring thaw. We lived for a year and a half in the float house, as it was the only accommodation that we could find at that time. We stayed in Honeymoon Bay for seven years, purchased land and built a house there.

In 1953, I received a beautiful Christmas card from my brother in England. He told me that shortly I would be receiving tickets to come to England for a vacation. The children (seven and eight years of age at the time) and I left for England in April of 1954. For five days we crossed Canada by train, and then sailed from Montreal to Southampton for another eight days. Although I was seasick across the Atlantic, the children thoroughly enjoyed the crossing. Because I had been ill on the trip, my mother was shocked when she saw me and asked, "What have they done to you in Canada?" We stayed six months and returned to Canada in November.

In 1956 Bob decided to take a promotion, and went to work as Personnel Manager in Tahsis, BC. Being pregnant with our third child, I had to stay in Honeymoon Bay. I also had to sell our home. Four days prior to our youngest son Donald being born in October 1956, my mother passed away. I had no idea that she was having heart trouble or even that she had been ill. I was grateful to have been able to visit her two years earlier. Bob resigned from Tahsis when the baby was born. He was told that a new mill was being built in Crofton and that they needed an accountant. Bob went to work as an accountant during the building of the mill and then transferred into the steam plant the following year. During this time I went to work in the Duncan office of T. Eaton Company. In 1965 we visited England on a charter flight organized by Eatons. I remained with T. Eaton Company for nineteen years. Bob and I are now both retired and enjoy a full and happy life with our family.

Barbara Walsh

"IT WAS A BIT OF A SHOCK
WHEN I CAME TO CANADA"

*Barbara Walsh is from Eastbourne in Sussex,
a seaside town on the English Channel,
a little bit like Victoria. She grew up the
youngest of four children.*

I used to enjoy living by the sea because we would go down to the beach all the time. We had a place called Beachy Head where we would walk on the rocks and watch the sealife in the pools left by the tide.

I graduated with my senior matric just about the time that war was declared. Then I took the civil service exam and started work with the civil service in the war office in Hastings, which is the town next to Eastbourne. I worked in records and we used to do posting for personnel.

My sister and I had a place in Hastings together and we stayed there throughout the war. We worked in a big old monastery that was converted to the war office. We had two Sealyham dogs (like little Scottie dogs, only they're white) and we were able to take them to the office with us because you couldn't leave an animal at home alone; it was a war concession, so we had baskets in the office for them.

We heard on the radio that war was declared. The sirens went off immediately after, and someone said that they were bombing Margate, which is an east coast town. But nothing happened, it was just a practice. They had issued everybody civilian gas masks and quite a lot of people put them on. It was a very frightening first experience, but after that things settled down. We had only the channel between us, and we didn't know what to expect. Naturally when the war first started, everybody rushed around buying up provisions and then of course after that everything was rationed.

Our town was bombed very heavily, because we were right on the coast and the Germans used to practise on us. We were kept on edge, so as soon as the sirens sounded we would take cover, either under a table or wherever we happened to be. If you were downtown, glass was one of the worst things. The plate glass windows used to cause terrible injuries. We had bombs falling in the garden. My sister and I lived just across the road from where we worked, and of course the Germans knew that's where the war department was, so they would come over and drop bombs there. The wind would take the bombs off course and sometimes towards our side of the road. You could hear the bombs whistling when they were coming down.

There didn't seem to be any crime during the war. My sister and I lived alone. We would go out at night and come home late, walking home in the blackout with no lights. We would go up to London on the train, and we would get into a carriage which was blacked out because all the trains were blacked out. You didn't have a clue who you were getting in with, but you never had that feeling of fear that someone might attack you.

We ate out mostly. There was a nice canteen at our office, and we had a club nearby. They had a lot of country clubs in England during the war, and they stayed open, so we went to the one close by for our meals. Then, of course, we didn't have to use our rations for that food.

I was an air-raid warden at night. In fact, sometimes I didn't go home, because we had an air-raid post under our office and I was on duty three nights a week. When the sirens went, we had to alert all the stations around, and then we patrolled what aircraft we could visually see. Also, when bombs were dropping we had a system in which we counted and could see how far away the bombs were. We didn't have many quiet nights once the Battle of Britain started in the fall of 1940. We were kept busy and it lasted all through the war. There were girls on ack-ack guns; they were on the gun crew that shot at the planes when they came over. Women also worked the searchlights along the coast, watching for the planes. We used to watch the planes fighting over the English Channel and quite a few came down around us. Sometimes you would see them come limping home, and then they used to do what they called a victory roll if they had shot a plane down.

I met my future husband when he came to our office and asked our Colonel if he could invite some of the office girls to a dance. Nobody really wanted to go, but a friend of ours came around twisting our arms, so we decided to go to be nice. We rode out in the back of an army truck and they took us to the village hall. When we arrived, there were no men, and there was supposed to be champagne and lots of goodies at this dance. So my future husband, who was the Sergeant Major at the time, had to go and rouse all the boys out of the pub. We ended up having quite a good time, but there was no champagne. I think we had cocoa and fish paté sandwiches. However the Sergeant Major, Norman, and I took a fancy to each other and we carried on seeing each other from that time on.

When I met Norman in 1941, he was in the Royal Artillery with the anti-tank guns. Anti-tank guns at that time weren't tanks; they were guns. They were guns that pierced the armour of the tanks. Because we lived in a restricted area you couldn't have cameras, so the local newspaper came and took the wedding pictures. We were married in a small church called Ore, and we had a fairly big wedding. A lot of the regiment came and, since the old parish church was adjacent to the grounds of our office, all of the office people came. We had our reception at a roadhouse which was in the same vicinity. There were about fifty friends and family at our reception. I have often thought about the wedding cake. I couldn't get white icing for the cake, so it had to be chocolate icing, for some reason. My wedding dress was actually an evening gown. I was going to be married in a suit but my sister said, "You can't get married in a suit," so we cut the bottom off the gown and put sleeves on it.

I left England from Liverpool. They bussed us to Waterloo, then overnight to Liverpool. I came over on the *Britannic*. There were about sixty war brides, and all the rest of the passengers were returning personnel. We were in the middle of the convoy but the submarines were around, and there were depth charges being dropped. All the English war brides were together but I didn't know anyone. Of course a lot of them had children. I was on A-deck, and it certainly wasn't luxurious. They had put bunks in. I think there were six bunks in our cabin and I was on the top bunk. During the day, the war brides with no children would stay away from the cabin as long as possible.

The food on the ship was very good. I think it was stocked with holiday food from Christmas. Anyway I loved the crusty rolls. We were so in awe of them because we hadn't had crusty rolls for many years.

It was very exciting to see all the lights of Halifax—a lovely and wonderful feeling. When we got to Winnipeg, we had to transfer to an ordinary train from the troop train we had been travelling on. We were put into a sleeping car and there were soldiers in it. We didn't like that at all; no way were we going to get into a bunk and undress with all these soldiers in the same car. We had been used to the troop train which we had all to ourselves. We sat up in the men's washroom all night because there were seats in it. We were not even aware that it was the men's washroom. All we wanted was safety! This must have been difficult for the men.

It was a bit of a shock when I came to Canada. I became very friendly on the train with a Hungarian girl who had been in England during the war, and also with another girl. As we three travelled across Canada, our spirits fell lower and lower, seeing the flat prairies go on and on. But it was March with no leaves on the trees, and the snow was melting. When I reached Regina, Norman's mother was there, and she was very hospitable. Norman hadn't come home yet, because the war had changed its course. He had gone to Holland to the war there. I guess I was a bit head-strong, but it wasn't for me to be in Regina.

I was kind of sorry that I had come. So I thought I would get a job. I went to the employment office, and they said "You have been in the civil service. Go and see the federal civil service," which I did, and they said, "We can't employ you in Saskatchewan. You have to live here for six months before we can employ you." But they got me a job in Ottawa with the Department of Finance, sending out the war bonds. That's where I was when Norman finally came back just after July 1st. I really enjoyed Ottawa. I didn't want to leave and go back to Regina. I was very homesick. In fact, I think I was homesick until I moved to Victoria.

I told Norman that I was never going back to Regina, but of course he had to go back. I didn't give up my job but I did go back with him. He was persuaded to stay on as an Army personnel counsellor, so I had to give up my job and live in Regina. But I wasn't very happy, and we had a bad time there. I had a thyroid operation and then I was pregnant. We lost our baby so we went back to England in 1947 for two years. We went back on the *Queen Elizabeth* which left from New York. It was very different going back, because when I came out, they had put bunk beds in all the cabins, but now the ship was back to its original purpose as a passenger liner.

Things were not very good in England after the war, but Norman loved England and worked for a motor company in Hastings. I had Philip our oldest boy in England. Not too long afterwards we thought we would come back to Canada. I said I would come back, but that I wouldn't go to Regina. I had relations in Montreal who we went to see, but we couldn't get anywhere to live. We ended up back in Regina and eventually had a very pleasant life there. The only thing was that the climate was bad. Norman was in the militia for many years, and I was busy with the Imperial Order of the Daughters of the Empire (IODE). Regina turned out to be a wonderful place to raise children because there were lots of things for them to participate in.

I have been back to England several times by ship. Once I took my three boys back for six months. Philip the oldest was fourteen, David was nine, and Jonathan was eight. They really enjoyed the trip, but it wasn't so pleasant for me because I had to keep track of them. Jonathan, particularly, was a real mad hatter and I was always afraid he would go over the rails. My husband was on a course at that time, and I thought I would be better off in England than staying at home waiting for him. The experience gave the boys a different kind of insight and a different kind of culture.

At the end of the war, I was presented with the Defense Medal for service with the air-raid wardens. In 1967, I was awarded the Centennial Medal for my work in the IODE. Norman and I celebrated our 50th wedding anniversary in 1992. Throughout the years, life has been very kind to us.

Anita Frocklage

"REMEMBER, IT MEANS YOU WILL BECOME A CANADIAN"

Anita Frocklage was born in Liverpool where she grew up in a big happy family. Anita was seventeen when the war started.

I worked as a waitress at Lyon's Corner House in London until war was declared, and then my mother didn't want me in London so she made me come back to Liverpool. I was very frightened but at the same time I hoped that we would win the war. I was at work when Chamberlain made the announcement that we were now at war with Germany. All I could think was, "Oh my brothers!" They were in the Merchant Navy then.

I went home and worked as a waitress at a big hotel in Liverpool. It was a lovely place. Before the war the hotel restaurants were so posh that they would never have waitresses—only waiters. Because I had experience, I was head of a section in the restaurant. While I worked at this hotel, I met many of the well-known actors and actresses who came to stay there during the war. I remember serving Michael Redgrave and his wife Rachel Kempson. They were in a play that was being performed in Liverpool. Then there was Joe Louis, the boxer, and even Mae West came there.

After I had worked at the hotel for awhile, people were being hired to work for the LMS Railway trains so my sister and I decided that we would do a stint on that. I got a job as a waitress on the train between Liverpool and London. It was nice because there was a lot of money in it, but it was actually very dangerous because of the bombing.

I remember one time we were on a train travelling between Liverpool and London when we got notice not to move because a bomb had been planted at one end or the other. We were stuck there while messages went back and forth but we never did find out if there really was a bomb. It was just one of those things.

It was also very frightening at the London end because, at that time, London was being bombed so much, and we used to stay overnight there. There was one time when my sister said, "Well we're not too far away from where we can go and watch *Gone With the Wind.*" So we went to the cinema. When it came to the part in the movie where Atlanta was all on fire, the noise of bombing began outside.

We really didn't know what to do, but because we knew we were watching a great movie, we actually stayed to watch it to the end. Then we headed to the underground for shelter, and when we saw the planes diving down to bomb the city, I said, "Well let's put our umbrellas up." Later, my sister always laughed when she remembered what I said. But even now, when I watch *Gone With the Wind* and it comes to the scene of Atlanta burning, the memories of that night come flooding into my mind. The bombing was always very frightening, and I would wonder what was going to happen to us.

The blackouts were very hard. Because of them, when I started to work downtown, my mother would meet me as I came home. She'd hold a flashlight for us on the ground so we could see where we were going. There was one time when we were very badly bombed at our hotel. I've never forgotten how the windows were all broken, and when I walked home there were live wires on the ground. It was pitch black outside, too. It's all like a dream now.

But I remember on this dark, cold night, mother was waiting for me at a corner of the long road where we lived. My mother was frightened that something had happened to me because of the bombing. Sometimes I would work longer hours at the hotel so she could never be certain when I'd come home, and we didn't have a phone either. I was so numb when I got home, mother got a bucket of warm water and bathed my legs to get the circulation back.

As a young woman, I loved to dance. I used to go out a lot to dances with my sister who was two years older than me. Sometimes, in the hotel they would say, "Well the soldiers are here and there's a dance coming on. Come back and dance." I was lucky because Liverpool had a lot of good dancing in big dancehalls with beautiful orchestras playing. I found the music to be excellent. It was the big band era—Glen Miller's type of music. One day my brother sent a telegram to my mother that said, "Arriving home with friend and lots of dirty washing." Because I was young and I was tired of the daily grind, I said, "Well I think I'll go to a dance tonight." So I went to the dance hall and returned home just after eleven o'clock that evening. My brother and his friend were sitting there, and my mother introduced me to my brother's friend.

I was really sassy so I looked my brother's friend up and down and asked, "So does this include the dirty washing that you've brought?" His shirt did look a little bit grey. He blushed so much. The friend was the kind soldier that had taken my brother under his wing in Montreal. His name was Fred Armstrong, and unbeknownst to both of us at this time, he was my future husband.

The next day, my brother wanted to take Fred to show him around during the daytime when there weren't bombs falling. Fred asked my mother, "Is it alright if I take Anita out?" She said, "Well it's up to Anita." My brother and Fred were with us for a few days and then they said, "We're going to get KP because we're staying so long." Before they left, Fred asked if he could come back again.

When Fred returned, he told me, "You know I was thinking about you, and I would really like to have a serious relationship. Your brother has met my family and knows they're okay. Now I've met your family and they're so friendly. They've made me feel welcome. But mostly I've been thinking of you all the time. Could be serious." I replied, "Well, I think you're right." I liked him—he was very handsome. But more importantly, he seemed so honest and sincere.

We started writing letters to each other. The next thing I knew, he wrote to say, "I've made arrangements with the Commanding Officer for us to get married." I said to my mum, "Oh gee, this is kind of sudden!" My mother said, "Well, you know, you better make up your mind." She wasn't too crazy about me getting serious about him but she said, "You're getting older now—make up your mind. Remember it means you will become a Canadian."

I wrote back to Fred and said, "Wait until I see you again." But he never got that letter, and then I got a letter from him and one from my brother that it had all been arranged with the Commanding Officer for both of them to get special leave. I was to arrange the wedding for June 9th! My mother was going mad trying to see about getting extra chickens and other food. My sister, who was living in Brighton, came down with a few chickens. They were going to do all the catering for my wedding. So we did get married in June of 1941, and we had a nice little wedding. A year later, our first son Geoffrey was born. While I was pregnant with our son we were badly bombed. I was living with my mum, and when I went into labour, she took me to the hospital. At this time, the hospital was being bombed and it was very scary.

My husband got special leave, and the next day he came in. He was so cute when he tried to visit me. I was in a big ward—there were twelve of us mothers breast-feeding our babies. Fred stood in the doorway looking over to where I was. All the mothers were shouting, "Get out!" He said, "Sorry ladies," and came back later to apologize. Of course it wasn't until after we finished feeding the babies that Fred was allowed to come in. He was only given twenty-four-hours leave so he had to return quickly but at least he got to meet our son.

The next day, we were so badly bombed that all the babies were wrapped in blankets, and the Red Cross took us in a convoy to Southport where my husband and I had spent our honeymoon. All the mothers and babies stayed in a lovely big home that had been given to be used as a temporary hospital. We were in a safer area because there was nothing there that the Germans would want to bomb.

Some time later, Fred wrote to me that he'd made arrangements so that I could come for a few days to Eastbourne near where he was stationed. My little boy was about six months old then. I wrote to tell him I didn't feel comfortable in coming because there was so much bombing and it was too frightening. He sent me a telegram that said, "Thank God you didn't come. The whole place was flattened to the ground." It had been badly bombed.

Late in 1943 I got a letter informing me that my husband, who had been wounded, was now in Canada. He'd been sent home. I was to be ready to be called upon to go to Canada. I was to destroy any mail that had my husband's address on it. I was also to take anything of importance to be stamped and sealed. It upset my mother to know that I would be leaving soon.

In July 1944 I received a letter that said I must go all the way to Scotland. It was a holiday week—what they call a bank holiday in England. My mother took me to the train. It was jammed. My son was nearly two years old by this time. I put him down on a seat, and I leaned out a window to look at mum until I couldn't see her anymore. All the time I could see her, my mother was crying but I couldn't let her know how bad I felt. When we reached Glasgow, the Red Cross was there to meet us. They took us to a nice hotel where we were to stay until the morning. The Red Cross worker said that she couldn't tell us the name of the ship. After we got to the ship next morning, what I noticed more than anything were all the soldiers. There were Canadians and there were German prisoners of war including an important commander going overseas.

The ocean liner's name had been changed. It was originally the *Empress of Japan*, and they changed it to the *Empress of Scotland*. We set off on July 31st, 1944. My son was only two and already quite smart in his own way, but I had quite a time with him. Because mum had looked after him while I was working, he'd grown very close to her. One day, Geoff told me, "You took me away from my grammy." Geoff also came down with croup during our crossing so I had to hold and comfort him a lot. We were together all the time on our trip across the Atlantic.

It took ten days to cross the Atlantic because we were constantly changing course to avoid being attacked. We eventually reached Halifax, and then my son and I had to take the train to Montreal. When we got there, my husband and his family were waiting. My husband hadn't been able to find a place for love or money, so we were going to stay with his parents.

It was hard for anyone to find a place at this time. Even one of my sister-in-laws who was married to one of my husband's brothers was still staying with my husband's parents. When my husband's family met us, my father-in-law stood there with this big ice cream cone for Geoff, who'd never had an ice cream cone before. My father-in-law said to him, "Look what I've brought you!" Geoff licked it and said, "I don't like that." So my poor father-in-law was stuck with it.

My husband didn't have a car in those days so we went in a taxi. It was nighttime, and Montreal was all lit up. Geoff looked out and exclaimed, "Look at all the moons!" He wasn't used to seeing city lights at night because of England's wartime blackouts every night.

Fred's family were delighted that my son could talk so well. He was my father-in-law's first grandson, so my father-in-law would take Geoff down to the basement, and they would play a game called "What's that?" My father-in-law would tell Geoff, "This is a hammer and this is a screwdriver." All these things were new to Geoff, so he loved that game.

Shortly after I arrived in Montreal, the war brides in our area started a group called "The Acorn Club." We arrived at the name "Acorn Club" by having a little competition to decide what we would call our group. One member said, "From little acorns the mighty oak tree grows." So we thought "Acorn Club" would be a great name. We used to meet regularly and celebrate special occasions together. Sometimes we would just get together in each other's homes. For all I know, we might have been the first war brides' group in Canada because this was before the war was over. We formed lots of close friendships within this group.

We stayed with my husband's parents for well over a year. It was 1945 before we were able to buy a house for ourselves. Our second son Doug was born in 1945. We continued to live in the same house until 1973. Our house was located very near to where the Olympics took place in 1976. It was a little two-bedroom cottage. Eventually, we built an extra room at the side of the house, and we had a nice big garden.

I had a very good life in Montreal, and the French-Canadian people were lovely to me. One day I said to my mother-in-law, "I'm going to get a part-time job." My husband worked for the T. Eaton company but it wasn't big money. Fred's family laughed at my idea of going to work. But I was determined. I thought if I could just get a little part-time position, serving lunch or something, that would suit me fine.

When I went in for an interview, the manageress asked me, "Are you bilingual?" I had just arrived a few months before but I said, "Oh yes." So she asked me, "Well what do you speak?" I replied, "Oh, English and Canadian." She laughed and said that it didn't matter.

In 1972, my husband died, and the following year, I moved to Victoria. My sons had already moved out here. Then I took an Early Childhood Education course, and found work at a little school here. I had always wanted to work with children. I also took courses in writing, gourmet cooking and even astronomy. There were a lot of men in the gourmet cooking course, and we had loads of fun. We used to eat everything that we cooked.

In 1976, I married my second husband, and we are very happy. Over the years, I have gone home to England a few times to the same house I grew up in. I always enjoy myself but usually after a few days I long to get back to Canada. After all these years, this is my home, my life.

Terry Bell

"I CAN STILL SEE THOSE HUNDREDS OF WOMEN"

Terry Bell grew up in Hendon near London.
During her childhood her family got together
regularly to entertain each other.
Life was very pleasant.

I lived in Hendon during the war, and worked at the General Post Office just by St. Paul's Cathedral in London. I answered the telephones taking local and overseas calls. We were bombed nearly every night because you know what a landmark St. Paul's was. But it didn't bother me, because I had three other girlfriends and we went dancing every night. We went out dancing with Canadians, Americans, the French and other servicemen from the different countries.

I guess being young, we didn't bother about the air raids. My mother and father were worried out of their heads, but for some reason we weren't. We had a good time, and wore tin hats when the shrapnel came down. Once a terrific bomb was dropped on Hendon. I happened to be home that night. All I heard was a swoosh; it was one of the worst disasters in London. The woman across the road was killed even though the bomb was three miles away. We lost all our windows, although my mum had pasted them with net so they wouldn't shatter.

We used to go down to Bournemouth to meet boys. We were there on the day the bomb fell on what I call the Pink Hotel. All these Canadians had just arrived and were killed. It was terrible. It happened at about ten o'clock in the morning. The four of us used to share a bed when we went on holiday; all we could afford was one room. I remember us all sliding under the bed when we heard the bomb come down. Then we went down later to the front, and we saw where they supposedly got the German plane that did it, but that was a bad one.

You know, where the boys were, the girls went, and it was all in fun. I was fortunate in having three other girlfriends, and when we were asked out, we always went together. Even if we paired off, two girls went together and the other two stayed together. I remember the Canadians: they used to say, "Well we came over here to save your lives; since we may be dead tomorrow, you should go to bed with us tonight." Well, we used to say, "If you feel that way, go pick that one up on the corner." We truthfully didn't go for that.

I was lucky as far as the rationing went, because I would eat at work. And if we could find some rich Canadians or Americans to take us out for dinner, we did. We said to these Americans one night, "We know where you can get a nice steak." So they took us to this place, and about three days later, we saw that the restaurant had been fined for selling horse meat. But the Americans had their steak.

One day I said to these Canadians, "Would you like to come home? We will have plenty to eat tonight because we have a rabbit." They said, "A rabbit—!" I thought, "Well, go hungry!" In my family we ate out regularly, and this helped to make the ration coupons last longer. We always seemed to have enough tea, that was the main thing. If old Hitler had done something with our tea, we would have capitulated right away. As long as they didn't take our tea away we would survive.

I remember a friend giving me a duck egg and I put it into my bra to carry it home in case I got searched on the way. If they had found a duck egg in my boobies, I would have got in trouble. I didn't like the duck egg anyway; it was too strong.

My girlfriend and I met my future husband and another Canadian on a train. We were going somewhere, and they were going somewhere, but they never went where they were supposed to go. They came with us instead. He was in the First Division of the Canadian Army, and very nice looking. But as soon as we got back to Canada he was a completely different person. Our courtship was quite a long one because I was in London and he was stationed in Aldershot.

We were married in Hendon in 1943. There was no wedding cake, because there was no fruit to make a wedding cake. I had a friend whose mother worked in a candy factory for export. Everyday she brought a teaspoon of sugar home in her bra, and that's how she was able to collect enough sugar for her daughter's wedding cake. It seems to me we got potatoes, mashed them and put in almond flavouring to make artificial marzipan to put on my friend's wedding cake. Some girls and I found a parachute, which could have been used for a wedding dress, but instead we made ourselves nice undies.

I was supposed to go to Canada, but then D-day was in the immediate future so it was postponed. I had to wait until my daughter was born.

By this time, the buzz bombs, the V-1 rockets, were coming over. I think England was just about at the breaking point. I was twenty-one and I had a baby so I was finally becoming mature and getting on to the serious side of this war; it had all been fun up to then. But when the family is not together and you have a young baby, with your husband in Canada, you might just as well get the heck out!

We left England from Liverpool. My baby was six weeks old and the youngest baby to ever cross the Atlantic in wartime. We left in the dark when the blackout was still on. I think we had a near miss when we were coming over on the ship. I can still hear them dropping the depth charges. All the food was bad on the ship because whatever hit us knocked out the electricity. I was nursing my baby, and with the food being bad the ship's doctor said, "Just go and eat peanuts." Apparently, peanuts are very nutritious. In England, we don't like eating peanuts.

We docked in Halifax, and I remember going into this big shed. You get off the ship, and come through a door. Then you see your last initial, and you go and stand under it. Forty years later, I visited where we docked in Halifax. This big shed was empty, and the pigeons were flying around, but you know, I can still see those hundreds of women and all those babies crying, tired and upset in a foreign land! Then we went through this doorway where the railway was, and we were put on the train.

I had never travelled, so before I left England I had asked a friend, what should I do? "Well," he said, "When you get on the train you give the porter five pounds, and you tell him when you get to the other end that you will give him another five pounds if he looks after you." So I gave the porter five pounds, and I had my bunk made up, morning coffee and afternoon tea brought to me. All the girls were saying, "Who the hell is she that she gets her bunk made up?"

When the train stopped in Winnipeg, there were people holding corsages. We hadn't seen a corsage for a long time. I said, "I'm not for here, I'm going to Vancouver." "No, you keep it," they said. They asked, "Do you have a baby?" and they gave me a layette, with little nighties with frills and embroidery around the neck and cuffs. There was baby powder, soap, things we hadn't seen in a long time. I thought it was absolutely unbelievable and very kind.

The train stopped often on its way across Canada, and at some places when it stopped there wasn't even a train station. But a war bride would have people waiting for her at that location. Some of the girls would say to her, "You're not going to get off here!" Some didn't get off but some did—four o'clock in the morning going off into the middle of nowhere.

You would fall asleep on the train, and eight hours later you would swear to God you hadn't moved an inch. I kept on saying to the old grey-haired porter, "Am I on the right train going to Vancouver?" He would say, "Yes, you are." Finally I realized I was in Canada when I got to Jasper. I saw the log cabin railway station and I saw the mountains. But up to then, I did not know I was in Canada. All I knew about Canada was it had mountains, Mounties and Native Indians.

When I reached Vancouver and saw my husband, he looked like a stranger. He felt like a stranger and he was a stranger! You know when I arrived, we wanted to be together, but we had no time together without family being around. We had no time to get re-acquainted, no bonding time. We went right to my mother-in-law's, and my sister-in-law was there as well. Later it turned out that I wasn't the type that should have married him, and we just didn't jell!

My mother-in-law was really no help. For one thing she had a girlfriend already picked out for my husband, and I don't think that I was quite her type. She had lived in England, and to hear her accent, you would have thought that she had never left there. If your mother-in-law is not nice to you, and your husband who supposedly really loves you will not go to bat for you, you more or less lose your marriage there.

One of the funniest things that ever happened to me occurred because of the difference in clothes in Canada. In England, you could always pick out the ladies-of-the-street by their makeup and the fur coats they wore. During my early days in Vancouver, my mother-in-law took me downtown. All the ladies I could see, including my mother-in-law, had all this makeup on and were wearing fur coats. I thought, "Oh my God. The place is full of prostitutes!"

My husband and I had the opportunity to go to Clayoquot Island just off Tofino on the west coast of Vancouver Island. So we went up there for a year. There were only eight white people on the island, although there were many native people. I wrote my father that I was expecting a baby, and that we were surrounded by Indians. He wrote back, "You come right home, my girl!" We didn't of course. It was educational living up there; I don't regret that one bit.

Our second baby was born in Tofino. We had this wharf that led out to where the cutter came in. Because it was a hotel, we sold beer, and we had a track that went down to the wharf to carry the beer. Well, they put me on this little track and gave it a kick. As I rushed down the track, I kept thinking, "I am going to have the baby any moment. Oh God, I'm going into the ocean!" But the cart stopped in time. We climbed down the ladder, boarded the boat and went over towards Tofino.

A naval mine had washed up on Long Beach, so there was a navy frigate in the dock at Tofino. The wharf was under construction, so I went up the cat ladder and across the deck of this navy frigate. But there were still about two feet between me and the wharf, and they told me to jump. That's when I decided that enough was enough. There happened to be a policeman on the dock, and he said, "Take her back, and I will meet her at the wharf and take her to the hospital," and that's what they did. I felt I was going to have the baby any minute. When I got round to the wharf and saw the policeman, I was so excited that I stepped right out of the boat and into the water, so he pulled me out and took me to the hospital.

Next we moved down to Sooke where my husband had property, and we thought we would build on it. In the meantime, he had to go into the hospital at Shaughnessy. So he took me out to Sooke, and I was stuck in some little trailer court with the high tide lapping at the door. The sink was no bigger than the ones on the ship, and I had to use this with two kids. I happened to meet the local policeman who lived next door, and he made arrangements for me to rent his guest cottage.

We had bought property with nothing on it. First we dug a hole for the foundation. Then my husband built a garage and I lived in that for three years. When I look back I don't know how I did it. Two children in a fourteen-by-fourteen-foot room, but you did it because you didn't know what else to do. The people were marvellous. My entertainment was the Women's Institute, the church, and the PTA. It was slow building the house, and my husband wouldn't go under the Veteran's Loan Association (VLA) at that time, because he had his pride, so we suffered because he had his pride.

In Sooke I went to work for the telephone office, and because of that I was able to finish the house. Then my marriage became so intolerable that I had to leave my husband and our home. The house was sold but I couldn't get a nickel out of it because it was under the VLA by then. I then borrowed some money from my employer and bought a house. I worked on the basement, built on the sundeck, made myself some money, and thought, "Hey, this is neat." So I kept doing it.

I rose above being put down, and I think I made something of myself. To help your husband you used your own money, and you worked alongside of him. I learned how to mix cement and build a chimney with a double flue. You helped do everything because you couldn't pay anybody to do it. The time we war brides put in was our investment in our futures, but many of us had to get out of our marriages and leave the results of all our hard work. There should have been a place for the girls to go for counselling if things didn't work out for them here in Canada.

When I had my problems, I was given the choice of going back to England. My brother was quite wealthy. He had a beautiful home and he was a bachelor. I knew if I went, I could go and stay with him. By this time I had three children. But I also have a very funny habit. If I want to talk to work out a problem, I go to the bathroom and shut the door and I talk to myself. Back then I said, "Do I want to go back there? I cannot see myself going to the shops every day for two pounds of potatoes and a bit of this and a bit of that. I can't see me polishing the brass. I can't see me putting milk on the front doorstep. I can't see me shaking out the rugs. I have my own car. I wouldn't have a car over there. I have a washing machine now, but I don't know if I would there. My brother's home is beautiful but it is fed by the coal fires every day." I kept thinking of all these things until I realized, "No, I have really been spoilt in this country. For one thing, I have a car."

When I went home to England to visit my sister, she was going to the store every day, for itty-bitty things, a little of this and a little of that, because they didn't have freezers. I said to her, "Why don't you buy a fifty-pound sack of potatoes? Then you won't have to go and get them every day. Why don't you try and live the way we do in Canada, instead of all this itty-bitty shopping every day?"

Well, she said, "There are two reasons, one is that I'm allowed so much money a week. You see, they work everything on a weekly basis, and I know what I can spend within that week. If I have anything left over, I am lucky, and it goes towards something special. But if I buy your fifty pounds of potatoes there's all my money gone for two weeks on one sack of potatoes, and I don't have anything else left to buy anything in the meantime. The second thing is, where would I put the sack of potatoes? There is no room to store them." So I thought, "No, England is a great place, but Canada is a marvellous place." I remarried for a second time, and we now enjoy our retirement years travelling and living happily ever after!

Evelyn Ashmore

"THERE'S THE CANUCK
HOLDING UP THE BAKERY"

---

*Evelyn Ashmore was born in Wimbledon
and grew up close to Merton Park. In 1939 she
started working for the Prudential Insurance
Company and was still there when
war was declared.*

The very first day of war, the sirens went off and that was a bit scary. Everybody really thought the Germans were coming, but it was a false alarm. The government was just trying the sirens out. After that, everyone had gas masks and we had to carry them around with us. Otherwise, life more or less went on as usual. In September, my firm was evacuated down to Torquay. Down there it was much more laid back. But while I was there, my girlfriend Joan, who was more or less a conscientious objector, became scared that she and I were going to be called up soon. She asked me if I would go into the Land Army with her. So there I was in Torquay in bed with the flu, and I receive this telegram saying, "Imperative you come this weekend." It was my last chance to join the Land Army so I had to get out of bed right away. And I joined the Land Army.

There was such a different feeling among the people of England after the war started. Before, everybody was very reserved and aloof to each other, but during the wartime the people were just marvellous. If you were in trouble or anything, somebody would come and help. The people in the shops used to put themselves out to help with the rationing going on then.

Of course, because I was in the Land Army, I was well looked after. I had my uniform and we were on a farm where we were well fed. In 1943 my father died. He was only fifty-five. So mother was left there alone. And it was really hard on her, so every chance, every leave I got, I was home. While at home, we used to have to go out and wait in queues for whatever food was available that day. I don't know how we managed really, and it's amazing to think back on it. We had no butter. We just got a little square of margarine, and that had to last us for a week. We never saw an egg. And I think eventually we even ate some horse meat.

When I joined the Land Army, I was a city girl who had had nothing to do with animals. Here I was suddenly landing on a farm with cows, and I had to get up at five o'clock in the morning and milk these cows. Then we used to help with the haying, and they had this awful filthy threshing machine that used to come around to thresh the wheat. And I had to help with that. I remember once standing up on this wagon, and a mouse ran up the leg of my dungarees! I just about collapsed. I don't know how I stood it but I did.

My friend Joan had a nervous breakdown because she really wasn't cut out for that kind of life, although she had talked me into it. So she finally got out and went to a secretarial job. I moved to a farm near Guildford, and that was a lot closer to where mother was, so I was able to spend more time with her. It was a smaller farm, and people were wonderful to me. They were really good. I was billeted in Guildford. The lady there used to keep rabbits in her garden so there'd always be something to eat.

I don't think anybody really thought anything of women going into the jobs that only men used to do. My three brothers were all called up together. My sister was married and living in Devon. She had children, so she was not called up. Then I went into the Land Army and never thought anything of the fact that I was replacing a man. I think women just automatically took on the new roles required of them for the war effort.

Everywhere my friends and I went, we'd cycle. We used to cycle from the farm into this little village. We'd go to the show and that was about it. But when I was in Guildford, they used to have dances. The lady I was billeted with and I used to go to dances on Friday nights. Those were the main things that we did.

In 1943 I met my husband-to-be, Roy, while I was on leave and just on my way home. I came to Trafalgar Square, where I was waiting for the train. Roy was standing on the platform, too, and he started up a conversation. When my train came along I said, "Here's my train." I got into the train, turned around and there he was following me! So we sat down and continued talking. At the end of the ride I got off, and there he was still with me. What was I going to do with him?

Finally I phoned up my mother, and I said, "I've got a friend here with me. Do you mind if I bring him home?" She was wonderful and said she didn't mind. I think it was only when we were walking up the street that I realized he was a Canadian. We got into the house, and my father was at the beginning of his illness, so he was in bed. I went up to see him. My mother had been up and told him ahead of time. So my father looked at me and said, "To think a daughter of mine could pick up somebody at the railway station." I protested, "Oh dad, he's lonely. He's come from Canada." But my dad told me, "There's places for men like that. They have the Maple Leaf Club." So he still wasn't very happy about what I'd done. But my mother liked Roy, and the three of us had tea.

I went back to the station with Roy and saw him off. The next night we arranged to meet and we went to the show. And it just started from there. Then my father had to move into the hospital in Surrey, and my mother and I used to go there to visit him. When we'd come back on the bus, there would be Roy leaning up against the wall of the bakery on the corner of our street. And my mother would say, "There's the Canuck holding up the bakery." He always seemed to be there.

Roy was with the artillery. He'd lied about his age and joined up before he was actually old enough. He came overseas in 1941. And I met him in 1943. It was October 1943 when he was sent to Italy. He wrote to his mother when we decided to get engaged. He asked her to buy a ring, and she did. She had a friend who was a minister back there who was coming to England. So she asked him if he would bring the ring over. One day at the billet in Guildford there was a knock at the door and here was the minister with this ring.

Roy was in Italy but I didn't know that at the time because they were sending all the information back to his mother in Canada. He was wounded in April 1944 and arrived back in England on the hospital ship on D-Day. He was taken farther up the coast, and I received a card telling me he was back in England. Roy was convalescing, and here I was still in the Land Army. Then one day when I'd been out to a show, I returned home to find this figure in blue standing at the billet gate. Roy was using a cane and was so thin that I didn't even know him.

We were engaged in October 1944. One night we were at the house of a friend of mine, and she suddenly asked, "When are you two going to get married?" Roy and I hadn't really thought about the wedding. In fact I had received a letter from Roy's mother suggesting that I come over to Canada before we got married to see if I liked it over there. Then I had a letter from Roy's sister-in-law who was married to his older brother, and she said, "Oh, go ahead and get married while you can. Don't wait to come over to Canada."

It wasn't many months later that we decided we would get married. It happened to be January 8th, a Monday, because this friend of mine who owned a fish and chip store asked when we were going to get married. It was going to be on a Saturday but she asked if we could make it on a Monday because then she could come when her store was closed.

We were married in St. Mary's Church, a very historical church in Merton Park. Horatio Nelson used to go to that church every Sunday. There's a plaque with his name where he used to sit. It's a lovely little church. We were married at two o'clock in the afternoon. My sister's husband gave me away because my father had died in 1943. It was a very small wedding, but Roy's brother was in England then so he'd come down. Roy didn't have anybody else representing his family, except for his brother. All my brothers were overseas but my mother was there and my friends came.

I don't know where my friend found it, but she brought this most beautiful wedding cake. From the black market it must have been! It was gorgeous. You know, with all the rationing going on, I could never have made one like that. Another friend had arranged for us to have a week's holiday down in Cornwall. Our train was to leave at ten o'clock at night so we would have to travel all night, and we would get there at nine o'clock in the morning. We had tea at the house, and then Roy and I went up to London to catch the train.

The train was full. Roy and I got into a first-class carriage. They had first-class, second-class and third-class carriages on those trains then. We got in, and we couldn't even sit together, it was so full. There was an American WAC on one side and an American WAC on the other side. Roy sat next to one, and I sat next to the other on the other side. One girl had a terrible cold, and she was sniffing and blowing.

At one of the stops, they opened the door and this fellow came in. He'd just come from the front in France. He asked, "Is there any room here?" And people said, "No!" All the seats were taken. So he just came in, lay down on the floor and went sound asleep. Finally, Roy and I reached our destination in the morning, and they sent a car to meet us and take us to our hotel. The hotel was an old farmhouse actually, and they had a lovely breakfast for us. Then we went to bed and slept all morning, I think. That was our wedding night.

Roy went back to Canada in February 1945; I received notification in April saying that I was to be on my way. And that was it. I had a kind of a strange fear. Here I was leaving my home and friends. Of course my friend that had got us into the Land Army was absolutely devastated that I was leaving for Canada. And I felt badly because my mother was alone as my brothers were still overseas. They hadn't returned yet, and I can always remember my mother seeing me off at the station. She said to me, "Well, I hope you know what you're doing." I said, "Well mum, I'm not always going to have you." And that was how I left.

Roy had really had no time to prepare me for what Canada would be like because he went back so quickly. He had only a month before he left. But my mother-in-law used to write all the time and tell me everything that was going on. When I was to leave, we went up to London first and then we stayed the night before getting on a train that took us to Liverpool. The boat was called the *Scythia*, a really old boat. I got on, and the first thing that I saw was this great big bowl of fruit on a table. There were bananas and all this lovely fruit which we had never seen all through the war. In fact, my niece who was born during the war had never seen a banana until her family came to Canada.

The food was excellent. There were two people to a cabin, and I was up on the top bunk because the lady down below had a child. The trip took eleven days, and we ran into some terrific storms. There were huge waves coming right up over the ship.

They were pretty tall, and they used to wash over the deck. Then one night while we were on the trip, we were told, "We're now passing through dangerous waters so don't undress." We had to sleep in our clothes. The ship had to zig-zag further down off course, because there was a U-boat following us, and this was why the trip took eleven days.

When we arrived in Halifax, the people were just wonderful. They made us feel so welcome. All the children came around cheering. Then we got off the boat and were put right on a train. I was going to Sarnia, Ontario. Roy and his brother met me at the station. When we got back to the house I met Roy's mother and father. They were the most wonderful couple you could ever wish to meet. My mother-in-law was English so she knew exactly what I was going through. Roy's father had emigrated from England when he was a child sponsored by Dr. Bernardo's Homes program. In those days, this program was sending orphans from England to work on Canadian farms. Roy's dad eventually joined up and fought for Canada in World War I, so he was more Canadian than his wife. She was very English. I don't think she ever lost it. But they were just the greatest couple.

We lived with Roy's parents for fourteen months while we were waiting for a house to become vacant. There were no houses available then. I found a job with a tractor company for awhile. It was something to do. Our next-door neighbours gave me a shower. And the people down at the bottom of the road gave me a shower too. I didn't even know what a shower was. When I went to the first shower I didn't know what was going on, and somebody said, "Well here's the guest of honour." I didn't know what they were talking about. Then the people next door gave us a beautiful dinner set. Oh, people were kind. It was amazing.

Our daughter was born while we were still living with Roy's parents. Of course Roy's mother helped a great deal with the baby. I didn't know what to do with this baby, but Roy's mother took over and looked after her. Finally we got this house, and fourteen months later our son was born. He was a "preemie." He wasn't supposed to be born for another two months. And he was born with cerebral palsy. In those days, they didn't even know what it was. It took them a long time before they realized what it was.

There were other children with cerebral palsy in Sarnia, so we shared information and got quite a group going. Then we put our son's name in to go to this home in London, Ontario. Meanwhile, in 1949, my sister and her family had moved from England to the West Coast of Canada. My brother-in-law, who was a doctor, suggested that we move out to BC because he thought perhaps there were more things available for children with cerebral palsy there. So that's how we came to move from Sarnia. Of course my mother-in-law was just heartbroken that we were moving so far away. We drove all the way with two children in the back of one car. It was quite a hectic journey.

I was also pregnant with our third child when we drove out to BC. We travelled through the United States for a time, but when we ran out of American money, we decided to cut back into Canada at Spokane, Washington. I remember we were in this old car on this dirt road. They hadn't any decent highways then. This was in 1950. We lost the grill on the front of the car, and then when we reached New Westminster and were going over the Patullo Bridge, the car lights went out. My husband was holding them by a wire to keep them on until we got to my sister's house.

Strangely enough, our third child was born in New Westminster on Christmas Eve. It was the same day as my husband's birthday and it was also my mother's birthday. We stayed with my sister in New Westminster while we were waiting for a house in Vancouver. Then we moved to Vancouver, and we lived there for thirty-six years. My husband worked for BC Hydro during this time, and when he retired we decided to move to Vancouver Island. Two of our children were living there—one in Cowichan Bay and the other in Mill Bay. This was ten years ago, and now all three of our children live on the Island. So my husband and I are happily retired in beautiful Cobble Hill on Vancouver Island with all our children close at hand.

Lillian Ambrus

"I THOUGHT, 'OH GOD,
WHERE AM I GOING?'"

---

*Lillian Ambrus was born in London and
raised in Bournemouth. She grew up the eldest
of six children.*

M y family has always been close. When I left school, I went to work in a nursing home and started training as a nurse, but my health wouldn't let me carry on. Then my sister and I worked in a factory and that went bankrupt. We then went to work in a steam laundry and we used to cycle there every day, and I was still working there when I met my husband.

I remember when war was declared, we were listening to the wireless and I felt a cold chill go over me just knowing we were at war. Rationing soon started and times were pretty hard. I never did spend a lot of money on clothing because I just didn't have it to spend. We always looked and never bought. It was kind of hard, but we never missed the new clothes. I helped my mum and dad with what little wages I had. I never thought of how little money I had, as long as I could eat and go to a picture show once in awhile. I didn't go out very much, and I never went to dances. We were more a cycling family and used to cycle to Southampton thirty-five miles away from Bournemouth.

Bournemouth was what they called an open town, a lot of the troops were stationed there. The German planes used to sneak in over the coast and drop their bombs and take off. We used to stand up in the window and watch the search lights. Mother was more upset about the bombs, as she had lived through World War I. They didn't really affect me in the first part of the war. I remember a Sunday morning when the siren went and we could see a lone German plane. We used to dress up for church, and the people would just drop in the gutter because of the bombing and machine guns. Not too far from where I lived, a bomb dropped on a house when this lady was having a bath. Her husband was outside puttering around when the bomb hit, and the blast picked up the bathtub and carried the lady far from the house. She turned upside down under the tub. Her husband was unhurt and started looking for her. She was found in the field, unhurt but in shock.

I met my husband Bert through an aunt. He was related to her by marriage and he was visiting her on this particular Sunday. My aunt had asked me to go over that day and cook dinner while they went to church. But she didn't tell me that they had company. I cooked dinner and was making pastry when two gentlemen walked into the kitchen. They were father and son. Bert's father lived in England. They didn't say anything much, just made fun of the flour on my nose, and then when my aunt and uncle came home, they introduced me. I was put to sit next to my future husband, Bert. After supper was over and the dishes were done, we played a game of darts. A laundry press had come down on my arm when I worked in the laundry, and sometimes my arm would go out. I couldn't hit the board with the dart no matter how hard I tried. Maybe I was self-conscious, I don't know. Anyway Bert went up to the dart board and said, "You're supposed to put it there." Before I could stop, I threw the dart, and it went right through his thumb.

Our courtship was very short. I was married Sept. 8, 1940, and I had my first baby Susan ten months later. We were married in the registry office, and we had a small family reception with my mother and aunt and the rest of the family. I was married in a suit with a spray of flowers. Bert had told me that if he was ordered back to Canada he wanted me to go, too, so it was done quickly, just in case. But we didn't get away to Canada until July 7, 1945. I travelled around England with my husband for awhile and stayed in a place called Storrington, and that's where my second baby Joy was born. When Bert went away and I was left alone, I would take off and travel back to stay with my mum and dad for awhile. When it was time to do all the paperwork to come to Canada, I moved back with mum and dad, and I left for Canada from there.

I was supposed to leave July 4th from Liverpool. Then at the last minute that was cancelled, and I had to leave from Wales. My mum, dad and sister came to see me off. Bert was back in England because he had been hurt in a lorry accident. So he was able to come to the boat, *S.S. Cavina,* to help me get settled for the trip to Canada.

I shared a cabin with another woman, an officer's wife, and her son. I put my baby in a cot on the floor. Towards morning I woke up and found the baby covered with cockroaches. That's when we found out it was a converted banana boat. There was no fresh water to wash the diapers in, so we had to wash them in salt water and hang them all over the railing. Those diapers!—you could never get them white again because they were so stiff and hard. I used to put toilet paper inside the diaper so it wouldn't rub the baby's skin.

We were late getting into Halifax because of a hospital ship which had to unload. When we did get in there was nobody to meet us. Someone phoned and a lady came. She took us to a hostel and gave us breakfast the next morning before we caught the train. On the trip across Canada we would get off the train at the various stations to buy little bits of things from the fruit carts. My daughter Sue had never seen a banana and she wouldn't eat them. A lady had dry pieces of banana slices and she said, "Give her some of these and when she eats them she will eat a banana," and she did.

My destination was Regina. My sister-in-law and her husband met us and took us to their place, and my husband joined me there. I told him I wasn't happy there because she had cockroaches in her house, too. So we went to Lipton, Saskatchewan, and visited some of the people my husband used to work for and they were very nice to us. He sent me ahead to Peace River while he went to Calgary to be discharged. One of his buddies in the war sold Bert a quarter section of land through his buddy. I rented a little two-room shack in Peace River and lived there. After my husband arrived he went to look at this quarter section to see what the buildings were like, but there was nothing we could live in. We had to stay in town for awhile. Then through the VLA (Veterans Loan Association) we managed to buy a farm with an old house on it across the road from the acreage.

We moved to the farm at the end of February, and a neighbour came and picked us up on a hay rack. We couldn't even drive the roads because the snow was so deep and I thought, "Oh God, where am I going?" When we arrived, the neighbour's wife was there in the old shack with something to eat for us. I can't say I was sorry we went, because it was an adventure, and there was something new all the time. I loved it on the farm.

We chopped holes in the ice to get water from the dam and I would melt the ice to feed the animals. When the nice weather came I picked wild raspberries, strawberries and Saskatoon berries. I had never canned a thing in England so I had to learn all that. I got used to it, and I liked it.

On the farm the men didn't like to go into town to get the groceries. So my neighbour and I would walk four miles along the railway tracks to the little train station and catch the train to town. Then we would come back with our groceries. Sometimes the men came to the station and met us. But one time they didn't and we couldn't get hold of them because there was no phone, so we walked the four miles home with the groceries. My neighbour broke her bag and sat on the tracks, so tired she could hardly go any further. I froze my legs and they came up in black lumps. But things like that we had to do and you couldn't give up.

My husband made this cutter, a small sleigh, and he built this little house on it and put a heater in it. I used to guide the horses to town eleven miles away, and because the roads were so bad it would take a long time to get to town. Sometimes you had to go into the ditch and cross the field to the other road. One time when it was getting near springtime and the snow was melting, my friend and I were on our way into town. This time the horses didn't want to go down the ditch as it was heavy pulling, and we tipped over. We had a crate of eggs we were taking into town, but none broke.

We soon found that the farm didn't pay at all, and so Bert was away working to bring some money in. Eventually we rented out the farm, but got very little from the rent. Finally everything was sold in 1961. We separated and I moved into Peace River. I went to work in a hotel, and Bert and I divorced.

I moved to Victoria with my second husband in 1978. I had originally gone to Victoria in 1976 to see my daughter and her new baby. I loved it because it was so much like England. I went back and told my husband. We came the next year for a holiday and decided that we would move out permanently. I didn't want to come until we retired, because we were both working and our house in Peace River was paid for. But my husband wanted to come so I had to give my notice at the hotel where I was working, and we came here in 1978.

I divorced my second husband in 1984, and when I turned sixty-five, I did everything I couldn't do when I was with him. I took dancing lessons with Arthur Murray and won a gold and bronze medal at competition. I went back to England for the first time since 1968, and I took my two girls because they had never been back. We went to a reunion of the Canadian and American War Brides while back in England. Since my retirement, I try to go back to England as often as possible to see family and attend War Bride Reunions. This year I am looking forward to going to England in May with other war brides, to celebrate the 50th anniversary of VE-Day.

Maureen Eggiman

"THE CEILING STARTED COMING DOWN INTO OUR ICE CREAMS"

Maureen Eggiman grew up in the small town of Badley near Leeds, England. When the war started Maureen was sixteen years old and working as a probationary nurse at a hospital in Bradford.

I can still remember it: the bad shock I had at the hospital where I worked. It happened one night when I was working on night duty. I wasn't really qualified. In fact, I had worked part of the day, and was supposed to get the afternoon off to sleep, then go back on duty at night. Instead, I had to go out with the ambulance, and pick up this man, Mr. Mawson. So I really didn't get much rest. About nine o'clock that night, he became delirious, and I was having a hard time keeping him in his bed. At that time I probably weighed about ninety pounds. The matron was a very devout Catholic, and she'd gone to a religious retreat.

I phoned a staff nurse and told her that this man was delirious and I was having a hard time managing him. So she said, "Alright, I'll get the nurse from the diphtheria ward to go and lock up, and I'll leave a note for the matron when she's come in." This man wasn't the only patient. There was quite a bunch of them, and about two o'clock, he settled down. Anyway, I checked him every few minutes, and he seemed to be alright.

Then I guess I went to check on another patient, and when I came back, he was dead. So I called the matron, and I said, "Mr. Mawson has died." She had the message but the matron never came to see me when she came back from her retreat. A nurse came over, and she stood on one side of the bed while I stood on the other. Then she started giving me the devil because I had said he had died. I wasn't supposed to say that. I was supposed to say, "He appeared to have died." I couldn't make a diagnosis. Apparently, he had a malignant kind of scarlet fever that they had never seen in years. And he had a really bad heart as well as pneumonia. I mean any of the three things could have killed him.

Then the matron told me to make sure his pyjamas were taken off because they belonged to the hospital. You see, in those days, if a patient died, you had to wash him and get him ready for the undertaker. Now I was barely eighteen years old. I'd never seen anyone dead. And the nurse said, "Now you can go make me a cup of tea." Well, I was the one who needed the cup of tea, but anyway off I went.

The next morning, I was passing the nurse's office, and Mrs.

Mawson was there. And this nurse was telling Mrs. Mawson how peaceful he'd been. She was with him when he died and he was so peaceful. He'd just gone to sleep. This was a real good Catholic hospital; they used to make us go to church all the time. I went home and told my dad. He said, "That's it. You're not going back." My supervisor tried to get me to come back. I was the best probation nurse she had. But that was it. No more. I started at another hospital.

I went down to the South Coast to a little hospital there. It wasn't a training school, just a little hospital. It was for infectious diseases. I was in Weymouth right on the coast. That's why I think most of my memories of the war are happy ones. Because the hospital was in a restricted area, there were so many troops and so few women that we got invited out to all the functions. In fact, we had one nurse who used to label her engagement rings so she didn't go out wearing the wrong ring for the man she was going out with.

You'd come off duty at eight o'clock at night and you'd be so tired. We were rather short staffed. In fact, I came off duty one night, and I was going to quit. That was it, no more. But the staff nurse had bought me a bouquet of flowers and put them in my room to thank me. So I thought, "Well I can't quit now."

We'd swear to God we were going to go to bed. We got off duty at eight o'clock, and by eight-thirty we were hightailing it down to the dancehall at the Regent. We had to be in by ten-thirty at night unless it was our days off. Otherwise you weren't allowed out after ten-thirty at night. When you were on your days off, you got one late evening a week. When you were on night duty, you got three nights off a month. And we worked twelve-hour shifts. We used to get two hours off duty during the day. Or if you were off at six— well that was the best part because you could go to the dance earlier.

At the hospital, we used to get a lot of men with the mumps from the torpedo boats. We didn't get the wounded soldiers, but our area was getting bombed and shot at. One night, the Thursday before Easter, the night before Good Friday, we'd gone down to this dance at the Regent, and while we were there, a raid started. You were so used to the air raids, it didn't fizz anymore. But we were sitting at the ice cream bar when some of the ceiling started coming down into our ice creams. We thought it was time to leave. This was April 1943.

It was not until July 1946 that my cousin introduced me to my husband-to-be, Fred. I'd gone down to Brighton on a Wednesday, and she phoned to ask if she could come to see me. I said sure. She said, "Well, I've got my boyfriend with me." I said, "That's alright." She came with this boy, and I thought, "My goodness, he doesn't look any more than sixteen or seventeen." He was in shirt sleeves. Then when I saw him later, he was all dressed up. He was a Sergeant in the Queen's Own. Well he looked older then, and I started seeing him.

During the following week, I saw Fred three times in the park. The fourth time I saw him, he proposed to me. When he asked me to marry him, I told my cousin, and she told me I was crazy. I asked her why and she said, "I've been trying for six months. And if he wouldn't marry me, I'm sure he wouldn't marry you."

The evening Fred asked me to marry him, I told him to phone me at six o'clock the next morning. At eight o'clock in the morning, the phone rang and he said, "I slept in. Will you marry me?" I said, "You're crazy." Well he was going back to his outfit that day, and he promised to write. That was the August weekend, and of course there was no mail so I thought, "Well he's gone back. I'll never hear from him again." And then the next day, I got three letters from him.

We were married August 12th, 1946, and in December that year I got a call on a Saturday that I had to leave for Canada on Monday. My husband had gone to Canada ahead of me on August 19th on the same boat that General Montgomery came over to Canada on. I came over on the *Sameria*. It was bringing war brides and taking German prisoners back. It was a pretty good trip. There were many kids. I guess there were a lot of forces on our ship as well. I remember sitting at the table in the dining room, and some of the senior non-commissioned officers would sit there. I guess the rest of the men had different seats, I don't know.

When our boat docked in Halifax, if I could have stayed on it and gone home, I would have. I know my dad's last words were, "If you don't like it, I'll send you the money to come home." I always knew if I really didn't like it, I could go home.

When we got off that boat, they were playing "Here Comes the Bride." Some of the war brides had four or five kids. And some of them were pregnant. I didn't even know if my husband knew I was coming because I had such short notice before I left England. Then we arrived in Toronto, and they were calling out our names. We were all laughing because men would come up and grab their wives and start hugging and kissing them. Finally they called my name, and this man came running up to me. I thought, "My God! Who is this?" It was so funny.

My husband and I went to Owen Sound, a nice town on Georgian Bay in southern Ontario. It has a harbour for big ships. We lived with my mother-in-law for a year. My husband had gone back to work for RCA Victor. He had worked for them before he went into the forces. RCA Victor had a factory in Owen Sound, and there were a few other factories including Keenan's. You know your toothpicks? Well, they come from Owen Sound. In fact, my sister-in-law is the office manager there.

After I had been in Canada for a few months, I found out how my husband had managed to get more leave just after we met. He was determined to marry me before he left England, and with the help of the Padre, Fred had been granted compassionate leave to arrange for me to have my baby (which was born one year and eleven months after our wedding). We were married without obtaining permission from his Commanding Officer. We had a hard time getting a marriage license but the registrar, who had spent about two hours trying to get a ruling on it, finally said he wouldn't refuse us a license because Fred and I were both over twenty-one. However he warned my husband he would get into trouble when he got back to the base. We met and married within twenty-one days time!

It was snowing when I arrived in Owen Sound, and it snowed

and it snowed and it snowed. I sat in a chair by the window, and pretty soon the snow was up to the window sill. Then it was higher and it was higher until you could walk on the snow banks and touch the telegraph wires. That was the winter of 1946-47. It was quite a shock.

I went to work at a hospital in Owen Sound. And then my husband and I bought a place in Hepworth about twelve miles out. It was forty-five acres. We had some chickens and some pigs, and some skunks. I worked until I got pregnant, and my daughter was born in July of 1948.

Later my husband went back in the forces, and we were posted to Chilliwack in 1952. Our daughter Kathryn was born in Chilliwack in 1953. Then Fred was posted to Germany, and I went back to Owen Sound. That was again in the wintertime. I rented a house there. I furnished it with odds and ends because I didn't know when I'd be going to Germany. I went to Owen Sound in September, and I was there until the following March when I took the children for a visit to England before we joined Fred in Germany.

We were in Germany for two and a half years before returning to Canada. We stayed another year in Chilliwack, and then my husband was posted to Germany again. The children and I went to England first, and my husband met the boat at Southampton. When they put the gangplank out, he ran up it and they chased him back down it. He could see the kids, and I guess he ran up that gangplank about five times, and they chased him down five times. They said I had to go through customs first. When we got up to London, all the men were meeting their wives with bouquets of flowers, and I asked my husband, "How come you didn't bring me any flowers?" He said, "These men all stayed up here getting drunk. I came down to meet you at the boat!"

I stayed in England for awhile, and then it was back to Germany for another three years. When we came back in December of 1960, we were posted to Petawawa, in Ontario. I hated it at first, but after ten years there, in 1970, we got posted to Valcartier which was even worse. Now we didn't want to leave Petawawa.

We'd bought a house. The kids liked it, and I loved it. I was working, and nobody wanted to move.

After that move, we were posted to Borden in 1972. That's where my husband retired in 1976. My husband didn't want to move any place, but we came out to the West Coast on a visit to our son. Later I came back again by myself to visit, and I said, "I'm moving to the West Coast." Nobody else wanted to move.

Three weeks after we moved to the West Coast, my husband said it was the best idea *he* ever had. We had over forty-one years together and seven children. My husband Fred died March 5th, 1988.

Maureen Eggiman on a mined beach at Ostend, Belgium, March 1945.

Beryl Tanner

"THERE WAS NO QUESTION
THAT I WOULD GO"

*Beryl Tanner was born and raised in Isleworth
which is in Middlesex, England. She was twelve
years old when the war started.*

T he day that war was declared, we were all at home and had the wireless on to hear the announcement. The first thing that my mother said to me after Chamberlain had declared war was, "Go and fill up the bathtub with water." I looked at her and I asked, "Why?" She replied, "Because they're going to poison our water." Well, I did as I was told, and I could see her way of thinking because we'd heard quite a few stories. Of course, the Germans never did poison the water, and it was many months later that the bombing started.

When the air raids did begin, my school was bombed so we had to share space with other schools. At first it was very difficult when the siren went off, because we'd end up in the air-raid shelter having our lessons. If you can imagine it, the poor teacher was at one end of a quonset hut trying to teach two long rows of girls. She didn't have any microphone so the sound system wasn't any good. The situation became more and more difficult, and it wasn't too long before the teacher and the students all decided they'd rather stay in school during air raids. Fortunately for us, our school was bombed at night when there was no one in the building.

Our home was also bombed. It wasn't completely destroyed but damaged to the point where we had to move to another house that was empty at the time. Actually when our house was bombed we were very lucky that we weren't in the front room where all the glass came in, or we would have been badly injured. All the furniture was pitted with glass and we found glass everywhere for years. It was awful to think of what would have happened to us if we had been in that room.

One of my more horrifying experiences was to do with a V-1 rocket. The V-1 rocket was a bomb that had wings and had an engine that powered it. The engine would stop before it dropped, and you had no idea where the bomb would drift and land. It depended on whether there was a wind or how strong the wind was. Because it made no sound you had no warning as to where it would land.

At this time we had an acre of land where my dad grew vegetables. We had chickens and rabbits as well. One day my father and my uncle were working on our garden which was quite a distance from our home. I was in the kitchen, and I looked out the kitchen door which was half glass, so that you could see through. Suddenly I saw a V-1 rocket coming and I just yelled at my mother and sister, "Duck!" I went right down and it landed in Hounslow High Street. The rocket hit Woolworths, and there were a lot of people killed because people didn't know it was coming. It also set fire to two or three big stores.

At the time of course we didn't know where it had landed. We could just hear the explosion, and we worried about my father and my uncle. Later we gave a big sigh of relief because dad got on his bike and came home immediately. He too had heard the explosions, and he didn't know where it had landed either. He rushed home because he was worried about us. It was quite a horrifying experience.

We always knew when an air raid was coming because our planes, the Spitfires, used to take off from the Heston Airport. Heston was an area close to our neighbourhood and the Spitfires were stationed there. When they took off you knew that there was a raid coming and the sirens would go off ten minutes later.

As far as rationing went, we were one of the more fortunate families because we had chickens and rabbits. We also had the land where my father grew vegetables. So really and truly, we never ever went without. I can remember towards the end of 1943, in order to get meat you had to be registered with a butcher. I did all the shopping for my mother, but it got to a point where I would go down on a Saturday and all I could get was corned beef.

This went on for about six weeks, and we were getting a little bit sick of it. I mean how many different things can you do with corned beef? So I said to mum, "I find it very interesting that there's a butcher up at the other end of Hounslow and he always seems to have meat. Whereas our butcher doesn't. I'm going to take our ration books and I'm going to register our name with him!"

That's what I did, and then I could get a roast every Sunday which of course we then rationed into the week. You had your roast beef on Sunday, your cold meat on Monday, and maybe shepherd's pie on Tuesday, and then whatever was left got mixed up for stew. There were five of us, and I was able to get what was known as a fair-sized joint. But I don't think I've ever bought a can of corned beef in Canada. I had enough of it in England.

I shopped for mum because she had bad varicose veins and queuing up was hard on her. The responsibility was shared between my father and I but I did most of it. It used to be delightful to get soap to do laundry. We had very hard water and mother liked to use Persil. Well try to find it! Easier said than done. But I would keep my eyes open and go to different shops. When I was lucky I would learn that a certain shop would have Persil and I'd scoot down into the shop because I always kept my ration books with me. Sometimes I was able to build up a little reserve supply for mum because I knew there would be times when it wasn't available at all.

Along with the rationing, we had what were known as points for canned food. Mother would say, "Get me a tin of sausage meat." Such an item came from the United States, and on the top there would be a certain amount of white fat which mother would take and use for pastry so we could have a sausage pie. This was one of the ways mum used to improvise with our limited food supply. I think that's why many of us are so thrifty now. We had no choice in the past.

After I graduated from school, my first job was in the office of a factory located in Hammersmith. That would have been in 1944. I worked in the costing department of the office. I'll never forget that when I had my interview, I was asked, "Do you know your alphabet?" And I replied, "Yes!" Then the interviewer said, "Good! Then maybe you can do the filing correctly." And I tell you when I first started there were stacks and stacks and stacks of unfiled papers! It was wild.

I had only worked at the factory office for six months when I managed to get a job at the hospital, which was much closer to home, so I could now ride my bike to work. I started off in the office of the hospital. I already knew how to file but I had to learn how to answer a telephone. Most families didn't have telephones in those days. My father used to say, "What do we need a telephone for? There's a telephone booth up the road."

I hadn't been at the hospital office very long when they trained me to work in the outpatient's department because hospitals in England at that time had just as many outpatients as patients that were staying in the hospital. They needed somebody to look after all the patients that were coming into the clinic. I had to make sure all their records were available. These patients were coming in for electrocardiograms or actually for any complaint that required a specialist's attention.

While I worked I still lived with my family and we always took our holidays together. We would stay at a boarding house or at least a place where your meals were served. My mother declared that she had to cook the rest of the year so for two weeks somebody else could cook for her. This particular year, we went down to a seaside resort called Boscombe which is in Devon. It was a lovely place and we had a lot of fun. I used to be roped into doing the entertainment after dinner because I've always enjoyed singing.

After the European part of World War II ended, a lot of the hotels were taken over for Canadian servicemen until they could be repatriated to Canada. I got to meet some of the boys because there seemed to be a shortage of females in that particular area. I would ask mum and dad, "Is it alright if I go off to the pub with some of the boys?" And they would say it was okay as long as I didn't stay out too late.

These pub outings were always enjoyable, and it was at one of them that I met my future husband, Fred. Fred and I hit it off but by then my holiday was coming to an end, and I had to return home. Fred came up the following weekend and stayed at my place. Things always happened very quickly at that time. I think it was due to the simple fact that you didn't live for tomorrow because you weren't too sure that there was going to be a tomorrow.

I met Fred in September, and we were married in November. It seemed automatic that if you were marrying a Canadian, you would move to Canada as soon as possible. But that wasn't true in every case because I do know of some war brides who wouldn't come to Canada, and naturally some boys were quite happy to stay in England. But as far as I was concerned, there was no question that I would go. You knew you were leaving your family, but there was also the excitement of something new. I guess I had an adventurous spirit, too.

After the wedding, I continued to work at the hospital until I received notification that I could travel to Canada. Finally I came over in June, 1946. I was notified to go to London to stay at a hostel before leaving. Mum and dad came with me to the hostel, and then I had to stay there for two nights. Later my parents were able to see me off at Victoria station. I had skedaddled to a phone while I was at the hostel to let my parents know where I was leaving from.

I took the train from London to Southampton to board my ship. There was so much involved in getting on board. You had to line up and check in with the purser. We had been standing in line on the ship for quite awhile and the ship had already started off when the girl next to me asked me if I was feeling alright. I replied, "Well, no." She said, "You're getting greener." From then on I was either lying on my bunk or up on the deck. I only made it to the dining room once. The doctor checked me out because they wondered if I was pregnant but I wasn't.

I travelled on the *Lady Nelson*, which was a hospital ship. Half of the ship was for the war brides, and the other half held the troops that needed care on their trip home. You were not supposed to talk to any of the troops. We had one girl who did fraternize with them, and when we got to Halifax, she was not allowed to get off the boat. But it was funny for me when the ship came into Halifax because I finally made it to the dining room and everybody wondered, "Where did you come from?" I was very hungry at that point after over a week of being seasick.

In Halifax, we were processed alphabetically so with my married name of Tanner, I had quite a wait but later I did have a delightful time on the train. They kept checking on me to make sure I was alright because I'd been so sick throughout the ocean voyage. I would respond, "Yes I'm fine—I'm on land!" We had a very nice porter, and we had a lot of fun. Our only complaint was how dirty the train was. Our seats made down into beds. Then they would fit tables between our seats so we could play cards and other games.

At first, I didn't know any of the other war brides on the train but we got to know one another as we travelled across Canada. I was going all the way to New Westminster in BC so I saw a lot of the war brides get off at their various destinations throughout Canada. It was very interesting when we got to Montreal. Usually when people were getting off the train, they had to put the steps down for them. But when you pulled into Montreal, it was just like getting off the tube in London—there was the platform right beside the train.

When we arrived in Winnipeg, there was a whole crew change-over. We were there for a few hours and we were told we had a certain amount of time to look around. It was an absolute scream crossing Main Street. There were about five of us and we were all looking in the wrong direction because traffic travels in the opposite direction in England. At any rate, we all held hands and scooted across. The only thing I can remember is a drugstore that we all went into and ordered a banana split. We'd all heard about these banana splits and had to try them.

By the time the train neared New Westminster the coach had become almost empty. I had been well prepared for the size of Canada. Fred had told me, "You're not going to get from here to there in a day!" When Fred finally met me in New Westminster, I took one look at him and asked, " Oh! Who are you?" I didn't recognize him in civvies. Then we proceeded over to where his parents lived.

We only stayed with Fred's parents for a couple of weeks. Fred was working on the stock exchange as a trader but he took some time off to get us settled. We started off with just a bedroom in a house that we shared with this dear lady. She was a character. We had the use of the house but the bedroom was our only private room. She worked, and thank goodness Fred came home early because, until he arrived, I would struggle with the wood and coal stove which, fortunately for me, did have two gas rings on one end. They saved my life! I really chuckled when I saw the washing machine. It looked like an old wash tub with a wringer on it, but at least it did run electrically.

I had quite a time in the house because I'm fairly tall and my husband was tall but the lady of the house was short. There was this lamp over the dining room table which she liked to have down far enough to hit me in the eye. So I'd raise it, and then she'd pull it back down again. Neither one of us ever said anything.

We didn't stay there too long because Fred had managed to find us an apartment in a building on the corner of Davie and Jarvis. I had a lot of fun going out and choosing furniture because there wasn't a lot of that available either. We ordered a bedroom suite which we had to wait for because there were only so many orders they could fill at a time. You have to remember that there wouldn't have been things such as furniture made during the war because all production was geared for the war effort. So after the war there was a severe shortage of everything that families needed to set up households. We chose a bed chesterfield and a big armchair so we were able to sleep on the bed chesterfield until the bedroom suite finally arrived.

I remember how it rained and rained and rained in Vancouver. Finally I went out and found a shoe store where I informed them that I needed a pair of wellingtons. They just looked at me as if to say, "What the heck is this girl talking about?" So I said, "Well, you know, what you put on your feet because of all the rain." They replied, "Oh you mean gumboots." Frustrated, I responded, "Well, show me whatever you have." So I got my gumboots, which I very much needed to survive in Vancouver where it does rain an awful lot.

Our first child Carolyn was born in June of 1947 at St. Paul's Hospital. We stayed at the apartment until we moved over to

Victoria in August of 1948. Carolyn was fourteen months old by this time. We moved to Victoria because Fred had been offered a job as manager of Victoria Photo Supply. It's gone now but it was a store on Douglas Street in the Sussex Building. Eventually we owned the store.

Our son Scott was born in 1950. While I was pregnant with Scott, a friend asked me if I was going to have a girl or boy, and I said, "Oh I'm going to have a boy." He replied, "You seem pretty certain." Then I assured him, "Oh yes—no ands, ifs or buts in *my* mind!" He said, "Okay, if it's a little boy, you'll get a thousand dollars." That was a lot of money in those days. He would give it to us for a down payment on a house. So, of course we got our thousand dollars, because we got our little boy.

In 1954, we built a house on Santa Clara near Elk Lake. Our daughter Denise was born in 1961 but things were not going well with our marriage. It all fell apart in 1967. When our marriage ended, I had to find a job, and I started out selling Fuller Brush products. It was not easy and I looked for another job. Fortunately, I was offered a job at Butler Brothers working in their readi-mix department office. I was responsible for all the invoicing and was also the assistant dispatcher. It was quite an undertaking, seeing as how I didn't know the first thing about concrete, readi-mix, gravel, etc.

I also became known as what they called a "women's libber" because I was now working in what had always been regarded as a male domain. "What! A female in the readi-mix department! You must be crazy." I actually ended up working at Butler Brothers for sixteen years.

Five years ago I decided to sell my home—it was a large house with a swimming pool and it was located on a third-of-an-acre of land. It was sold within a month which rather floored me. Then I was unable to find anywhere else to live because the houses on the market were being instantly snapped up. I can remember one night that I cried myself to sleep and wondered, "What have you done, you stupid fool. You had a beautiful home and now you don't have anything."

Beryl Tanner

The next morning after church (God always answers your prayers you know), I was riding around and spotted the house that was perfect for me. I made arrangements to buy it and I still live in it today. Although I'm now retired, I keep very busy doing what I most enjoy which includes looking after my granddaughter, doing volunteer work for my church and of course serving on the executive of the Vancouver Island War Brides.

207

Nancy Pittet

"IT'S ALL AN ADVENTURE
WHEN YOU THINK
ABOUT IT"

Nancy Pittet was born and grew up in Paisley, Scotland. Paisley is an industrial city situated close to Glasgow. Nancy was fifteen years old when war was declared.

T he day that war was declared, it was such a shock. You cried. You were scared. You were frightened because you didn't know what to expect. And then you realized that members of your family would be going to war, like my brother Bill, who was eighteen. My brother Jim, who was married, went and joined the Army. My oldest brother was already in the regular Army. You knew that it was going to happen, but all of a sudden there it was. The blackouts began and gas masks were issued to everybody. You had to carry the gas mask with you wherever you went.

You were taught a lot of things. You were taught about blackouts, to keep your windows completely covered. No light showing whatsoever. People taught you about shelters. We had a shelter built in our backyard. We lived in council houses which were like little apartments. People showed you how to build the shelter so that it was partly under the ground; that was where you would go when the air-raid sirens went.

The first siren was the most scary thing I ever heard in my life— that moaning sound. Once the siren went, you were to get up and go to the shelter. Of course, everybody was supposed to take their gas masks with them. You also took a kettle so that you could have a cup of tea if you were there too long. A good cup of tea, and you were alright.

This particular night, we were going to the shelter, and we could hear the planes. That was the worst part. We could hear these planes droning overhead, going steady. We were seven or eight miles away from the shipyards, but still it was close, and the shipyards were a target. I don't know what happened, but all of a sudden we heard this bomb coming down. And it's the eeriest feeling you ever had. It was whistling over you, and you could hear it. And we were all looking at each other, scared, and saying, "Well, is this it?"

You're frightened for your life. And then all of a sudden, nothing. It just didn't explode. So we all looked at each other, "Good! Nothing's happened after all." But, a block away, there was a group of homes together. It was at the very end of the block, and this bomb came down and sheared the end of the building off.

The one set of apartments was gone. The next set of apartments was fine. But this one set—it was as if they had been cut off from the top. There was one man who had grown tired of waiting for the "all-clear." He went back into his apartment, and they found him dead in his chair. He was the only casualty from that air raid. Another time they hit a first-aid shelter, and that was bad—there were many casualties.

Mother would say, "Now if the siren goes, everybody be good and don't get upset." Then she'd be the first one to be ready! I thought, "Good, mum!" We used to have one little kettle that we called the "all-clear" kettle. When the "all-clear" would come, we'd say, "Oh good!" and then put the kettle on to boil.

We did a lot of skating. There was myself and my three girl-friends who were sisters, and our mothers were our chaperons. They came along to the ice rink and watched us skate. We loved it. It was a big indoor rink. And then we learned to dance on our skates. So I danced with the three sisters. Oh, we had so much fun. I still like skating.

When I was seventeen or eighteen, I could either join the forces or go into the Land Army. But you didn't want to go far away from home. So my girlfriend and I went to work at a munitions factory in Lindwood. I remember we had to learn a lot of new things. We were working on the breach locks of the guns, so we hoped we did a good job. We also learned how to use a comptometer for measuring and how to file the edges of pieces of steel.

I had never been on night shifts in my life. We worked different shifts—two 'til ten or ten 'til six in the morning. The night shift was a little difficult, especially when you had to take the bus to work. I enjoyed the work because it was different. You felt that you were doing something important, and that you were really contributing to the war effort.

It was quite a big factory, and they had overhead cranes. We had to wear white coveralls and a little hat to make sure all our hair was in and covered. I remember that we had such a nice boss. He was so patient with us because he was working with girls who had never done anything like this in their lives. He was a wonderful man. I can still see him. He had nice light brown hair. He wore glasses, and he had a mustache.

Once I fell asleep for a few minutes. We were on night shift, and we weren't used to it. My girlfriend nudged me, "Nancy, you're going to sleep!" And our boss said, "It's alright. You'll get used to the shifts." So you learned and carried on. It just seemed unusual for women to be doing so many things they'd never done before. It was good in a lot of ways.

I had been working at the munitions factory less than a year when I met my husband-to-be, Gabe. My girlfriends that I had grown up with had all met Canadians and married them by this time. Gabe came with a friend to visit my girlfriend's family, and my girlfriend invited me over, telling me there were two nice Canadians visiting. So I went over and met him. And I kind of liked him. He was really nice.

It's so funny to remember being introduced to Gabe. And you know my first thoughts were, "Well he seems nice." I looked into his eyes, and he had such kind eyes. Yet I didn't want him to think that I was going to be bold.

Gabe asked me to go to a show with him, and it was *Gone With the Wind,* the classic movie. Then after that, he asked me if I would like to go out with him again, and I said yes, I would. We met in August 1942, and we were married in March 1943. In the meantime, Gabe left Scotland and went back to England where he was stationed. He then went overseas to Belgium and Holland, and finally the border of Germany.

I don't remember much about my wedding. I just remember going down the aisle with my dad, and he was so nervous. I was telling him in a low voice, "Dad, just take your time, take your time." Then we had a nice dinner at the co-op hall, and our minister came, which was pleasant. We didn't go on a honeymoon because Gabe had to go back the next day.

After that, I saw Gabe briefly when he came home on leave. Then he went to Europe, and I didn't see him for quite a long time. That was the hardest part. It was about nine or ten months. I was no longer working because I was pregnant. Gabe got a forty-eight-hour pass and came from Aldershot, England, to visit me. They had told him the baby was going to be born.

Gabe came in on Sunday and he could only stay overnight with me because he had to leave the next day. But he did get to see his son before he left. Raymond's birth was kind of scary for me. The first one is a bit frightening. I had the baby at home, and a mid-wife came. I remember her being very, very capable. Raymond was born at seven in the morning.

I stayed with my parents until it was time to go to Canada. On the 29th of February, 1946, with my little son and pregnant with my second baby, I was at the Paisley train station.

One moment, you're standing on the platform. You're all talking, and then all of a sudden, it's final. Boom! You've got to get on that train. And it's almost like you want to grab your family and hang on forever. I can remember hanging on to mum and hanging on to dad. My brother Bill was there, and he had a little baby girl. She was a little older than Raymond. Bill walked to the end of the platform, and he was the very last one that I could see, standing there waving. I remember I was crying and crying when I left on that train.

Oh, you know, you have so many mixed emotions. You think, "Oh my gosh!" But then all the girls were in the same coach, and we were all crying. There was none of this stiff upper lip stuff. You're leaving everything you've ever known, and that's when it hits you. And then all of a sudden, I thought, "I've got a little two-year-old here. Come on! Shape up!" So then you start talking and laughing and saying that we're going to see daddy. But he really wants his granny and grandpa. And I want to see mum and dad.

We caught another train in Glasgow, and from there we went to Liverpool. My son and I stayed overnight at a hostel with other war brides and their children, and the next day we were all taken to this big ship, the *Mauretania*. It was the biggest ship I had ever seen. She's the next in line for size, I think, after the *Queen Mary* and the *Queen Elizabeth*.

The voyage was very good, and five days later we landed in Halifax. From there, we travelled by train. We had a nice train ride, and then we came to Winnipeg—a very crowded station. All you could see was a sea of faces, and I thought, "How am I ever going to find Gabe?" Then all of a sudden this man comes towards me. He looks great in a tweed suit, a nice overcoat and a hat. I didn't recognize Gabe at first because I'd never seen him in civvies. And then of course, Gabe picked up Ray. It was splendid, their meeting.

From the station, Gabe, Ray and I went to a hotel. We stayed overnight there, and the next day we caught the train to Cardinal, a town close to where Gabe's parents lived on their farm. Cardinal turned out to be twenty-two houses, a hotel, a general store, and a barber shop. Gabe had told me what it was like but you cannot visualize it until you see it. There was a lot of snow, more than I'd ever seen in my life. Gabe's brother, Marcel, was there waiting for us with a team of horses and covered sleigh to take us to the farm.

I thought, "Oh my Lord, where am I going?" Then after a short journey, we came to a halt. That was the frightening part. You're thinking as you go along, "What if they don't like me? Well, what can I do about it? It's too far to go back." I was happy with Gabe but I was wondering about his family. And yet I knew they were nice because Gabe's mother had already been writing to me. Then we went into the farmhouse, and I saw Gabe's mum busy at the coal and wood stove.

There was a Coleman lantern hanging in the kitchen, while in the living room—oh!—she had a big table set for dinner that night. My sister-in-law, Denise, was there because her husband was just out of the forces, too. She was Gabe's younger sister, the same age as myself. Then there were two young brothers. As I came into the kitchen, my mother-in-law and my father-in-law and the two young brothers greeted me. And then all the others including Gabe's oldest brother, Joe, and his wife Anna.

So you're excited, and it's so cosy and warm. And, ah, Gabe's mum had a beautiful dinner prepared for us. Everybody was lovely, and when they greeted me, of course, out goes the hand to shake theirs but I'm kissed on the cheeks again. I told Gabe, "I was a little worried because your mum was very reserved." But they were all so warm. Unfortunately, my Scottish accent wasn't quite as easy to understand!

We had a lovely dinner, and afterwards we went into one of the little bedrooms. Gabe's mum had made a quilt for us. It was made from different materials, from coats and things like that. She put it on the bed and said, "That's a little gift for you, Nancy." Then she had a photograph of my mum and dad. Oh, when I saw that, the tears flowed. My in-laws were a terrific family. I soon called them mum and dad too. Mum taught me so many things because I wasn't a very good cook, and I couldn't sew very well. She was a wonderful seamstress and what a cook!

There was no running water on the farm, and they used coal-oil lamps because mum and dad were at the end of the line. But they were to get their electricity within six months. In the meantime, I was initiated to the coal-oil lamps, the Coleman lantern and the coal and wood stove. The next day Gabe's mum said, "Nancy, I'll be washing today." I said, "That's fine." Then they brought in snow, and I was looking at this snow, wondering what it was for. So I asked Gabe, "Why are they bringing in snow?" He said, "Mum likes soft water to wash clothes." Very intelligent, wasn't I?

Everything in Canada was so different to me. The closest neighbour here was a mile away while in Scotland the closest neighbour would be from one wall to another. So you know it was quite an adjustment. Gabe had tried to prepare me. The joke during the war had been that some of the Canadian soldiers had gopher farms. It was just a joke but still you wondered where you were going and what you would see. After a time Gabe told me there was no place for him on his parent's farm, and we would live in the city. We stayed with Gabe's parents for two months, and then we moved to St. Boniface.

Just after I arrived, I said to my husband, "You know I never before appreciated water running out a tap. I haven't got running water here." He said, "Oh yes there is. There's two pails. You see them there?" I told him that I did. He said, "You run to that pump, and you come back." So I learned the art of carrying two pails of water.

When I moved to the village I learned the art of cooking on a coal and wood stove which was mammoth to me. I'd lived in the city all my life and had all the conveniences. I asked Gabe how to adjust the temperature and keep it there. "Well Nan," he said, "You put the wood in, and if it gets too hot, you open the lid and take out a piece of wood." He was joking, of course. I looked at him, and I said, "Gabe!" Anyway, I had to learn there's green wood and there's dry wood. And I did.

One day, I asked Gabe, "What are you going to be?" He said, "Well, I like woodwork so I'll be a carpenter." So that's what he did, and he's worked hard ever since. Over the years, we've lived in Manitoba, Alberta, and finally British Columbia. Gabe has been in the brush-cutting business, and I have helped him run first a hotel and then a hardware store. And we have eight wonderful children who paid my way to Scotland so that I could revisit where I grew up.

You're always Scottish inside because you were born there, and I guess it's there to stay. But on the other hand, you're in this country. You accept this country as being very good to you. It's been wonderfully good. I've been in Canada for so long now that I've been here longer than I was in my country of origin. But I'll always have that longing for the country I came from. That will never go away. Yet I'm very proud and happy to be Canadian. It's a learning experience from the start as you travel through different bits of your life. It's all an adventure when you think about it.

I've never ever regretted coming to Canada. It's a wonderful country, and I was made very very welcome by my in-laws. Gabe's mum taught me so much, like cooking, canning, sewing and gardening. And Gabe's parents taught me how nice it was to see a family pray together, as they did. A great beginning.

Muriel Clark

Muriel, on right,
with friend.

"THE ONLY THING THAT GAVE ME AWAY WAS THE ACCENT"

Muriel Clark was born in South Ealing, the youngest of five children. When war was declared, she was fourteen and living in Ruislip, not far from London.

I worked in London during the war, and I certainly didn't like passing the people who were in the underground for shelter from the air raids when I was catching the train. I used to catch the workman's train up to London in the morning because it was cheaper. When I arrived there, people were in the underground from the night before, and when I was going home, they were all coming in again with their blankets to stay the night. It was actually very depressing. You would go to work one day and find that your favourite restaurant had been bombed. But you lived with it. It was uncanny when I think about it. How could I have been so calm? I wasn't when the war broke out and the sirens began. I started shaking all over. My mum said to me, "Just pull yourself together, this is a war and it's going to last." From then on, I smartened up and realized this is life, and I had to live with it. I went dancing just about every night in the week, even in the blackouts. We lived our lives, we really did, and enjoyed life as much as we could.

My sister had a baby when the Battle of Britain was on, so I went down to visit her in Bognor Regis on the coast. We were all under the table shelter when I said, "I have to go to the bathroom." Her husband said, "You can't go outside, there is shrapnel falling everywhere." But he took me out, and of course there was shrapnel falling on the garbage cans and everywhere. It was a rough night. It was so rough that my mum and dad came and got us the next day.

I remember that it was pretty tough finding food for the family. Mum and dad kept a couple of chickens, and even in the air raids one would come in and sleep with us under the table. Yes, we slept under the table. In order to keep a chicken you had to give up some of your meat rations. You couldn't keep both, and my dad used to keep rabbits as well. It was weird: mum always seemed to make something out of nothing. If there was ever a queue for anything, say for oranges, my mother would tell me, "You want oranges, you go line up for them," and that's what I did when I had a craving for oranges.

I remember I had a china doll made in Germany, and this lady in a queue said she wanted to get a doll for her little girl for Christmas. Well, you couldn't buy a doll anywhere during the war, so I said, "I have a doll. I have washed her face so much that all the colour has washed off, and I have cut her hair so much that it doesn't curl anymore. But it does have a bonnet on and it has clothes. Would you like it for your little girl?" Oh, she just thought it was wonderful. I said I was going to Canada, and I couldn't take it with me.

My parents moved down to Reading in 1943. I didn't want to go because once you gave up your job you had to go wherever the unemployment office put you. When I went to the unemployment office, they said I would have to work in a factory that made shells. I didn't want to work in the factory because some of the people who worked there had had fingers and hands blown off. Then they said I could work in the planning and progress office, so I was really glad.

I met Syd, my future husband, at the factory hostel, where the Irish people and others that worked at the factory were housed. They used to have dances at the factory for the workers twice a week, and they would bring in the Americans, Canadians and the British servicemen for the dance. Syd was with the Canadian Scottish—from Victoria.

I met Syd on the 24th of May, and D-Day was the 6th of June. He was so busy being a pay-sergeant that he never made it to many of the dances, but I had people bringing me messages from him: "I will get there as soon as I can get a day off. Can you get a day off work?" I had to phone in sick, something I had never done, but if he was getting a day off, I had to have a day off too. So we went up the Thames and rented a punt. Then he came back for supper. I saw him once or twice more before he went overseas.

The men were not supposed to tell anyone when they were going overseas, but Syd and I had agreed on a code to let me know when he was going. In July, about a month after D-Day, Syd phoned my neighbour, to tell me the code we had agreed on. I had just come home with my cousin from the show, and she asked, "Would you like to see him before he goes?" I said, "Yes, I would love to see him." We got a bus, then a train; it took forever, and we didn't get there until about eleven o'clock that night. We went to this army camp that was in the middle of nowhere. When we got there, they were all in the dance hall, so we stayed at the dance for awhile and my cousin met this other fellow and danced with him. He wasn't going overseas at that time.

After the dance we walked and walked, trying to find somewhere to stay. My cousin said, "If we can find a firehall they will put us up. She was in the fire service and knew they would help her. But we couldn't find one. We walked until four o'clock in the morning and it was drizzling rain. We looked like a couple of drowned rats. Syd said, "Let's go in this air-raid shelter," but I said, "No way." Finally we sat in a bus shelter for a long time. Then Syd said, "I have to get back to camp, so why don't we all go back. I know there's an empty tent there. You can stay in there and Cliff will arrange to see you off the camp in the morning." Well, we went into the tent and sat on the cot. We couldn't sleep, we couldn't even relax. There was a kit bag there and I said, "Oh dear, he is going to come for his kit bag and will see us in the tent."

The next morning all these guys got up, and we just hoped that nobody would come near the tent. I said, "Wait until the *News of the World* gets a hold of this—two girls found in an army camp." Finally Cliff came and said, "I'm going to take you where you can see the fellows going away on the trucks." My boyfriend was going with his tin hat and knapsack. We were waving and he actually saw us. Then we went back in the tent until nine o'clock, just to stay out of sight. We stayed until we could get off the camp very discreetly. Cliff came and brought us a couple of chocolate bars and said, "I think it is safe for us to leave the camp now." So we walked and walked. We had to walk to Aldershot, since the buses did not start running until twelve o'clock. I phoned my mother and said that we would be home as soon as we could get transportation. We did finally get home, about three o'clock that afternoon.

Syd came home on leave in February and he wanted to get married, but I said no, I wanted to wait until my twenty-first birthday in July. I said, "We will get engaged and then get married on my birthday." The war came to an end in May, and Syd got leave in June. He had written and said, "Don't bank on it but I might be home in June."

My mother had a three-tier cake made. Everything was mock this and mock that, but it was a lovely wedding cake. We were going to be married on the sixteenth of June 1945. I had to order flowers and invite whoever could come on such short notice. I didn't know until Syd actually arrived home on the thirteenth if he would make it. He had been to London buying me a diamond ring. From that day on, we were lining up for food. We went to Aldershot twenty miles away to try and buy food for the reception. I had a beautiful second-hand dress which had belonged to a Canadian girl. We read in the paper that this Belgian lace wedding dress was for sale. I went to see about it and it was three pounds. My mother gave me the three pounds to buy it. I said, "After I'm married I will sell it again and give you back the money," and that's what I did. The bridesmaids' dresses were all hand-me-downs.

We were married at Christchurch in Reading. It was a nice wedding but not a big one. The only way we could get down to Somerset for our honeymoon was to take a train at five-thirty in the afternoon, and we weren't married until three o'clock that afternoon. We didn't enjoy too much of the reception before we had to leave in order to get to the train station on time. We had a lovely week in Somerset before Syd was to go back to the continent. He packed all his things, and we said good-bye. Then he didn't go. It came over the radio that the Channel was closed for fog and he couldn't get out. They did this many times.

Then Syd came home in August. He had six weeks furlow and instead of taking it in Canada he took it in England. That six weeks went on and on and on. He would report and they would say, "It's not your turn today," and again he would come back home. He had to travel quite a ways, but he would be there when I came home from work. He got on a ship to Canada at the end of

October. He returned to Victoria and went back to work for the *Victoria Colonist.*

My mother and my brother and his wife came to see me off on the train to London on April 14, 1946. My mother just stood and cried! We stayed in a hostel in London for three days, then went by train to Liverpool. From there we all boarded the boat. I came on the *Letitia,* and the night we were to sail, all our stewards went out on strike. So we had to help ourselves to food. All those white rolls, ham and fruit cocktail. . . . I had never seen anything like it before. A lot of the women were pregnant and it was really crowded. The way they carried on, you would think they were having their babies. We didn't know if they were having them or not.

I travelled with one girl all the way to Victoria. But I was scared to death coming through the mountains. The train was right on the edge of the mountains, and you could look back and see the end of the train coming along the edge. My husband met me in Vancouver. He had booked a room at the Georgia Hotel. Then we went to a party at the Vancouver Hotel, and some people were playing poker. I had never played poker in my life before. I didn't

No. 2 Canadian Hospital Ship "Letitia"—Capt. G. K. Baillie, O.B.E.

really know the worth of the money, and here I was winning all this money. We had a few days in Vancouver before we came to Victoria.

I used to go to a War Brides Club in England, and they told us that when you arrived in Canada, the best thing to do was to fall into their ways: "Don't try and say we do it like this, that we call a garbage can a dust bin. If you fall into their way of doing things, you will get along a lot easier,"—which I found quite true. I never said "pram." Even though I felt silly saying "buggy," I nevertheless did. The only thing that gave me away was the accent. I would go into a store and they would say, "And where did you come from!" —even though I said "store" and not "shop" and "cookies" instead of "biscuits."

I thought Victoria was beautiful. I painted a rosy picture of Victoria in letters back home. You could walk down the street and see all the mountains. So my dad gave up his job on the Great Western Railway when he was fifty-seven and they emigrated to Canada. Most of my family came out to Canada to live, but I have one sister still in England. We all survived the war; we are a fortunate family. We were all scattered, but we remained a family, and we often have family get-togethers.

Syd eventually wrote his civil service exam and went to work for the post office in Victoria. I delivered the rural route mail in Victoria for a number of years. My route was Gordon Head and Cordova Bay—all by car, six days a week. I would go in at five in the morning and sort all my mail. I would then deliver it and be home by twelve noon. I went through quite a few cars, and I have been in many predicaments on my route, but I really enjoyed my job. In 1972, we moved to Duncan, where Syd was the postmaster until his retirement. We have three sons, Ian, Steven and Michael. I always used to say that when I married, I wanted to have a little boy and call him Ian David, and I got my wish. My mother is ninety-seven years old now, and she also lives in Duncan. This year Syd and I will celebrate fifty years of marriage.

Margaret Brown

"MOVE ALL THE WAY
FORWARD, RIGHT DOWN TO
THE FRONT, PLEASE"

Margaret Brown was born in Glasgow. She grew up in a large close family that enjoyed lots of love and laughs. Her parents dedicated their lives to their children.

There was a little paper shop across the street from my aunt's. On a billboard there it read, "Britain declares War." I didn't know the real meaning of it, but it was kind of scary. I went to school until I was fourteen, and then I got a job in a shop where I handled the ration books. It was sad in a way because you would have some people come in and they would be ahead in their books because their ration books weren't sufficient. I used to cheat a little because we would sit on bags of sugar for our tea break, so if someone came in and asked if we had any more tea or sugar and if I knew the store had it, I would give them some extra. If a dozen ketchup sauces came in, we could not put them on the counter, or there would be chaos, so our boss would divide them among the staff. The boss let us make up our own orders of groceries, and we used to give some to the neighbours because they knew I worked in a grocery store. We never really wanted for food because the boss would always give us extra if the store had it. My mum's cupboards were not bare. I felt sorry for people living alone or with only two in a family. But mum had eight ration books so it worked out really well and we didn't suffer. We were on coupons for our clothes as well, and whenever I gave the customers a little extra sugar or butter, they would slip me some coupons for my clothes because they knew I liked dancing.

The policeman who directed traffic would come in on a rainy day with his big black cape. We knew there were groceries under his cape when he came out of the back room with our boss. Our shop was in a poor district of Glasgow and we used to sell our broken biscuits. The little kids would come in poorly dressed and would ask, "Have you any broken biscuits?" I would look at their little faces and I would break the biscuits deliberately under the counter, and then put them in a bag.

One Saturday night my friend Nessie and I were closing up the store and our boss said, "You can have an extra dozen of cracked eggs each, take them with you tonight." We came out of the store and were rushing for the street car when my eggs went up and the whole dozen broke. All we could do was laugh. So the dozen that Nessie had, she shared with me.

The Germans bombed Clyde-Bank Shipyards. Although they didn't hit the shipyards, they got the houses. Our windows were cracked and shattered from that bombing. My older sister Mary was working on the streetcars and she was there in the Clyde-Bank bombing. I will always remember her coming home. She was just screaming in absolute shock; my dad had to slap her across the face to bring her to. She had run from her streetcar after her driver had deserted her and it was everybody for themselves. It was her nerves that were mostly affected, and it took time but she came around. She was off work for quite awhile.

My girlfriend and I used to go to the shows and dances. Basically we had no fear of the bombings; the Scottish people have a great sense of humour, and their spirits kept them up. We saw the funny sides of it. One time my girlfriend and I were coming back from the show in the blackout, and the police stopped us and asked for our identity card and gas mask. We would be trying to find them in our bags with this tiny flashlight.

After working in the shop I always wanted to go into the forces because my girlfriend Cathy was in the ATS (Auxiliary Territorial Service) and she always looked so nice in her uniform. But my dad said, "No forces and no ammunitions." My mother said, "If you volunteer for the streetcars that will let you off from being conscripted," so at eighteen years old, I was a streetcar conductress. I wore a uniform and I used to shine the buttons, and wear my dad's shirt and tie and a conductress hat. I really thought I was queen of the road, because I was conducting this whole streetcar, saying, "Move forward, please. Move all the way forward, right down to the front, please."

Although my job was in town, I didn't know the town well. We weren't allowed in the town very often during the war, because of all the different soldiers. So I didn't know the streets too well. If someone asked me to let them off at such and such a street and I didn't know it, I would run upstairs and ask someone else where the street was and run back down and tell the person.

On the streetcars I never collected all the money either. There were poor little kids who just kept looking out the window. I would go up and down saying, "Fares please, fares please," and if they didn't give it to me I would not bother. If it was a busy time and I saw a little old lady wanting the streetcar or a man with a coal dust streaked face, who had been working hard all day, I would say, "I will take you, you and you." My heart went out to the people. I would often use the same ticket for many soldiers who came on. I would say, "I will take that ticket," and then would give it to the next one that got on. That way some could have a free ride.

I loved dancing so much that I didn't like working on Saturday nights. I lived for dancing, ballroom dancing. I used to go on my day off in the afternoon and then go home, change my dress and go again that night. On Saturday night all the soldiers and others would want to be let off at the beautiful big dance halls. I used to say to the driver, "I have a headache." It wasn't very nice but he didn't mind. He would say, "Okay Margaret." I would put "Depot Only," in the window, and we would run the streetcar into the depot. Then he would help me to count out my money and then I would go home, get changed and go dancing. There would always be a spare conductress to take over, so nobody suffered.

The streetcars would start at four or five in the morning and of course it was blackout, so my dad, even though he was working, would get up and take me along to the streetcar depot to see that I was fine. Then if I was working late at night, until eleven or twelve, he would also meet me. We lived in the tenements. They were called a "close," and when I came home from a dance during a blackout, I would call to mum and dad from the street of the close, and they would come and meet me. I thought that was funny because all the neighbours could hear me call.

My mum and dad and all the family would go to the air-raid shelter. We had this dog that used to sleep at the foot of my bed and we wouldn't move, so my mum and dad would send one of my brothers over to get me. But I didn't have any fear; I thought if I am going to be killed, I am going to be killed in my bed.

There was a family who didn't live far from us. They were strong Irish Catholic and we were Protestant. They had a son whom I had known since I was fourteen; his mother and my mum became friendly. When we came of age he wanted to get engaged. I told mum and dad that if they wouldn't let me marry Andy I would go to "Gretna Green" (run away). They knew I really loved Andy and wanted to marry him, so mum and dad must have talked it over and said I could marry him.

Andy, who was in the Seaforth Highlanders, had developed appendicitis and was in Drumond Military Hospital, an hour's run from Glasgow. His sister Cathy and I decided to go and see Andy on our day off. So we left our house in the morning and went into town to catch the bus. As the bus was coming out of the bus station, it stopped to pick up another passenger, Bob. The bus was full so he had to stand. He asked Cathy and me if we had a light and I said, "I'm sorry, I don't smoke." So Cathy gave him a light and he gave her a cigarette, and I thought maybe they had hit it off. He asked where I was going and I said, "To the military hospital to see my boyfriend," and he said, "Oh that's strange, I was in there and I'm going up there to see my old buddies." He was stationed in England but was up in Scotland on his sick leave.

When we reached the hospital Bob kept following us, even when we went in to see Andy. Bob would go away for awhile and then come back. The wards were large and there was a table down the middle of the room with flowers on it. He would sit on the corner of the table, and every time he looked over he would wink at me. Andy asked, "Who is that?" and I said, "Don't worry, it is just some Canadian we met on the bus and we will get rid of him when we are outside." The visiting hours were from two to four, and when we came back out, Bob followed us and got on the bus, still giving Cathy cigarettes and still chatting to us.

We came into Glasgow and got off the bus, so I said to Cathy, "Let's go and brush our hair and when we come out he will be gone," so we killed a lot of time in the ladies' room, and when we came out Bob was still there. He said, "Don't mind me, but I'm here on leave and I don't know anybody so I would like to take you kids to a show." I started to say, "I'm sorry," but Cathy said, "Oh, I think that will be fine," so anyway we went to a show with him. When we came out of the show, it was about nine o'clock, and he took us into this fancy restaurant. We were sitting in this expensive restaurant, and I could see all these girls who I called gold diggers, taking the guys for their money, and I felt sorry for Bob. When they brought the menu I could see that they had scratched out the prices and put higher prices in, because of the Canadian and American soldiers in there. Cathy asked what I would like and I said, "I'm not really hungry," as I kicked Cathy under the table. I said, "Let's go home, I don't live far from here and we will buy fish suppers at the local fish and chips shop, and my mum will give you a cup of tea." So we went out in the black-out, got on the streetcar, stopped for the fish and chips and went up the stairs to my mum's. We still were not introduced, so I asked, "By the way, what's your name?" and he said, "My name is Bob." I said, "I'm Margaret and this is my boyfriend's sister Cathy." When my mum opened the door, he took off his cap and I took it into the bedroom. Mum followed me and said, "Who's that?" I said, "Mum, he's just a nice Canadian boy. He doesn't know any-body here, so I brought him up for a cup of tea. I hope you don't mind." She said, "Oh no, he is some mother's son." Just before eleven o'clock at night mum said, "It's getting late, you better see Bob to the streetcar." So Cathy and I went down and put him on the streetcar. He didn't ask our last names or ask the number of the close, or the name of the street. We thanked him for taking us to the show and we said good-bye, and we didn't think we would see him again.

When we got back home, the eleven o'clock news came on: the war was over. All the street lights came on and the blinds went up, and there was music in the street. Cathy and I pleaded with mum to let us go back out, as Cathy was staying overnight with me. We saw Bob through the crowd with another girl. Everyone was mix-ing and we were dancing with two English sailors, just having a good time.

For three months after this, I never heard from Bob. Then I came home one day and mum met me at the door and said, "Margaret, I have a big surprise for you. Look who's here." Bob was sitting in the big chair next to the fire. I said, "How did you ever find our house?" and he said, "I have been in lots of houses looking for you." All he knew was that I was a girl called Margaret, with dark brown hair. A lady was cleaning her stairs as he came up our close, and he said, "Is there a Margaret living up here with dark brown hair," and she said, "No, I don't know anyone," and as he was just ready to go away, she said, "Oh yes, there is a Margaret Bell living here, just try that door." When he came to the door my mum recognized him and brought him in. The strange part was that I had broken off with Andy on the Monday and this was Friday.

So I went out with Bob for five days. Then, in my mum's hallway, we had our arms around each other saying good night, and he said to me, "Let's get married." I got the giggles so much I couldn't stop laughing and I said, "I don't even know you, Bob, never mind marry you." I thought it was so romantic when he said, "We will spend the rest of our lives getting to know each other."

In the bedroom I was sharing with my younger sister Ina, I told her that Bob had asked me to get married. My sister was excited and asked if I loved him, and I said, "I love his little mustache (he still has it to this day) and I love his accent, and I love his manners." She said, "That's it, you're in love." My mum and dad thought I was too young, that I didn't know him and would be going too far away from home. I said, "Mum, if I stay here I am only going to end up marrying Andy and we have been off and on over this silly religion." I asked Bob if he was Catholic and he said, "No, does it matter?" and I said, "In Scotland it does." So I said I would let him know the next night. The next night I told him I would marry him and he went back down to England, and I didn't see him again until I was in the church for our wedding. We just wrote letters for the next three months. I couldn't understand his writing and so mum had to read his letters to me.

On the day of the wedding I was sitting under the hair dryer, and I asked the lady what time it was. She said, "It's five o'clock." "Five o'clock, I'm getting married at six," so I had to run from the hairdresser's. Mum met me in the street and almost dragged me into the house to get dressed. When we got to the church, some of our neighbours and friends were expecting me with Andy and you could hear the people outside gasping when they saw Bob.

I had a white wedding in a little church and our reception was held in a friend's house. We were married January 4th, 1946, and I didn't go down to England until February. We had a short honeymoon for just a few days, then Bob went back to England. Bob was from Vancouver and he was in the Army with the Engineers. His father, who was also in the Army, went over in 1939 when war broke out. Then Bob volunteered at seventeen and a half to get in his father's regiment, and surprised him in England.

I got lost getting down to London to be with Bob. I had never been away from home before. Some of my family and neighbours came out to see me off. I took the ten o'clock night train, "The Flying Scotsman," and we arrived in London in the morning. Mum said not to go near the soldiers, but the whole train was packed with soldiers. Then she saw this woman and asked her, "Would you mind taking care of my daughter? She is to meet her husband in London." We sent a telegram, but Bob didn't get the telegram so he didn't meet me. Here I was with my little case, hungry and tired, and there was no Bob. He was in Haslemere and it was a short bus ride out of London. I couldn't find the camp, so I was completely lost. I just sat on my case by the roadside and bawled and bawled. I didn't know there was a house behind the large hedge. Then I heard this voice of a lady who said, "Are you alright, dear?" I said, "No, I'm lost, I was supposed to meet my husband and I have never been away from home before and now I am lost." She said, "Come in, dear, and have a wash up and a cup of tea." She was a very nice lady. It was a beautiful home with a maid and a butler. She gave me tea, a boiled egg and toast, and she was very concerned about me. Then she got her private car and took me to the camp. But it was the wrong camp and she left me there thinking it was the right one. So I was still lost. Finally, the military took me to one of the officers. They put me in a Jeep and found Bob. I asked Bob if he had received the telegram and he said he hadn't.

We rented a room to stay in, and after I had settled in I decided I would get a little job during the day. I saw on the post office notice board a help-wanted notice for nurse's aides. I thought, "I'm going to apply for this," so I went out to this beautiful expensive nursing home. The matron took a shine to me and gave me the job. I was only working there a few days when the matron asked me if I would like to live in. "Oh," I told her, "I can't, I'm married." "You're married. You're too young!" I said, "I will bring my wedding pictures tomorrow." So she said, "I will tell you what I will do. There are nurse's quarters here that we don't use anymore. We used them during the war; it's dusty but if you and your husband clean it, you can live there rent free." You can imagine my excitement: electricity, heat, plus my wages. I worked from nine in the morning until two in the afternoon. We wore the nurse's uniform with black stockings and white aprons. A light would go on to tell which room needed help. Usually all I would do was brush a lady's hair, change the flower water and make sure they took their pill. That was where we stayed until we came to Canada.

I went to visit my parents in August because I was leaving for Canada in September. Bob arrived in Canada a week before I did. It was sad leaving Glasgow on the train. They were playing on the bagpipes, "Will You Not Come Back Again." All the soldiers were holding back the relatives and friends. I never saw my dad cry in his life before that day. You don't realize how far you are going. My mum couldn't come to the station. She just fainted in the house and one of the neighbours had to stay with her. After I had shed all my tears at the station, I got the train to Southampton. I met this girl, Molly, from the north of Scotland on the ship, the *Letitia.* We became good friends on the trip over and had lots of laughs.

She asked me where I was going and I said, "Vancouver," and she said, "Well I'm going to Saskatoon. You stay with me even after we get off the boat and on the train." Well I didn't know there was the CPR (Canadian Pacific Railway) and the CNR (Canadian National Railway) so I went on the same train as Molly. The Red Cross lady asked my name and she said, "Oh I don't have your name on my list." Everywhere we stopped, the Red Cross nurses would go off duty and different ones would come on duty but I was on nobody's list across Canada.

I had a little case and so did Molly, as we were travelling casually in slacks and sweaters. I had a nice little suit and hat in my case because I wanted to look nice to meet Bob's family. We were sitting there and the porter said, "Saskatoon." It came right on us like that and poor Molly didn't have any time to change. She said, "What am I going to do, Margaret? I am not dressed." I told her they were going to love her just the way she was. I remember watching her meet her husband and his parents, and I thought, "I'm not going to get caught like Molly did." So I took my case and went back to the bathroom and got all slicked up. I was sitting there when the porter came along and said, "My, you do look pretty, are you getting off soon?" I said, "Yes, the next stop, Vancouver." He looked at me and said, "It will be three more days before we arrive in Vancouver." Molly had told me it was the next stop!

When I did get into Vancouver all dressed up, there was nobody to meet me, and I started to cry. I knew I was pregnant, and I thought Bob was married to someone else, or had a girlfriend and didn't want me. I was terrified. The Red Cross nurse came to me and gave me a cup of coffee. Someone said, "We should phone the other station," and sure enough Bob was waiting for me there. I was supposed to come on the CPR and I came on the CNR.

I didn't know what to expect when I came to Canada. I thought I would see cowboys. The prairie seemed so flat, it just went on for miles and miles. I couldn't believe it was such a vast country or that it was all one country. I loved Vancouver because it is a beautiful city. Someone had told me in Scotland that Vancouver was a beautiful spot. The first thing I bought in the store in Vancouver was this big doll for myself. I took it home and said, "Bob, this is for the baby." He said, "It's kind of big for a baby, isn't it?"

After the war there were no jobs and no places to live. So we lived with Bob's mum until almost the time the baby was born. Someone told us there were rooms in the old Vancouver Hotel, that the soldiers had taken it over. So we went down and got a huge room on the third floor. It had a big fancy bathroom and we were to go down to the cafeteria to eat. The rent was very reasonable.

Bob couldn't find work and it was really bad. It was the first time I really *wanted* in my life. We used to go down to the Salvation Army for a grocery voucher. We were really, really poor! One day he would try and drive a taxi and the next he worked digging a ditch. We had his grant from the military when we were staying with his mum and we bought a crib and things for the baby. His folks didn't have a lot of money either. They had a large garden and would bring us things from it, but they couldn't give us money. I think we needed to learn a lesson, because when Bob did get his gratuities from the Army, we were eating in restaurants. I didn't know the value of the money, and to be honest we did go under a bit and then we hit bottom. It was a good lesson. I would not write back and tell my mum, because I knew she had fainted when I left, and she might have said, "I told you so, you are going too far away." I knew they wouldn't actually say that, but it was in the back of my mind.

Our daughter was born on February 2, 1947. The doctor said it was going to be a boy because it had a strong heartbeat. His name was going to be Robert, but she turned out to be a girl, so we named her Roberta Lee. Four of us went to a show the night before she was born. My friend Isabelle, her husband Gordon, and Bob and I were sitting up in the balcony when my pains started. There was a big clock there and I was watching the time. I said to Isabelle, "Come to the bathroom with me, I think I am going to have my baby." She was so interested in the show, she said, "Oh Margaret, you get so excited, it's only piles!" I started to get fidgety. Bob noticed and said, "You alright?" I said I was having pains. "Pains! Let's get out of here." He took me to the hospital in a taxi, and I was like Cinderella because it was almost twelve o'clock at night.

Then Bob went away and I was really scared, I was terrified. They put me in a bed with the sides up; that was the labour room. I could hear this other woman screaming and I said, "Could somebody help that poor woman." I didn't think I would be next. "Can't you give her something, she is in terrible pain." I felt so sorry for that poor woman. I started to cry, sobbing my heart out, I was so scared. I remember the doctor coming in and saying, "You know you are a rosy-cheeked healthy little Scots girl, you are going to be fine." They put me out towards the end, and my daughter was born at nine o'clock the next morning.

When I was leaving the hospital, the Sister said to me, "Well Scotty, we will see you next year." I said, "No, not me." But sure enough, twelve months later my son was born. When I was taking my son home, I said, "Please don't say a thing about next year." We had two cribs in the one room and I had to do my washing by hand in the bathtub. The skin would rub off my hands from scrubbing Bob's rough army socks. I didn't even get a scrub board until Bob's mum got me one. We ran lines across the bathroom and I would open the window to dry the clothes.

My son was breach, so I had a worse time with him. After his birth I had two miscarriages. In three years I had two babies and two miscarriages. I received blood transfusions with the miscarriages, and very nearly died with the second one. I wanted to die in a way, if you know what I mean. I thought, if this is married life. . . . We lived in a rented wartime house, with two babies, and I lost two babies and Bob didn't have a job. We couldn't keep up the rent, but we weren't the only ones. We only had wood fires, so I used to wear my heavy coat and sweaters, with no heat.

I had written my mum before I had the second miscarriage and said I was really, really homesick, not telling her what happened. She booked our passage. My little son could travel free, but for my little girl, who was two and a half, we had to pay half fare. We didn't have much but we sold what we had. I didn't leave Bob: we left on good terms, but the sad part was I couldn't take my little boy with me. After the trip was booked I had a severe miscarriage. I couldn't lift my son Jim, so I had to leave him with Bob's mum. I took my little daughter. It broke my heart, but I couldn't have made that journey on the train and boat with him.

I came out of the hospital at the end of August and went home in September, so it was fast. Bob had said, "If you go home to Scotland with Bobbie, I will try and get a job. Then Jim and I will follow. You gave my country a try so I will give yours a try." But the next thing I knew, the Korean war broke out and Bob volunteered. He re-enlisted and his thinking was maybe he would be sent to Germany. He would be quite close to Scotland and the family would be reunited. But because of his combat background he was sent right to Korea. So I stayed with my mum and dad. My mum, dad and I went to a travel agent to arrange to fly Jim over. We could have gotten him flown over even though it was a lot of money, but Bob's mum would not let him go. I think she was scared that if she let him go she would lose her son. Her excuse was that she would make herself sick worrying about Jim travelling over alone. I didn't hold that against her, although at first I did, but we became good friends.

I was separated from Bob and Jim for two and a half years. Bob came home from Korea, and he still wanted to come to Scotland, but by then I was homesick for Canada. So I decided to give Canada another try and came back by boat and train. By then I had gotten my strength back. When I first returned to Scotland I was really run down and thin, but mum took me to a doctor and they built me up. I then went to work and worked for the two years that I was over there. I worked for Remington Rand Typewriters, and the money was fabulous. Bob sent me money every month, so I was banking it away. Mum felt better this time when I left. She said, "Margaret, if you go this time, don't be afraid to come back if it doesn't work out for you." But we never looked back. Bob was in the Army in Calgary for five years, then we were transferred to Victoria, where he remained in the Army until retirement. We stayed together and I don't regret it.

Mavis Watling

"WE ALL HAVE THAT THREAD THAT RUNS RIGHT THROUGH US"

Mavis Watling was born and grew up in the little market town of Selby in Yorkshire. Mavis was thirteen when the war started.

M y friends and I were the teenagers on the block, you might
say, when war was declared. I can remember a group of us
talking about it, and we were all full of bravado. If the enemy
came here, we were all ready to fisticuff them! Of course, my parents were worried because they had three sons coming to the age
when they would be called up. My eldest brother was called up
and he was nineteen years old. He joined the Navy and his ship
went down to Java. This was where the British Fleet really took a
beating, and he was killed when his ship was blown up there.

During the war my mother wanted to go to work, so she asked
me to look after our house and do the cooking. At the same time,
I also took a commercial course—shorthand, typing and bookkeeping. My training got me a job at the railway telegraph office,
although I never used any shorthand and I never did any bookkeeping, but I did use my typing. I enjoyed my work, and I met all
the railway workers. The reason for that was because there was a
shortage of matches at this time. There was always somebody coming in for one of the tapers we had ready for them so they could
light their cigarettes. Of course, everybody smoked in those days.

Being the communications office on the railway, we had to be
open twenty-four hours a day. This meant we had to work weekends; we actually got only one weekend off every three weeks.
Otherwise, we worked steadily because the office had to be kept
open. At six o'clock in the morning, I would go to work from
Selby, and check all the street clocks on the way. I also used to
cycle quite a bit. I had a racing bike, and I would "swish" straight
down the main street in front of the Abbey, turn right near the
park, and there you were at the railway station.

I worked three different shifts, six to two, two to ten and ten to
six. The night shift was easiest, because there were so few trains
going through for which we had to send out the word to the next
station that a train was on the way. Our office was important
because we were keeping the communications open.

Selby was surrounded by airfields, and there were these big
bombers that we could see going by at night. We had the big
Lancaster bombers. The airmen would come into our town for

dances but they were a pretty tight-lipped lot. I don't know but maybe it was because they were really feeling this brush with death every night. There were always some of them missing in action.

One night, my mother came rushing into my bedroom and awakened me to say, "The town is on fire!" I looked out the window, and sure enough there was a big fire there. What happened was that one of the returning airplanes with an Australian crew in it had crashed into the church spire, and then it had gone into a new subdivision. It killed pretty near every person in one family, except the daughter who was not sleeping at home at the time. It was a real tragedy. The father was a first-aid man, and he was telling them how to treat his burns. He was burned from head to toe, and later died.

Selby was for the most part not hit by bombing but I remember one night when a few bombs were dropped on the outlying farms. Right on the coast of England, there were three miles of anti-aircraft guns, so not many enemy planes got through but the odd one did. This one enemy plane had followed the train because the pilot could see the light from the fire in the engine. And when the train stopped, the pilot figured that was the station. The engineer knew this, and that's why he stopped the train outside the town. When the pilot dropped his bombs, they didn't do any damage because they only landed in the farm fields.

Another thing that I remember about the war was taking a basket around. Everybody had a basket that they held in front of them, and there'd be sticks of bread in them. There were no bags or no paper during the war. When we first saw a loaf of bread without anything on it, everybody said, "Doesn't that look awful!" And yet, you know, within a week we were used to it. This is a thing that has stayed with me all my life. During the war, there weren't any bags or other things that we now take for granted—you just had to do without. So if there is anything that I can't have here, I just think back to the war, and I forget about it. In many instances it isn't important because, believe me, you really can do without things.

One night, I was at a dance; that was where everybody met people. But I think the English dances were different from Canadian dances. In England, there were lots of dances where you changed partners. You didn't just go with one person and stick with him the whole night. There were plenty of dances where you would all be in a circle, and you'd turn and face the next person and dance with him. And there were plenty of ladies' choices where you'd just go and pick somebody to dance with. It was quite normal; you didn't have to wait until you were asked. And another thing, too, was that girls would dance with each other. In fact, I've been to dances where you danced with your grandmother; you danced with your aunt; you danced with a little four-year-old. No problem!

The Saturday-night-hops were full of soldiers from all over, including airmen—airmen in particular—because between York and Selby there were aerodromes scattered all over the place. It was just a small hall, but we had some great times at those dances. I was standing with a group just talking, and there was one boy I'd gone to school with who was a real prankster and joker. He asked us, "Would you like to meet my Canadian cousin?" And we all said, "Oh go on. You don't have a Canadian cousin." But he said he would take us to him.

Standing behind the crowd, all on his own, was my husband-to-be, Trevor. And sure enough, he had the Canadian emblem on his shoulder, and he still had his hat on. It was a tam in those days. So we brought him forward to the group, and because I had spoken to him when we had gone over to meet him, he asked me to dance. We danced, and then because we all went the same way home, he walked along with me and asked me if I would like to go to the pictures the next night. I said okay, and that's how we met. This was towards the end of the war.

We got to see each other only when Trevor was on leave, and that wasn't enough time to really get to know each other. But we became engaged, and then he was in Germany when he was shipped back to Canada. I wasn't actually sure that I wanted to come all the way to Canada. And we weren't married yet but I decided that I would come. I thought I would come out and see if I would like it in Canada. Because we weren't married yet, I felt that I could come back if I didn't want to stay.

But once I saw Victoria, I fell in love with the city. So many war brides have come to really crummy places. I came to the best place, and I recognized it right away. It felt right up my alley. There were so many English people here, I felt right at home.

While I was still in England, Trevor and I wrote to each other, and I stayed with my job at the railway office. I didn't go through the same process as the other war brides because I wasn't coming out as a war bride. I was not yet married to my husband, and my way wasn't paid to Canada. Although Trevor offered to help, I preferred to pay myself.

I had to save up my money, and finally in 1948, I came over on the *Aquitania* which had previously brought over a lot of the war brides. I stayed in a cabin with three other women coming out on their own too. They were also coming out to see what it was like in Canada. After arriving at Halifax, I got on the train to Vancouver. Coming across Canada, what amazed me was when you'd see a little cabin in the bush and a great big red car in front of it. It was amazing to me because cars were few and far between in England during the war. There were a lot more cars in Canada—a lot of everything. You've no idea. You just have to live it to realize just what it's all about.

On the train, I was befriended by a Scottish couple who were going up to Port Alberni on Vancouver Island. We had a berth each, and they were beneath the top berth that I was in. I became very friendly with them. Then when we finally arrived in Vancouver, there was nobody there to meet me. And the funny thing was that I remember somebody way back in Halifax saying, "You'll be on the CPR instead of the CNR" or vice versa. Even though I had worked on the railway in England, it didn't register that there could possibly be two lines going right across Canada. I just thought it would be two sections. So Trevor was waiting at one station, and I arrived at the other station.

Funnily enough, I didn't panic. I thought that, well, if worse comes to the worst, I could turn around and go back. This Scottish couple said, "Well, we've got a little bit of time. We may as well wait until we see if he comes." We'd been waiting for about half an hour, and then they said they had to go to the ferry. I told them I would walk with them to the exit of the station, and whilst I was saying goodbye, I suddenly saw this red-headed fellow with his broad back, and I thought, "My God, that's him!" I just yelled, "Yahoo!"

The funny thing was when we got to Nanaimo on Vancouver Island, Trevor's dad was waiting for us in his little black Austin. We all sat in this black Austin, and his dad tried to turn the car around. All of a sudden, he said, "Oh, my goodness, I'm in the wrong car!" He had got into somebody else's little black Austin! The other car was open because in those days people didn't lock their cars. That was so funny.

We drove from Nanaimo to Victoria. Trevor had actually built two rooms on to his parents' place, and we lived in these two rooms—they were our bedroom and sitting room. There was also a little room at the bottom of the stairs that was our kitchen. When we were first married, my husband was just completing his apprenticeship as a sheet metal worker, but we didn't have to pay rent while we were living with his parents. We saved up enough money for our first house, which was in Vic West.

Canada hadn't experienced the austerity that we had gone through in England. In England, it still lingered on for quite some time after the war until the economy gained momentum. After arriving in Canada, I saw this blonde woman walking along. She was wearing a yellow suit, and I thought, "Oh my goodness, she's in her pyjamas!" But it was this sunny zoot suit. And I thought how lovely it was. It was very bright and sunny. And all the colourful flowers in Victoria made life feel a lot brighter here than it was in England at that time.

In 1962, we bought half an acre of land, and Trevor built the house we're living in now. He still likes to make things, so we've steadily improved the house over the years because I like to paint things, too. I do a lot of the painting and varnishing. And

Trevor with his draughtsman skills helped me design the curtains that I made for our windows. So we both help each other in our projects.

We have five daughters, which was a surprise to me, coming from a family with three brothers. My husband and I have lived an industrious life. We both are avid gardeners, and like to get out in the soil and muck around. I always feel like Orpheus in the underworld, because I come out very dishevelled but I love it.

I have been back to England many times over the years, and Trevor and I have also been able to go on several cruises to other parts of the world. You hate to say it, but if there's one advantage to being brought up in wartime England, it made us all very thrifty and innovative, and I think that has kept us in good stead all our lives. We used to say, "I always have two pennies in my pocket to rattle around." In other words, you were never broke. You never emptied your pockets completely.

I was young enough that the war didn't fall on me as it did on my parents, who were in a different position. You were busy working, and we didn't really have the bombs that happened down south in England. We were pretty safe in Selby except for the rationing. But of course there was the terrible thing—that you were losing a lot of your friends.

You do come out of it with a stronger appreciation for life. Nowadays you often hear about how people push themselves to their limits when death is so final. Well, something like the war really brings it home to you. Your own peers have gone missing because of the war. We saw the pictures of the holocaust in the papers, and they're imprinted in my mind forever. People can't comprehend it now, and yet you see things happening in the world that are related to it. The atrocities are going on but you have to be there to see it—and feel how frightened you can be. Here we don't think that any minute we're going to get killed.

During the war, women showed what they could do. Employers had to take the women into the ammunition factories, which was the type of work only a man would do before. Then it was known that women could do the work equally well. In fact, better, because they had more patience and their fingers were quite nimble. And women were in the Land Army. Working on the farms had always been a man's job. Now there were all these Land Army lasses, and were they ever a bunch! They were well fed. They were rosy-cheeked. They would go into a pub and down a beer better than the men! I still remember this blonde woman with her hair flying, and she was so husky. Well, they'd been working really hard, ploughing fields and milking cows.

War brides share all these memories, and the Vancouver Island War Brides are a great group. One thing that I found out is that it doesn't matter whether you come from London or you come from Yorkshire, we're all very similar. We all have that thread that runs right through us. I can recognize it and they can recognize it, which gives us a common bond. It doesn't matter if you come from Scotland or Wales or Ireland because we're all the same. I love the Vancouver Island War Brides—we're a great support group for one another.

Joan Bedford

"I WALKED IN, TOOK ONE
LOOK AND CRIED AND
CRIED"

---

*Joan Bedford was born in
her grandmother's house in London.
With her older brother, she grew up in Southall,
a suburb of London.*

We slept in the shelter every night during the Battle of Britain, which was very hard on my mother, who suffered from heart disease. Once, a land mine went off about a block from where we lived, and my mother's sister, her husband and daughter were buried for twenty-four hours. The next day incendiary bombs were dropped around us. It really was a dreadful experience.

My grandparents had been evacuated to Cornwall, so my mother decided that she and I should join them. Our next door neighbour, Mrs. Kidman, said she would come with us to Cornwall and look after my mother. We were there six weeks, when the neighbour went into Plymouth to do some Christmas shopping. She caught a meningitis germ and died three days later. My mother felt guilty and decided to go home again. We arrived in London on New Year's Day and mother's nephew was killed that day. My mother went to bed and didn't get up again. When she died in November 1941, my dad said, "We'll never have to sleep in the shelter again; if a bomb drops we won't hear it." Mother, wanting to protect us and keep us safe—felt we should sleep in the shelter.

If the air-raid siren blew when we were at school, we thought it was fun. We had to march across to the concrete shelter, and here we played "Truth-or-Dare." Toward the end of the war, when I was getting a little older, we went to lots of dances, and there were many boys in uniform. It was fun being a teenager in England at that time.

I went to work at Hoovers in their Special Products Office, as a junior secretary to the boss's secretary. It was a large drafting office. They were making bomb carriers in the factory instead of vacuum cleaners. I earned two pounds a week.

In December of 1944, my girlfriend Beryl, whom I knew from Greenford County School, invited me to Gloucester for the weekend. She was working for an architect in Quedgeley, about three miles out of town. We went to a tea dance at the Cadena Gardens in Gloucester. A young Canadian Airman, Ed, asked me to dance. Before the afternoon was over, he asked if he could find a friend for my friend. That was easy! The four of us went for supper. There was no transportation so they walked us three miles home. Then they had to walk to their own base, three miles the other side of Gloucester. Ed asked if he could see me again the next day, and we went to the movies. He came to London to see me the following weekend; then he was transferred to Yorkshire. I thought I would never see him again. But I did. Ed came from Yorkshire every weekend (not always with a pass). I knew when he didn't have a pass since he would always ask the patrolling MP (military police) for the time, so they would think he had a pass.

One weekend Ed brought his friend Jack to London for the weekend. The secretary that I worked for was twenty-six, and loved to shock us with her stories about being out with American boys. She overheard me on the telephone trying to get a date for Jack. She said, "Joan, I'm not busy tonight I can come with you." She was my boss so I had no choice, but to say yes. We had a great evening, but when she tried to take Jack home with her, I stepped in and wouldn't let him go with her. Jack still teases me about not letting him go home with her.

In February 1945, Ed asked me if I would marry him. Then he was sent to Egypt and Italy. In July his brother Jack arrived in England from France and came to stay with my dad and me. A few days later Ed phoned to say he was in Bournemouth, and how about getting married on Saturday? His brother and I made all the arrangements, and we were married on the 21st of July. The family had all been saving fruit and eggs, and my aunt made a cake. I borrowed a beautiful wedding dress from one of the girls at work. At the wedding ceremony his brother asked Ed, "Have you got a ring?" "No," he said, "I thought you had it." Well they didn't have a ring. My girlfriend's mother took off her ring and lent it to us. We were married, and as we walked out of the church she asked me for the ring.

We arrived at the hotel in Bournemouth at five in the morning. There was no one there so we sat in the lounge for awhile, then left again. No one knew we had been there. The following night we stayed at a bed and breakfast. When Ed got up in the night, he had to unbolt about six doors to go out to the Loo. Ed was being transferred to Torquay, so I left to meet him there. The porter directed me onto the wrong train, a non-stop train to Plymouth. I then had to find my way back to Paignton. I finally arrived about seven o'clock that night, totally exhausted. I had travelled all day with not even a cup of tea! I arrived at the bed and breakfast and burst into tears. I was sitting having some tea when Ed came in with his friend Jack. And do you think Jack would leave? We were supposedly on our honeymoon. Five days later I returned to London and learned Ed was being sent back to Canada. It would be a year before we saw each other again, and by this time we had a son whom we named Bryan.

I left my home in Southall on the 4th of August 1946. We boarded the *Letitia* in Liverpool, with five hundred crying girls and five hundred babies. Bryan was a very good baby. There was another English girl named Molly in my cabin. The other fourteen girls were Dutch; they were pregnant and ill the whole eight days. Molly and I said goodbye in Halifax, but we have always kept in touch. On the train, I met another war bride, Mary, with her baby, Ian. He was ill with jaundice and Mary and I walked the aisle with him. When we arrived in Vancouver, our husbands were chatting to one another. Since then we have been the best of friends.

Soon after, Ed's mum and dad moved up to Kelowna, so they rented us their house. It cost us twenty-five dollars a month. We had two girls in the following two years, Linda and Janice. Then we moved into a very old house that Ed's dad had bought during the war. There were rent controls then, and we had to take the tenants to court to get them moved out. They were given six months to move but wouldn't tell us when they were leaving. I was expecting my fourth baby when we finally moved into the house in October 1950. The house was filthy. I walked in, took one look and cried and cried. We spent the next fifteen years restoring it. We were opposite a park, and the school was across the road. We were very happy there.

When our fourth child Keith was born, they told us he wouldn't live because he had a malformed heart. He was a joy for the six years that he was with us. Brenda was born in 1954 and she loved her brother. When he died, and they did an autopsy, they said that, medically speaking, Keith never should have lived. We had two more sons, Stephen in 1960 and David in 1963.

At that time I had taken a little job working for a catering company in Vancouver in the evenings. We worked in all the wealthy homes, and it was a lot of fun. I knew everyone who was anyone.

Ed and I always liked looking at houses. In 1965 we found a beautiful home in Vancouver with five bedrooms and three bathrooms. We bought it fully furnished, for sixteen thousand dollars. We were very concerned about the mortgage, which was going to be one hundred and eight dollars a month. Bryan was working at the bank by this time making one dollar an hour, and Linda was in residence at Vancouver General, taking nursing. We moved into that gorgeous house and lived there for ten years.

Then Ed had the opportunity to move to Victoria with his job. We bought a beautiful house in Oak Bay and moved over here with our two sons, who were still in school. Unfortunately, we put urea-formaldehyde insulation in the house, which made Ed and me very ill. We had it removed, but it cost us twenty thousand dollars, so we decided to sell. We sold it when the prices were rock bottom. We rented a house for a year, until David graduated from the University of Victoria and moved to Ottawa. Then we bought this little house. We had lived here five years when Ed died, two weeks before his seventieth birthday. I discovered I couldn't live alone, so I had two university students stay. Now my granddaughter is living with me while she attends university.

Audrey Sawchuk

"GEE, YOU KNOW
EVERYTHING
IS BIGGER HERE"

---

*Audrey Sawchuk was born and grew up
in Cardiff, South Wales. After graduating from
school, she took an apprenticeship as a
seamstress and continued to live with her
family. She was seventeen years old
when war was declared.*

All through the war, being a seamstress, I made parachutes. There was this one particular time that I was working, and somebody said there were going to be some presentations made at lunchtime. When I went up to the lunchroom, three airmen were sitting on the stage that we had there. I hadn't heard anything about this at all, but there was my cousin sitting with these other two airmen.

They read out who had worked on the three different airmen's chutes, and I had not done anything on the other two, but only on my cousin's. When any airmen jumped, they reported it to the firm that made the chutes. It had to be an emergency jump. Then the firm would present these airmen with a stein, a tankard with the day and the date of their jump and the firm's crest on it. We often had airmen come after they had made an emergency landing, and this day, of course, they got a silver stein. My cousin actually made a joke out of it when they toured the establishment afterwards. As he passed me, he said, "It's a good job it opened or my mother would have been over to see you!" But of course it was nothing to do with my work anyway, because the airmen all had to have packed their own unit. He was just being cheeky.

Our firm took over one of the big stores in Cardiff, and that's where we were working during the war. Sometimes we worked twelve hours a day, from eight o'clock in the morning to eight o'clock at night. Some of the people had no experience. They were training people who had never sewn, because they had to have more workers. The parachutes that we made were not only man droppers but supply droppers as well.

At the beginning of the war, parachutes were made with raw silk. A lot of it came from Japan but then when Japan entered the war, nylon was invented. So after that, it was all nylon material that we used to make the parachutes. We were told nylon was made from coal, fresh air and water. Our work came to us all cut. There was a cutting room where they did all the cutting.

We used industrial sewing machines. They are much heavier than the ordinary sewing machines you would have at home. And they are all powered of course. They are much more powerful

Audrey Sawchuk's (neé Summers) Work Pass for the British Parachute Company.

than even home electric machines. I worked on a double needle most of the time but I also took a first-aid course and became leader of the first-aid squad by the time I was eighteen. I had to be available for anything that happened in the workplace because often there were accidents.

The first year of the war was quite quiet. Then we had bombing, but not like London or Coventry. Still we did have quite a bit of bombing. I can remember going into work one day and finding my sewing machine missing. And I asked, "Well, where's my sewing machine?" They had taken it out, evacuated it temporarily, because there was a time bomb next door. Mine wasn't the only one. I said, "Well, I think *I'll* leave for awhile too!" There was no communication as there would be now to say, "Don't come into work yet." You went in and found that this was what was happening.

You heard the siren when the air raid was on and then waited for the "all-clear" to go. But you didn't know until they hit where the bombs would land. You can hear a bomb coming, you know. It screams as it comes down, and then "BOOM!"; everything shakes for awhile, and that's it until the next one comes along.

I enjoyed the work that I was doing. Our firm had a wonderful choir, and I was soloist for the choir. We had a dramatic society that used to go around giving little concerts here and there for relaxation and relief from the war effort. Our firm also had a discussion group that used to discuss many things. One particular topic was housing after the war. Our firm entered into a competition and won the prize. Our employer, British Parachute Company Limited, organized and sponsored all these different activities.

While I was working during the war, my mother took care of all the shopping and cooking. She had my dad, too, and my dad was on one shift while I was on another. I was working six to two, and my dad was working two to ten. One of my sisters was doing clerical work from nine to five-thirty. And my other sister was still in school. She was younger than I by four years. Can you imagine trying to cook for us on our different schedules? If we all ate together, our rations would go so much further. But everybody was going in and out for different meals at different times, and my mother had to cope with it all. I often think about it now when I feel overwhelmed. It was certainly a full-time job for my mother because we were so stringently rationed.

But we were never hungry, never. On the continent, it must have been dreadful for the French, Belgian and Dutch. Even in Germany, people were hungry. But while rationing made our diets very monotonous, I was never hungry. And I don't know of anyone who was. Our bread was brown but it was very good bread. Milk was also good. I don't think we were rationed with milk.

I met my husband-to-be, Ed, at a dance. I wasn't going to go that night, but my sister said to me, "Oh go on! Go to the dance. You just never seem to do anything much these days. You don't dance." So I went to the Astaire Ballroom, and Ed was there with another fellow whose name was Ed also. I'd never been out with Canadians or Americans before, so when they both said their name was "Ed," I thought, "Oh sure." My husband-to-be, Ed, said to me, "You don't trust me, do you?" I replied, "Not as far I could throw you." And he was rather a large man! But he said, "No, but you will."

That night, Ed danced with me, and he wanted to take me home but I refused. I said, "No, I live way out from here, and you would never find your way. And there's no transportation back anyway." All the trams and buses stopped at eleven o'clock. And then I snuck out. I really did. I snuck out on him. But when I came out of the cloak room, there he was standing, and he said to me, "You thought that you were sneaking out on me." I told him he could come around to the bus stop but he wasn't going home with me. So he said, "Well we'll see." He came around to the bus stop with me, and the bus came by too full to take any more passengers.

Now I had a long walk ahead of me unless I could catch a tram. I ran around the corner, and I did get on the tram but he got on with me. I said to him, "You've got to get off this tram because there's no transportation back." But he sat down, and he argued with me until I really promised that I would see him the next night. I had no intentions of going out with him but he said, "I won't get off until you promise to see me tomorrow night *on your honour!*" So I did. I said, "Well, alright then, I'll see you at seven o'clock in town."

I went out with him the next night. I didn't tell my mum and dad that he was a Canadian. I just said that I was going out with an Army corporal but my dad saw me in town. So I really caught it when I got home! I was raised in quite a strict Christian household. It was not like it is now. So when I got home, my mother was really cross.

My dad didn't say very much but my mother remained quite perturbed. I told her not to worry about it because it was nothing serious. And I really believed that. I really did. Ed wasn't in our area very long before he was posted to London, and then from London to Scotland. He came back on three leaves, and that's when things got serious.

We wrote to each other all the time, which Ed never does now. He never puts his name to anything. I have to do all the writing for the family. Yes, back then he wrote quite regularly, and came on leave to see me. I was twenty-two when I met Ed. I only knew him from September 1944, and then we were married in April 1945.

I was fortunate in the fact that I had a white wedding and my two sisters were bridesmaids. We were rationed in clothes as well as food. I had my own, and some of the family gave me some of theirs. Everything was rationed—stockings or a coat or anything. But I did have a white wedding. A friend of mine who was a dress-maker made my wedding dress and my bridesmaids' dresses as well. It was considered unlucky to make your own dress.

I had a bouquet of pink tulips, pink carnations and white heather. My bridesmaids were in very pale lavender, and I've always, just always, loved violets. They grow the big hybrid ones in Wales. So my bridesmaids had big posies of those huge violets and white heather. It was really different but then I am too. We were married in St. Saviour's Church in Cardiff.

Then we went on our honeymoon—all four days of it! We just went to a local seaside resort in Wales. It's called Portcaul. It's on the Bristol Channel but it's edging into the Atlantic so the water is much more turbulent there—the waves are a lot higher. We left on Saturday afternoon and we were back Thursday. And then of course Ed had to go back to camp.

I was given the address of the Canadian Wives Bureau in London, and they would send me books on Alberta, because Ed was born in Alberta, and books on British Columbia, because he was living at Buckley Bay, BC, before he volunteered for overseas service. A lot of people seem to think that some of us war brides married just to get to Canada. Well that was not my intention. You gave up all your family, and we were a very close family. You also gave up your friends which you had known all your life, and everything you knew.

The war was over only a month after Ed and I were married. Ed was in the first contingent back to Canada because they were going to have leave and then get trained to go to Japan. But by the time Ed had finished his leave, the war with Japan was over because the United States had dropped the atom bomb in August 1945. I had to apply to come to Canada through the Canadian War Brides Bureau in London, and I did that but it was a year later before I could follow Ed to Canada. I arrived in time for our first wedding anniversary.

My mother and my sister went with me to London where we were met by a fellow from the Army, an officer from the Canadian Wives Bureau. Mother was crying, and they didn't want me to go. They didn't want me to go any more than Ed's family wanted him to marry overseas. But of course my family just carried on. Ed and I were married, and that was it. My father said goodbye to me in Cardiff because he had to go to work the same day.

I stayed overnight at a hostel with other war brides in London, and we went down to Southampton in the morning on a bus. There we boarded the ship which was the *Aquitania*. We were on the ship overnight, and we sailed the next day. I was seasick all the time. When we got into Halifax, we were called in alphabetical order to go and claim our one trunk. One trunk, one suitcase, and one hat box were what I had. You were only allowed that amount. I think we were allowed a maximum of 600 pounds. Now that sounds like a lot but you just pack one trunk and one suitcase, and it adds up.

Our train dropped off war brides all the way across the country. There were twelve hundred of us that got on the train in Halifax, and when we got to Vancouver, there were fifteen of us left. All the way, it seemed to be snow, snow and more snow. The prairies were just covered in snow.

One night when I had to get up and go to the bathroom, I asked the porter why the train was stopped so long. The porter said that the train had arrived late, and a war bride's in-laws had gone home. They had to wait for the in-laws to come back, since war brides had to be signed for before we got off the train. And of course they weren't going to just drop the war bride off and leave her alone at a remote station. The in-laws finally came back with a horse and sleigh to pick up that war bride. It was two o'clock in the morning.

It took two whole weeks from the time I left my home to the time we arrived in Vancouver on March 28th. Nowadays, you can fly the same distance in eight and a half hours. In Vancouver, my husband was waiting for me—kind of. We got off the train, and everyone seemed to find someone but me and one other girl who was going to Powell River. It seemed like ages but really it was only a few minutes before the crowd parted and there he was. Ed had a great bunch of flowers. I just dropped everything I had in my hands, and Ed didn't even see me until I bumped right into him. After he'd signed for me and claimed the luggage, we went out-side and my brother-in-law, sister-in-law and their little boy were waiting outside. They stayed overnight at the York Hotel with us and left the next day. Then we had a proper honeymoon in Vancouver for ten days.

After our honeymoon we caught the ferry over to Nanaimo, and stayed with my sister-in-law in Nanaimo for a little while until Ed found somewhere for us to live, and that was hard because there was nothing to rent and nothing to buy. You ran after it but it was always sold before you got there. First we lived in a motel in Royston, and then we rented a little place for awhile. In Septem-ber we bought the little cottage in Buckley Bay. We lived there for eight years. Then we built the house that we live in now, and we have been there all this time.

When I first arrived, Buckley Bay looked wild to me, really wild. And it still does, really, when you look at Britain and then at Buckley Bay with all its trees and the water. It was strange but I liked it. I thought it was all green and lovely. You're young and you kind of take things more in your stride than when you're older.

We bought a second-hand car in Courtenay. Ed was logging when I first came but he had quite a lot of experience pile-driving wharfage, bridges and such, so we eventually started our own company. It was really funny when I got married because people were not used to the name "Sawchuk." They'd never heard the word "Sawchuk" before. I got called Sawchurch and Sawshoot and Sawshook and all kinds of other names. My maiden name was "Summers."

There were a few neighbours around. Hyslop Ingham, who now lives in Victoria, lived right opposite, and she and I were quite good friends. She had children, and eventually I had my first daughter and then my son, and we used to have birthday parties together and all that sort of thing. There was another lady by the name of Uma Webster who lived nearby, and she had six children. But there weren't all the houses that there are now.

I remember when I hadn't been here very long yet, and I walked out of my back door and saw this huge cat. I thought, "Gee, you know everything's bigger here." So I just looked at it, and it walked by and down to the beach. When Ed came home, I said to him, "Gee, you know I saw the biggest cat today." He asked me, "What was it like?" I told him. He said, "Well don't you know that was a cougar?" We war brides had a lot to learn, believe me. Everything seemed so much bigger to me here, it didn't occur to me that I was looking at a wild cat. And it did just walk by. It took awhile to adjust and get used to things.

On the whole, people accepted me. They were all telling me how lucky I was to live in "downtown" Buckley Bay, which I suppose I was in a sense. I felt that some people were quite patronizing. But most people were friendly. I'd been a soprano soloist all my life. The word soon got around, and I was asked to sing for various charity events or weddings or whatever. When I was young I had been in a choir and took voice training as well. I didn't ever play piano or anything but I always sang.

My first child was born in 1949, and I went home to Wales that year. They used to tease us at the tourist bureau because we were booking for three, and we were only two at the time. Before I emigrated to Canada, my doctor had made me promise I wouldn't tell the rest of the family but he said my father wouldn't be here much longer than three years. So when I left England to join Ed, I told my mother, "I'll probably be home in three years." But I didn't tell her why, and I never ever told anyone, only Ed.

Ed and I drove from Buckley Bay to New York in our car, and went home on the *Queen Elizabeth*. We left in November and didn't come back until March. My daughter was a year old the day after we got home. It was a great Christmas and a good four-month stay with my parents. But then I wasn't able to go home again for about fifteen years because we were building a business and a house as well as raising a family. You can't do everything.

But we did get back home in 1949, and not very many war brides did so soon after the war. I was determined to do that. That was the last time I saw my father. George VI, King of England, died in February 1952, and my dad died on the first of April the same year. I didn't get home again until 1965 but ever since then we've gone home quite regularly, every three or four years.

Although I am proud of my Welsh birth and upbringing, I have lived in Canada much longer than in the land of my birth, and I am a proud Canadian. Canada has been good to us, and we war brides have been good for Canada, bringing our talents with us and raising our families to be good Canadians. The Maple Leaf Forever!

Personal Narratives:

(The following stories, unlike
the earlier oral histories, were written
by the war brides themselves.
They have a distinct literary quality.)

Yvonne Wiseman

"I WAS BLISSFULLY
UNAWARE OF WHAT LAY
AHEAD"

Yvonne Wiseman was born in Goodmayes, Essex. The older of two girls, she was always keen on the theatre and loved to go up to London to the shows.

I was working as a VAD (Voluntary Aid Detachment) in a military hospital in Penshurst, Kent, when I first met my future husband, John. He was, without a doubt, the worst patient we had. Completely uncooperative. Whenever a doctor or nurse would ask him how he was, he'd answer, "When am I getting out of here?" He had a deep-rooted objection to hospitals. In spite of his behaviour, I was attracted to John. I learnt that he was attached to the 59th Newfoundland Regiment, stationed in Tonbridge, about five miles away. I searched my memory as to what I knew about Newfoundland. It wasn't much. A rugged island off the east coast of Canada, and codfish. Once John left the hospital I didn't really expect to see him again, thinking he probably wouldn't show up as an outpatient. But he did, mainly to see me, though I never knew this until later. He was rather a reserved man, except when he was riled or talking to doctors.

Eventually John asked me for a date; we agreed to meet on my next evening off, at a spot on the main street in Tonbridge. As luck would have it, I was late getting off the ward that particular day. I pedalled hard, up hill and down dale and arrived very hot at our rendezvous, ten minutes late, and no sign of my date. I thought that surely he could have waited; he must realize I might not be able to get away on time. I watched and waited but still no sign of him. By then I was mad, figuring I had been stood up. So I mounted my bike and cycled the five miles back. When John showed up the next week for his treatment, I was all hoity-toity and ready to show I didn't care a fig. But he was ready for me. His maxim was "the best defence is a good offence" and he greeted me with "What the hell happened to you last week?" It turned out that patience is not one of his strong points. When I didn't arrive on time, he, being a very punctual person, decided I wasn't going to show up. So he wandered off up the street, met some buddies and stopped to talk. Eventually he returned to our meeting place, just in time to see what he thought was the tail-end of me, disappearing over the hill on my bike.

So we arranged another date, which led to others and eventually our marriage. John had been on manoeuvres the three preceding days and had to rush across London for our wedding. My life altered completely from then on.

We had a real "war wedding." John made it with only minutes to spare. My mother was convinced I was going to be jilted at the altar. No white gown and flowing veil. We never had coupons for such frills, but I did wear a very pretty green dress and a cute little hat. I suddenly remembered while kneeling at the altar, that the sole of one of my shoes was wearing through and in full view of the assembled gathering. But it was too late to do anything about it. Strange things flit through one's mind at inappropriate times. Our reception was in a Lyon's Corner House in London with just the regular menu to choose from. Not even a wedding cake. But we were used to shortages in the war and it didn't seem to matter much.

We went to a London theatre after the reception and my new husband slept right through the show. He had only had a few hours sleep during the previous three days and was dead tired. After a short honeymoon in Torquay, we returned to Tonbridge.

When I learnt I was pregnant, I left the VAD and took two furnished rooms in a house owned by an elderly couple in Tonbridge. I had only a gas ring for cooking but when John could join me for a meal, they allowed me to use their kitchen range. They were nice people but I gave them an awful scare one night. I had been to Seven Oaks that morning on the bus and it had been a bumpy ride. On my return I started leaking water and was feeling apprehensive. I went to the natal clinic where a doctor was very brusque with me. I told him I was losing water but he just told me to come back on my regular day. I returned to the house and that evening about eight-thirty, I started having pains. I stuck it out for a couple of hours then called the lady of the house to phone for a doctor. He came very quickly and our daughter was born at twelve-thirty just after midnight, two months premature. She arrived into the world on sheets of newspaper which had been spread out to protect the bed. I was transported by ambulance to a hospital in Tonbridge Wells where the maternity section turned out to be from Guy's Hospital in London, evacuated from the bombing. Hazel, as we called our firstborn, was in an oxygen tent for the first six days. She weighed only four pounds fifteen ounces, and was so tiny, her little head could fit into the palm of my hand.

John was now in Worthing on the south coast. Although I got word to him, he was unable to come up to see us. Plans were in full swing for D-Day. He eventually got a few hours off and came up by motor bike when Hazel was three weeks old. When he arrived he could stay only an hour. He thought our daughter looked ugly and was a funny looking squirt. Just as he left to return to Worthing, the air-raid sirens sounded but instead of the usual drone of the German bombers there were strange cranking sounds in the night sky and sudden explosions. Nobody could make out what was going on. Nurses wheeled the baby cots into the hallways by the walls. I remember it well. Hazel had the hiccups. It was the first night of the V-1's or the doodlebugs. Soon afterwards, this area of Kent became the second line of defence for London, where these horrible weapons could be shot down before reaching the city. They came over day and night and we would watch these unmanned missiles, hoping the engines would not cut out, because then they would fall and explode. I was out once when that happened and I ducked into the nearest shelter— a telephone booth. Rather stupid I thought afterwards, being enclosed by glass.

In July 1944 my husband's regiment went over to France and I became one of those wives left behind, to await letters and hope for his safe return. Activity in the air increased with the doodlebugs. It's strange the degrees of fear one can have. One night when the sirens went, I heard the German bombers overhead and thought, "Thank goodness, it's only an ordinary air raid, not those doodlebugs." Hazel slept in a karry-kot and when a raid was in progress we huddled under the table until things quietened down. We had many disturbed nights.

Hazel had to be fed every three hours. She took an hour to feed, and more often than not, she would bring it all up. Feeding, keeping her clean and washing towels and clothes was a full-time job. Things were getting pretty rough around our area and the Government decided to evacuate women and children to safer places. So on the 4th of August '44, a crowd of us boarded a train and we were shipped to Somerset. Lorna, a friend of mine, came with me and we were fortunate to be billeted together. We were in a small village called Ditcheat, and a very kind and understanding couple took us into their home. It was really marvellous how people rallied round, opening their homes to complete strangers. They gave us a bedroom each and another room downstairs which served as a kitchen-dining-living room. It was heavenly to be away from the air raids and to go to bed at night in peace and quiet.

My friend Lorna had her baby son in November and in the New Year decided to join her parents at their home near London. Things had improved by then and an old office friend of mine, living in a flat near Leeds, suggested that Hazel and I move in with her. Soon after we settled in at my friend's home, John came home on seven-days' leave. It was wonderful and went all too quickly. He was quite enchanted with Hazel who looked totally different from the tiny morsel of life he had first seen. Then he was once again back at the front. By then the tide had turned in the war and for our little family it ended on VE Day, the 9th of May '45.

John had come through safely but not entirely unscathed. He suffered blinding headaches and blackouts periodically for a number of years, caused by a shell exploding too close for comfort. It was late July before he finally joined us in Leeds, and we then awaited our instructions for our journey to Newfoundland and a new life. It was a happy period. Hazel had started walking in August, and when it was time to leave, she was toddling quite nicely. We bade farewell to our friends in late October, and headed south for our voyage to Canada and a rendezvous with the future.

I guess the adventure of being a war bride really started when John and I and our eighteen-month-old daughter boarded the _S.S. Queen Elizabeth_ in Southampton, England in November

1945, bound for Halifax, Nova Scotia. The liner had been stripped to accommodate thousands of troops, returning them to their homeland. It wasn't a voyage of luxury but it got us there safely. We will never forget our early morning arrival into Halifax harbour. It was full of boats large and small, with sirens blowing and horns blaring and every kind of noisemaker imaginable being used. Cheering crowds and flags waving, all there to welcome home the soldiers. It was an impressive moment when the national anthem was struck up and thousands of male voices joined to sing "Oh Canada." As the tug edged us in closer there was a rush to one side of the ship for a better look at the welcoming crowds—and then the PA system suddenly bellowed forth, urging us to move back to the opposite decks. The mighty ship was listing.

That evening we boarded a train for North Sydney. There we embarked on the *S.S. Burgeo* for the night crossing of the Cabot Strait to Port aux Basques. I was blissfully unaware of what lay ahead, but not for long. It was a dreadful night, blowing a full gale. Evidently not unusual for this stretch of water in November. I swear we went across like a submarine. The ship was tightly battened down and our cabin grew hotter and hotter. There was a big brass hook on the door so we used it to latch it open and let in some air. Unfortunately during a massive roll of the ship it was wrenched off. The bunks were screened by curtains hung on brass rings. So all that night, when the ship rolled one way, the door swung back and the curtains slid down the bar—and when we rolled back—so did they. Both Hazel and myself were horribly seasick all night. I was also expecting our second baby, which didn't help. Wouldn't you know—my dear husband slept peacefully through it all. I guess it was minor compared to the barrages of war. We were two hours late in arriving and there were times when I never expected to see land again. We then continued our journey, a twenty-seven-hour train trip across Newfoundland.

A few days later the demobbing process was completed in St. John's and my husband was once again a civilian. We travelled to John's home in Hearts Delight, an outpost in Trinity Bay. John's dad was with us for a short while but being ill he had to return to the hospital for treatment. The house in Hearts Delight had a lovely position facing the sea, but was also open to the weather, as I later found out. It was old, large and cold, and not modern at all, although we did have the convenience of the well being in the pantry, which was a help. No sinks, no bathroom or toilet, and oil lamps for light. John did manage to fix up a chemical toilet in the outside porch but a trip out there was, to put it mildly, hardly comfortable. There was a range in the kitchen and a Quebec heater in the hall. These two appliances were the only means for cooking and heating. They were fired with wood. John had to leave for St. John's in early January to attend a course at the Demonstration Farm to prepare him for farming.

Before he went he got in a supply of wood to tide me over the winter. This was put in an outside barn and I brought it in as needed. As the weather became colder, so did the house. I abandoned the upstairs bedroom and fixed up the front parlour for sleeping. Most of the furniture in the parlour I moved into the kitchen to make it more cosy. When my father-in-law later returned he said the house looked like a monkey puzzle. Maybe so, but it gave us a degree of comfort in two rooms at least. It was a severe winter, the worst for fifty years on the east coast. Cold winds and masses of snow. By then I was getting somewhat unwieldy, carrying all before me. It became quite difficult to cope on my own and one day, while I was trudging outside, I missed the path and landed up to my waist in the snow-filled ditch and had to be hauled out. Eventually some friends of my husband took Hazel and myself into their home for a month until John's dad returned in late February from the hospital.

Our son Roy was born in Whitbourne Cottage Hospital on Sunday the 28th of April '46. His birth was completely opposite to that of Hazel. Whereas she entered the world two months ahead of time, Roy was in no hurry. He was a week overdue when my labour pains started. The district nurse attended me and by morning she was growing concerned. Roy was "stuck" and she was going to need some assistance. She dispatched a local taxi to

Hearts Content, a distance of eleven miles to fetch a doctor. The driver came back alone. The doctor was out on another case and could not come. So the district nurse somehow bundled me into the taxi and we set off for Whitbourne—thirty miles away over an unpaved road, with Roy still refusing to enter the world. He was eventually born that evening with the aid of instruments.

In late June after John had finished his course, we sold the house in Hearts Delight and travelled to Deer Lake in the west coast area of Newfoundland. We stayed for the summer with John's brother Bill, his wife Dot, and their nine children. It was a new experience and like living in a hotel, with so many people coming and going.

In September we took up residence in Cormack, the area selected by the Government for those returning veterans who wished to take advantage of the Agricultural Resettlement Scheme. Each applicant was allocated fifty acres, ten acres of which was cleared, plus a cow, a horse and some pigs, also some farm implements. But most importantly we were given a house to live in. Just two rooms were completed; it was up to us to finish the rest ourselves. We were young and in love and ready to conquer all.

Preparations were made for the coming winter. John dug a well outside for our water supply. A good barn had been built and we fitted it with stalls and got in a supply of hay and oats. In the house we had the kitchen range which was our only source of heat and the only means for cooking and heating water. We needed a large amount of wood and I learned how to use a bucksaw and differentiate between green and dry wood.

In the house our furnishings were sparse. Just essentials for our two rooms. We walled off an area for the two kiddies. Our clothes were hung on nails driven into the wall, as we hadn't any closets. Personal washing and dishes were done in bowls and the laundry on a washboard in a big tub. When it became too cold to hang out the washing, I hung it on a line stretched across the room over the stove. Oil lamps were in use again for lighting. It was all very primitive. The phrase "being thrown in the deep end" aptly described our lifestyle there.

So the winter advanced. I had thought Hearts Delight was cold but it was nothing compared to Cormack. The temperature dropped lower and lower, and it became harder and harder to heat the house. The kitchen was the only place which was warm and we stoked the fire at night to hold in some heat. One morning when I was late returning to the bedroom to make the bed, I found loose ice in the hot water bottle, which was still under the bedding. We had never heard of insulation back then. For our food supply we went to a small store in the "Camp" which was in the centre of the settlement. This involved us walking in, hauling Hazel and Roy on the sleigh, a distance of five miles there and back. We also had moose meat, frozen and bottled, and my husband snared rabbits. I made our bread and also learnt how to churn butter.

To help out financially, a contract had been secured for the farmers to cut birch wood for railway ties. So John used to get up at five-thirty in the morning to feed the horse, harness and attach the sleigh ready for the day's work. After breakfast he took off and I was left to cope with the usual chores of the day which included seeing to the cow and pigs in the barn and mainly trying to keep us warm. There were times when I came in from outside almost crying with the cold. I would put down the oven door and lodge my frozen feet on it. I can still recall the pain of them thawing out. For two months that winter the temperature never rose above zero Fahrenheit and dropped as low as thirty degrees below. Our well froze; it hadn't been dug deep enough. So we had to go down to a fast running brook a quarter mile away for our water supply, using the horse and sleigh and a big wooden barrel which we filled and hauled back home.

Eventually the winter came to an end, and it was time to prepare the land and put in our first crops. We worked hard, tending our plants, and attempting to make the house more liveable inside. Everything was coming along well and we anticipated a good harvest of potatoes and a fair return for our labours. Then on August 22, the temperature nosedived during the day and that

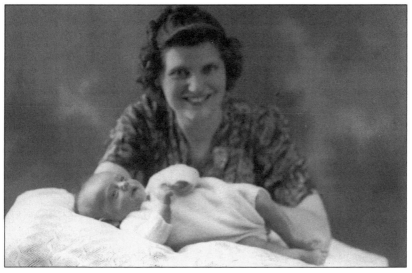

Yvonne and daughter Hazel, England, 1944.

Yvonne at Cormack farm, Newfoundland, Winter 1947–48.

night we had a hard frost. A sorry sight awaited us the next morning. All our thriving potato plants were limp and black. The frost stunted their growth. Then a further misfortune befell us. Arrangements had been made for us and the other farmers to ship our produce by rail, but the railway went out on strike and there was no other means of getting the produce across the Island. So our community of hard-working farmers had to truck the results of our labours into Corner Brook over forty miles away, and peddle our wares around the stores and houses there. It was a sad end to the first year.

Our second winter in Cormack was not as hard as the first. There were heavy snowfalls but the temperatures were slightly higher. We had worked on the house, and now had a living room with an oil stove and some comfortable furniture. A bathroom of sorts was fitted with a chemical toilet. It seemed a palace now. I was getting hardened to the life and our two children were older. When spring finally came we prepared once more for planting with renewed hope and vigor. Remembering the frost damage of the previous year, we decided to go mainly for cabbages, thinking they would be safe from the vagaries of the weather. All went well until one day in September. A hurricane from the Caribbean decided to make a bee-line for our settlement. It was frightening. Torrential rains and hurricane-force winds. When the storm passed it left a scene of devastation. What really suffered were the crops. Our rows of "safe" cabbages were blown right out of the ground and strewn around in a saturated mess. Once again our hard work had sustained a crippling blow and to cap it all, our cow died.

We did some hard thinking as winter loomed ahead, and came to the conclusion we weren't cut out to be farmers. Our savings were badly eroded. We couldn't see any economic benefit by continuing and not much of a future for our children. We figured if we didn't get out then, we never would. So early in 1949 we "threw in the towel" and decided to seek our fortune elsewhere. We were still young and in love but we hadn't conquered farming.

We decided to go back to England, licking our wounds and

wondering what to do for the best. We went to stay with my grandmother for awhile on the Isle of Wight and it was so good to be back in a temperate climate again and to have such things as running water, bathrooms and electricity. John landed a job as a woodsman on a large estate in Bedfordshire, and a house went with the job, which suited us just fine. The area was quite lovely and rural. Hazel started school there and I used to cycle in daily with her on the back of my bike. John's pay was not very much, so I helped out by working in the fields for a local farmer, picking peas, radishes, marrows and other vegetables. We stayed there for two years, but again a decision had to be made as to where it was leading us.

So, it was back to Canada and Newfoundland. John went ahead to get a job and a base for us. I returned to the Isle of Wight with the kiddies to my grandmother's for the summer. I worked in a hotel to maintain myself financially and not be a burden on my grandmother who looked after Hazel and Roy while I was working. John laboured in the woods in Newfoundland for awhile, but then travelled to Toronto and got a job there. In October we again set off across the Atlantic to join my husband. We stayed the winter in Toronto and come spring we returned to Newfoundland (we were devils for punishment). We settled in Corner Brook, ran a restaurant for a number of years and bought a house. Then it came time to move again. Hazel and Roy needed better schooling, so it was back to Toronto.

When John retired in 1972 we bought an old, dilapidated house in rural Ontario. It could be "nostalgia" because this house too was bereft of modern conveniences. We worked on that house for years and eventually a very nice residence replaced a rather sorry beginning. John developed health problems and we decided to move to a warmer climate. We now live on Vancouver Island in a comfortable home with every convenience and close to all amenities. We have been married for over fifty years. Like most couples we've had our ups and downs and faced many changes in our life together. However, neither of us has ever regretted making that second date all those years ago in Tonbridge, Kent.

Jean McLeod

"WE DROPPED OUR BIKES AND ROLLED INTO THE DITCHES"

Jean McLeod was born in Littlehampton, England. Eighteen years old when the war started, Jean served in the Land Army from 1942 to 1945. She became engaged to Norman McLeod, a Canadian soldier, in 1943.

O n a very warm day in August 1944 one of the Land Army girls, Joan Springhall, and I decided to take a hiking trip to Scotland. We took a train to Carlisle, and hitchhiked from there, sleeping at the YWCA, which cost two shillings a night for bunk beds (which of course we were used to) and included tea and toast for breakfast. We went to a trucking yard to hitch a ride to Glasgow, and ended up hanging on to ropes as we rode on top of a load covered with a tarpaulin. We weren't allowed to ride inside the cab because the driver had a duck sitting on the seat!

We had on our Land Army uniforms, so that helped us get rides. We each had a small army haversack, a change of underwear, socks and shirts and our green sweaters. We hitched a ride to Loch Lomond and used our ration coupons to buy bacon, eggs, tomatoes and bread. The shopkeeper gave us a biscuit-tin lid, and we cooked our supper over a small fire right beside Loch Lomond.

The next day we headed out on a main road. We didn't know where we were going. We got another ride in a truck—inside this time—and were dropped off at a crossroad. The driver said we could get a ride to Penrith so we started to walk and walk. No rides in sight, and it was evening so we called into a farm. We asked if we could work for a couple of days for a meal or two; we said we would sleep anywhere. Well, we were amazed that they welcomed us with open arms. Supper was ready—meat and potato pie, raspberries and cream. They were an older couple with no children of their own.

The family already had a Land Army girl, Betty, and two Italian prisoners of war working for them. The Italians slept upstairs above the kitchen, very quiet lads who had been there a long time. The next day, after Joan, Betty and I did a few chores, the family lent us their old bikes and we went off to Ullswater Lake. We took a ride on a steamer and had a lovely day. The farmer's wife had packed a lunch for us. On the following day the farmer drove us into Penrith to catch a train back to Carlisle. I shall never forget those wonderful people.

The following year, my fiancé Norman wrote to say he would be coming home for seven day's leave and would I get things ready to be married, so I really had to get a move on. My sister who lived nearby said she would make the wedding cake and have the reception there, and she made arrangements for St. Peter's Church where she knew the vicar.

I got a week's leave from the Land Army. Mum and I went to our nearest big town, Kingston, to buy cloth. I had all my coupons, and I bought a deep aqua suit, brown suede shoes, gloves and purse. I made my hat by using the crown from mum's old hat and sewing aqua and rose felt flowers around the front and sides of it. My underwear was bought on the black market—terrible, I know, but I was desperate. Norman was bringing his friend to be best man, but at the last minute he couldn't make it because his leave was cancelled. I asked a neighbour's son, who was a British Army officer home on leave, to be Norman's best man.

Jean McLeod with Land Army buddies, 1942.

Norman had to go to London to get a signature on the marriage certificate. He sat in the outer office for nearly three hours. When the Brigadier came out, he told off the CWAC girl for making Norman wait so long. He said, "You don't keep these young men waiting when they have come back from the fighting lines." Norman was infantry, Loyal Edmontons.

About our wedding day, April 23, 1945, I can't say I recall very much. I was so tired after all that racing around. My brother-in-law gave me away, since my dad had died after we were bombed in London during 1941. I vaguely remember walking down the aisle at St. Peter's Church and sitting at the reception at my sister's house. Leaning against a sideboard and hearing the drone of voices around me, I dozed off. Somebody woke me and said, "Have a piece of wedding cake, Jean."

Everybody came to the train station to see us off on our three-day honeymoon. We were going to my sister's cottage at Ferring-by-the-Sea on the south coast near Worthing. By the time we arrived, a neighbour had been in and lit the fires to air the cottage out. At the back door was a box of groceries, including vegetables and a dead rabbit. I had eaten rabbit stews, pies, etc., but I hadn't the foggiest notion how to cook this rabbit. It was a good thing that Norman was from northern Alberta. We laughed all the time as Norman skinned the rabbit and then I stewed it. I guess it was my sister's idea of a joke. But we never let her think it was anything unusual.

When we arrived back home, Norman had to return to his outfit, which was in Holland at that time. I went back to Woking to work in the field, but we knew it wouldn't be long before he'd be back in England again. I never had any doubt that we would win the war. I've always been an optimist.

I managed to obtain a transfer to work for my brother-in-law who was a market gardener. His market garden was one of the largest in England. His lorries took produce to Covent Garden in London. He was the first to have irrigation in his fields and machines to wash vegetables, and later on, to pack vegetables in cellophane. He was a good kind man, and I loved him. He had about fifty Land Army girls working for him, plus his own farm workers and gypsies who were given an acre of land for themselves.

One time, whilst I was working for my brother-in-law, Joan Springhall and I were cycling home at the end of the day. We were going down a road with trees on each side, and a small plane came up the road towards us skimming the tree tops. We started to wave because we thought it was a Spitfire, one of our planes.

Suddenly, there were tracer bullets firing at us from each side of the plane. We dropped our bikes and rolled into the ditches. It must have been a German Messerschmitt—pretty scary! We reported it to the air-raid warden who said the plane must have been lost. Its real target must have been Vickers Armstrong Aircraft factory which was in Weybridge, the town next to us. And we were in our Land Army uniforms so the pilot probably thought we were regular Army.

At this time I was living with my mum, and my friend Joan was billeted with us. In fact, we had four bedrooms, and during the war, you were ordered to take in lodgers if you lived outside of London. Mum provided bed and breakfast. She liked doing it. She missed my brothers, and my dad had died. It was a crazy mixed-up world. Now I realize how frightening it must have been for mum.

Norman came back in late June 1945. He had asked for a six-month extension before going back to Canada. All the Land Army girls gradually went back to their own homes. Joan Springhall married her British lieutenant, and went to live in Cornwall. I'd love to know where all the Land Army girls are now and how they're doing.

Norman was stationed in Aldershot. Every morning he left on the six o'clock train, and I used to get up to make tea and toast and jam for him, and also take a cup to mum. Then I became pregnant, and later I had neuralgia in my face. The doctor came each evening to give me a shot in the arm so I could sleep. I thought I was going mad. I used to sit up in bed, holding my face and rocking back and forth. This went on for weeks.

Finally I went to a dentist. He took one look at my gums and said all my teeth must come out. I had pyorrhoea of the gums— what a shock. Here I was only twenty-five years old and newly married. Poor Norman. Poor *me*. Even though I was pregnant, the doctor and dentist said that my teeth must come out. So I went to the local cottage hospital for two days. It took a long time to get used to dentures. I lost my baby—guess it was all too much for me. We were going to call her Dawn. I could never understand why I had pyorrhoea. I had perfect teeth up to this time.

Norman went back to Calgary, Alberta, in March 1946. I got a notice to be prepared to go in August on the *Aquitania*. That was cancelled, and then a telegram arrived advising me to be under the clock at Waterloo Station at twelve noon on June 6th. My mum, sister and sister-in-law came to the train station in Walton-on-Thames to see me off. There were lots of tears, and I was tempted not to go. Then I thought of dear Norman.

I went with other departing war brides to an old house on Seymour Street around the back of the Cumberland Hotel. We could hear the parade and celebrating going on. It was the D-Day anniversary but we weren't allowed to go and watch. I guess they didn't want us all disappearing at the last minute. By the way, I was pregnant again—nearly six months along. We stayed overnight in this dark, dismal house—masses of us. Two-tier bunkbeds, guess who was in the top bunk. Babies crying, most of us weeping, too. The next day we went by train to Southampton to board the beautiful *Queen Mary*—what a sight! Two thousand war brides, a few civilians and MacKenzie King, prime minister of Canada at this time. We all asked, "Who's he?"

The state rooms had four to six two-tier bunk beds. I managed to get a bottom bunk this time. I pal'd up with a June and two other Jeans. We were told to come to the dining room after we settled into our rooms. First, we all went up on deck to wave goodbye to the folks on the docks as we sailed on the outgoing tide. The dinner that evening was fantastic. We had never seen so much wonderful food since 1939—turkey and all the vegetables that go with it and white dinner rolls. Apple or peach pie and cream—I can remember it to this day. The waiters were laughing. I guess they had seen it all before.

Well, that was the last meal I had for five days. I was seasick and six months pregnant, and I was *still* trying to get used to my dentures. I was a sorry sight! I wanted to die. The stewards brought me crackers and ice water. Everyone said, "You've got to get up on deck. Fresh air is what you need." I could just picture myself rushing to the rail to throw up, and my teeth going too! Could you imagine me meeting my husband's parents without any teeth?

Well, I survived the trip and finally came up on deck. When we docked in Halifax, it was drizzling, a miserable day. Not many people were there except for a few VIP's to meet Mr. King, I guess. By this time, folks were getting a little weary of war brides. The Red Cross people were there to sort us all out in groups to go onto the train. We felt like refugees, which I guess we were in a way. We hadn't been able to wash or bathe because there was only salt water on the ship.

I felt so sorry for the girls with babies and small children. The Red Cross people were marvellous, however. They were so understanding. I wanted to cry on their shoulders. But you know, we British—stiff upper lip and all that. Ha! Ha! It wasn't funny at the time though. Once we got on board the train, everyone seemed to settle down. It was very hot, and we were told not to open windows because of the cinders and dust blowing in. After we had got out of the city, it was better. Lovely country.

It's funny but I can't remember having meals on the train. I know I must have but it's a complete blank. And I had missed four and a half days of food on the _Queen Mary_ already. Oh, by the way, I was assigned the top bunk, "berth," I should say, again. In Ontario, we stopped at a small place to take on water. Three of us dashed across the road to a little general store to buy chocolate bars and cigarettes, and I bought a cheap pair of red canvas sandals to match my red smock. We almost missed the train. And was the porter mad!

My three pals, two Jeans and a June, were in different coaches. One Jean was going to Saskatoon, the other to Vancouver, and June, who had been a model in London, was dropped off at a remote stop somewhere in Saskatchewan. I saw her out the window—a very slim girl clutching her hat and wearing high heels. She had regular luggage and a hat box, as only a model would have. Nobody was there to meet her, but the Red Cross would not have left her there if somebody hadn't been on the way. There was just a dirt path leading to the train tracks. It must have been a cattle loading stop. I do hope everything turned out alright for her and the two Jeans. We should have kept in touch but one never thinks of that at the time.

I desperately needed a good wash. Each time I went to the washrooms, girls were rinsing out nappies. All the basins were being used so I crept down to the washroom at five o'clock one morning and stripped to the waist and went to it. The door opened, and the porter walked in. He said, "Good morning. It's a lovely day, isn't it?" He took his white jacket from a hook and walked out. I was standing there with my small towel clutched to my bosom and my mouth gaping.

The train journey went on day after day. We all thought Canada was such a vast country. And it was still very hot. I noticed huge red barns with white trim and tiny farm houses. I finally arrived at my destination, Edmonton, and said goodbye to the girls and the little ones. The Red Cross nurse helped me and gave me a hanky trimmed with lace. I gave her a kiss and thanked her.

I saw Norman and his mother and grandma. Lots of kissing, hugging and crying. Then Norman's mother asked me, "What would you like to do first? Have a rest or maybe a meal?" They were staying at the Leland Hotel. My response was, "Please, can I have a bath?" What bliss. I must have soaked for half an hour. After I had dressed in my same dirty clothes, I went to find the others. Then we all went to have dinner. The waitress put a plate of food in the middle of the table, and Norman passed it to me. I said, "No, I haven't got my plate yet." I thought it was for all of us! What a meal! But I also thought what a waste it was, because I could only eat half of it.

After my arrival in Edmonton, Norman decided to stay in the Army; his first posting took us to Calgary. Over the years, we have also lived in other parts of Canada, including Ontario, the Yukon and British Columbia. Wherever we went, we enjoyed ourselves and had great adventures on the many camping trips that we took with our three children. All in all, it's been a good life, and I am truly thankful I still have Norman—together we have come a long way. I'm very proud to be a war bride and live in this beautiful country.

Jean Kirkoff

"VALERIE? THERE'S NO VALERIE HERE"

Jean Kirkoff was born in Farnborough, England. She and her younger brother grew up in a lovely house with twenty rooms.

W e met at the Rex Cinema, December 29, 1940, in Farnborough, thirty miles northeast of London, during a Laurel and Hardy film. He offered me a cigarette, and liking what I could see of the tip of his nose in the glow from the screen, I accepted. He was a Canadian soldier named Harry. He walked me home in the blackout after the picture show. He asked my name, and I told him my fantasy version: Valerie. (Valerie, my heroine, solved the mysteries with her dog Flash, in my childhood books.) At my gate, Harry invited me out on New Year's Eve—though we hadn't yet caught a glimpse of one another.

When he called for me on New Year's Eve my house was in wartime darkness. My father answered the door, and Harry asked for Valerie. My father said, "Valerie? There's no Valerie here." I tore down the stairs to contradict him. We then took the bus to Aldershot, five miles away, with only tiny glowlights to light our feet, and a pencil light when the bus conductor took our fares.

From the bus we entered the unlighted foyer of the theatre. We saw another movie in the dark, after which we walked home down Queen's Avenue in the blackout. Our relationship took a downturn when Harry fell into a construction hole. I had difficulty helping him out without falling in myself in the darkness. Before I knew it, my stockings had fallen, too, in the struggle to get Harry out. What with the wartime rationing of elastic, my garterbelt was less than effective at coping with my exertions. I said to Harry, "Turn away while I hike them back up." "Why?" he said, "I can't see anything anyway."

Finally we had our first real look at one another in a lighted hotel dining room over a late-night supper. Four years later we married, eventually having three children, Patricia, Frank and Fred, each five years apart. I laughingly said that they were our five year plan.

[Jean's story was the winning entry in the Victoria Times-Colonist *Valentine's contest, Feb. 14, 1992.]*

Jean Sharlow

"WE WERE AFRAID TO GO
TOO DEEP INTO THE
TUNNELS"

*Jean Sharlow was born in Surrey.
The family moved to West Wickham, Kent, in
the early thirties.*

I t was May 1941 in Croydon, England. "There's a good show play-ing at the Rex at Hayes," I said. "Okay, let's go then," said Bill. "We can most likely get home before the air raid starts." Bill was my Canadian soldier fiance and we were planning to be married in July.

The movie was enjoyable, and we left the movie house just as it was getting dusk. England at this time was on double daylight sav-ing time; this was to enable its workers to travel home before the nightly air raids started. We were standing at the bus stop, when the air-raid sirens started to wail. Although these sirens were an everyday occurrence, sometimes even up to a dozen times a day, a shiver of fear always ran down my spine, with the rising and falling of the siren's wail.

What should we do? Our choices were to stand and wait and see if the bus would come (sometimes they stopped running in air raids), or take a train. This too was risky, since railways were good targets for the bombers, they too were inclined to pull over when the bombing got heavy, which we found out later would have been fatal.

The distance to home was about three miles if we took the short cut, a foot-path alongside the railway tracks. After walking briskly for about a half mile, we heard the unmistakable throb of a German bomber. Searchlights swept the sky and our heavy anti-aircraft guns got into action.

It didn't take us long to realize that this was no ordinary air raid. London seemed to be their target, and judging from the blood-red sky over London, they were getting it. Biggin Hill, an Air Force base, was only a few miles away from us, and bombers that were turned back by the heavy gunfire, jettisoned their bombs all around us.

Things got very hot. Bombs were falling all around, and the screaming whine they made as they fell to earth will ring forever in my ears. Bill said, "We just can't go on. We must seek a shelter." Shrapnel from our guns was raining down in white jagged lumps. This time we had two choices. The footpath we were on had a high fence on either side. To the right were the railway tracks;

they are electrified in England so this was out of the question. To our left was a school, at which two years before I had been a student. We clambered over the school fence and started searching in the total blackout for the air-raid shelter that we knew every school-yard had. At last we found it, and were horrified to find that the door was padlocked. As we stood there trying to break in, a bomb whistled down dangerously close. We threw ourselves on the ground; it had hit the railway tracks, and debris showered down all over us. Bill started throwing himself at the door and finally it gave way. Once inside we edged cautiously into the dead black underground tunnel, found a bench and sat down. We were afraid to go too deep into the tunnels, as no one knew we were there and if the entrance became covered, we would never be found.

The relentless bombing went on for what seemed like hours and hours. Suddenly there was a lull, and we sensed that something had happened. We found our way out of the shelter. The moon had come up, and our wonderful Spitfires were giving the German bombers chase. Bill said, "Let's make a run for it." I agreed. Never before or since have I moved so quickly. We covered that last two and a half miles in record time. As we ran through the familiar streets, we were shocked to see so many of the houses in ruins. Not a hundred yards from our house was a small crater blocking our way. We edged our way around the rim. Imagining my family would be out of their minds with worry about me, we ran straight down the garden path to the air-raid shelter, at the foot of the garden, and burst in. "Were you worried about us?" I asked my mum. "Oh no," she replied, "I knew you would be alright—you were with Bill."

Bill and I were married at St. John's church in West Wickham, Kent, on July 19th, 1941. We managed to have a white wedding in spite of the rationing, my mother had set aside some white and blue taffeta, enough to make a bride's gown and two bridesmaids' dresses. Bill's brother Leslie, who was in the Calgary Highlanders, was his best man, and my sister Betty and friend Molly were my bridesmaids. Owing to the rationing, our wedding cake had no icing, only a decorated cardboard cover. I think most of Bill's regiment, the 92nd Battery of the 3rd Field Regiment Royal Canadian Artillery, attended. They sent a gun carriage to take us to the reception. A guard of honour plus the military band was outside the church.

The bombings continued in our district, and in 1942 I returned to my mother and father's home to help my mother look after my baby nephew, whose mother was hospitalized after being injured in a bombing. I saw Bill on his leaves as often as he could get away.

In the spring of 1943 the ship, the *St. Essylt,* on which Bill was travelling to the invasion of Sicily, was torpedoed. It was in a convoy of five ships; three of them were sunk that same night. When rescued from the water, Bill was taken to Algiers and later he rejoined his regiment. It was months before I learnt what had happened; those were bleak and unhappy days of waiting for news. I was expecting my first child Michael. When he was born on December 9th, 1943, my mother sent Bill a telegram through Cairo, to tell him he had a baby son.

In the spring of 1944, the buzz-bombing started—it was terrible. Our district was so badly hit that we were advised to leave if possible. I went with my baby, my mother, my sister, who was still in a body cast, and her son to Doncaster in Yorkshire. My mother had a cousin there and she took the five of us in. Oh, what peace! We returned home some months later to wait out the end of the war.

When the war ended on May 8th, 1945, the relief was enormous. Our street had a street party for all the children, and we all took something to eat that we had saved. I am sure it was the first party for most of the children. Bill returned from Holland around May 12th, and in five days he was on his way back to Canada.

It was the following February 1946 that I started my journey for Canada. When I glanced down at our little boy dozing beside me on the train seat, I thought, poor little chap, uprooted from the only home he had ever known, and now going to a daddy he had only met once, and another set of grandparents. How would we settle in this huge strange land?

It seemed ages ago that my son Michael and I had said a very sad and tearful goodbye to my family, friends and neighbours who had gathered to wave us off on our trip to Canada. Our first night was spent in a large house in London. It was here that we met some of the twelve hundred women and children who would be travelling on the *Mauretania* to join their husbands and fathers in Canada.

Early the next day we were on our way by train to Liverpool. It was getting dark by the time we reached the dockside. I will always remember looking up at this huge ship, which seemed to have hundreds of lighted portholes. We trudged up the gangplank, and after many lineups, and much paperwork we were assigned to a cabin. Much to my surprise there were ten of us sharing a cabin, six women and four children. We soon settled down into a routine, helping each other with the children. For mothers with babies, it was very difficult; washing had to be done in the hand basin in sea water. After five years of rationing we enjoyed the meals very much. The children saw and ate a banana for the first time.

The month was February; it was cold and the sea very rough. Seasickness took its toll. I found that by keeping on the deck as much as I could, it helped overcome the feelings of sickness. I would wrap a blanket around Michael and myself, and find a sheltered spot to sit full of thoughts about our future life. How my life changed by going to a dance, meeting and falling in love with someone from the other end of the world, and now here we were heading for Vancouver.

Eight days later we arrived at Halifax. An efficient system had been developed to get us through customs, and onto the bride train, taking us to our various destinations. Mine seemed far away, and of course it was. My husband Bill, now discharged from the army, was working in Vancouver. We had decided that Michael and I would stop for a few days in Alberta, to meet my in-laws, who were anxious to meet their daughter-in-law and their first grandchild.

The days on the train were similar to those on the boat, except that now there was a strong feeling of excitement, as we all drew nearer to our destinations. The porter in charge of our coach kept us all laughing with his tall tales of life in Canada. Of course it was deep snow all the way.

The coach was beginning to feel quite lonely, since at every stop women and children disembarked into the waiting arms of their new families. It was a great temptation to go right to Vancouver, where Bill awaited us in a rented basement suite. As we drew close, my anxiety grew and grew. Would they like me? Would we recognize each other? How I wished Bill was with me.

The porter told me the next stop was mine. I gathered my possessions together, and stepped onto the snowy platform. I could see a small plump lady racing towards me; as she drew near, I said, "Hallo, Mother." A smile broke over her face. "Oh Jean," she said, "I thought you would never get here." A huge man in a checked mackinaw strode up and swept his first grandchild into his arms, and suddenly we were surrounded by family and friends. The warmth of that greeting assured me it was going to be alright.

Bill was on the phone as soon as we stepped into the house. "You can stay four or five days," he said, "Then come to Vancouver." But it didn't quite work that way. After five days of parties, shopping and bridal showers, first Michael and then myself came down with the mumps. Bill said, "Enough is enough," and managed to obtain a leave of absence from his job to come and get us. We arrived in Vancouver, and we later bought a house. We had a second son Stephen and we lived in our home for thirty-nine years, before moving to Victoria, where we are very happy.

Rosemary Bauchman

"YOU LUCKY GIRL, I WISH I
WAS GOING WITH YOU"

*Rosemary Bauchman was born in a
Cotswold village in Gloucestershire.
As a mature student she went to university and
earned a BA. She is the author
of six published books.*

T hank God, no more air raids! Shortages and austerity would no longer be excused with the flip "Don'cha know there's a WAR on?"

Demobbed, the boys and girls would all go marching home again, tra-la-la; back in Civvy Street they'd find that golden future of their dreams. Having finished their fathers' fight, they confidently expected the dawn of a thousand years of peace.

For four years I'd shared these dreams; marrying a Canadian had not substantially changed them. Serving with the WAAF I found my life was full of immediacies. I didn't give much thought to a future in a new land. But when my injured Spitfire-pilot husband was found unfit for flying duties and whisked back home, the picture altered. Bereft, I eagerly filled in forms pertaining to my own journey to Canada and spent a lot of time wondering what it would be like.

Being stationed near home I used to spend my weekly day off with my parents. As I cycled thirteen hilly miles through familiar lanes, it was unbelievable that soon I'd be leaving them forever, to go to far-off, snowy Canada. The concept had no reality in soft Cotswold twilights and on early mornings with the bird choir in the hedges tuning up for spring. But as the wheels of officialdom gained momentum, I went to London for interviews with the Canadian Civilian Repatriation Department. I was directed to a doctor for a medical check-up, to a photographer for Entry-Permit photographs, inundated with information about Canada and directives concerning the impending voyage. Everyday routine gradually acquired a miasma of "for the last time," though it still seemed incredible that soon my days would not be bounded by Reveille and Lights Out, that I would be able to forget parades, PT and passes.

I felt I had encountered an insurmountable problem when I discovered I could not get my discharge from the RAF until I received my sailing orders. Like most worry, this was needless; when the vital document finally came, all clearances and formalities were accomplished with such dispatch, all farewells, both glad and sad, were taken so swiftly, that I found myself standing at the

Main Gate of the station watching the new jet aircraft chalking doodles in the sky while I waited for a taxi, and dazedly asked myself, "Is that really IT?"

Between standby and actual sailing there developed a precious hiatus, a full, sad-happy week at home when I see-sawed between elation and heartbreak: one moment riding high at the thought of being reunited with my darling, the next in tears over parting from my family and home, the English way of life. I wanted the impossible; I wanted both.

It was a week of goodbyes—"You lucky girl, I wish I was going with you!" Everyone made some such remark, everyone professed to envy my going to Canada. Right up to the last minute there was the lifeline of letters exchanged across the ocean—all cryptically worded because of security regulations and the censor's scissors. My husband knew I'd be arriving soon, but dates, times, places, names of vessels were taboo. He was stationed in Halifax, where I'd almost certainly dock, and he assured me he'd be there to meet me, with bells on! Still in the RCAF, there was a chance he might be posted to British Columbia. That prospect thrilled me. For years I had corresponded with my dead brother's friends there, and knew more about the West Coast than I did about my husband's native Nova Scotia.

Then came the dreaded moment of parting, the hired car at the door. Mother admonished, "No tears, now, if there were no partings there'd be no meetings," while her own eyes brimmed over. Dad made a production of stowing my luggage before catching me in a gruff, wordless embrace . . . Waving, waving, until we turned the corner . . . My sister and best friend seeing me off at the station, repeating the formula, "You lucky thing, I wish I was going with you."

The landscape passed by in a watery blur. My saturated handkerchief poked in my pocket, I set about repairing my face before alighting at Bristol where I had a four-hour wait for the train heading north. At battered Templemeads station the glass roof was in shards, offices and waiting rooms boarded up, but the tracks were clear. Makeshift booths displayed the "BUSINESS AS

USUAL" signs that sprang up like flowers after air raids. Among these I found a magazine stand where I bought a story about Canada which engrossed me until the train for Liverpool steamed in.

I found a seat, doors slammed, the train gathered speed . . . Goodbye, Somerset. . . . chug-a-chug-chugchug through a patchwork of fields stitched with stone walls and hedges . . . chug-a-chug-chugchug . . . Goodbye Gloucestershire . . . numb, cold, I watched the western counties slip away as the day wore on. Close on midnight we reached the terminal, Liverpool station, shadowed and chill. Canadian soldiers, wearing armbands like shepherds, were herding travel-weary females into groups. Only my reflexes made me turn at an excited cry, "Jeff!"

"Jeff" I had been throughout my service career, and despite my civvies, Jeff I still was to the two smiling girls whose warm greeting started my spirits on an upward spiral. They had travelled all the way from Devon on the same train. If only we'd known, we would have been company for each other. Never mind—we'd be together crossing the Atlantic.

We went by bus through Liverpool's black streets to a hostel where we were fed and bedded down. Waking to a familiar pattern of feminine chatter, I needed a moment to relate to my surroundings. After breakfast, we were well-briefed, cosseted; even the snags had all been anticipated and smoothed. Then a time-killing walk in the pale February sunshine among the blitz-scarred streets. The proud people of Liverpool counted every bomb-demolished house a triumph. But blitzes were a thing of the past. Crocuses and aconites were brightening the sooty gardens. Was it spring yet in Canada?

Leaving the hostel in high spirits, we bussed to the dockside. The Port of Liverpool was humming in high gear despite devastated wharfs and sunken vessels. We boarded the *Pasteur,* a one-time French luxury liner, one hundred strong. From Yorkshire moors and Devon's coast, from Stepney, Mayfair and Blackpool came teachers, barmaids, ex-service women, nurses, chorus girls, fresh-checked young women and plump matrons, a pot-pourri of

Britain's daughters. Escorted by tugs and seagulls, we set sail for Canada that day, slipping out of port in the waning afternoon. Goodbye, Liverpool ... goodbye, Lancashire ... goodbye, England ... Oh, England, England ... Goodbye ...

Land receding and lifeboat drill, its purpose emphasized by a speck thrumming in the sky. Gun crews sprang into action, swinging the guns after the plane, all heads swivelling apprehensively with them. "Relax! It's one of ours!"—broke the tension, we went below. Was this tall *Pasteur* a luxury liner? Converted, it was the epitome of austerity: stripped, crowded, none too clean. A cabin designed for six, now crammed with pairs of narrow bunks in tiers of three, slept thirty. At that we were luckier than most of the returning servicemen who slept on the decks. The one lounge was small and packed, it served all the officers on board as well as the "brides."

The green rolling Atlantic seemed to go on forever and ever. Then on March 6th, at twilight, there was a clatter of footsteps in the passageway, an eager young voice crying—"Girls ! Girls! Come and see CANADA! Quick!—There's snow and trees and little houses and LIGHTS!" We crowded on deck, excitedly vying with the returning men for vantage points for our first glimpse of Canada—the eastern shore of Nova Scotia—just discernible in the dwindling light. We tore ourselves away and went below for dinner. Seated at the table, a thrill rippled through the assembly ... The ship had stopped! Soon, in an indelible moment, a swirl of bagpipes heralded a file of kilted soldiers, threading their way between the tables, piping a royal welcome. Pent-up emotion broke under the impact of the plaintive music, and the atmosphere was charged with tears and laughter. Abandoning the chef's best efforts, we rushed aloft to see what we could of Halifax.

Optimistically, I scanned the dock, not that I really expected to see my beloved there. But we'd be together soon. My heart skipped—maybe even tonight! That hope was soon squashed. The loudspeakers told us there would be no disembarkation that evening. I started to pack and then I was called for by two young RCAF officers of the Women's Division. They told me my husband had been posted to Vancouver the week before, and they had wired him for instructions. "He wants me in Vancouver," I told them confidently, waving my precious letters to prove it. They borrowed the letters, promising not to read the intimate bits, and departed to see what could be arranged. Later I was elated to be informed that I was to proceed with the other west-bound brides by special train to Vancouver.

Few slept that night, and while the cheery goodbyes of those going to the Atlantic provinces echoed through the passageways before dawn, the rest of us got up, did final packing and impatiently paced the decks until at last we had the word to go. We trundled ashore into the vast immigration sheds where rambling enclosed walkways frustrated all our attempts to catch a glimpse of our new country. Purses bulging with our new money, we completed formalities and sat around, sipping cocoa, smoking, making small talk while we waited to board the train. At this eleventh hour I was paged and looked up to see the same two girls in air force blue. They had come to tell me that I wasn't going to Vancouver after all. A telegram from my husband had arrived, directing them to send me to his home in Nova Scotia.

I was stunned, incredulous. There must be some mistake, I insisted. He wanted me in Vancouver just as much as I wanted to be there. They showed me the telegram—there was no arguing with that. The bottom dropped out of my world. He didn't want me. The dam broke.

My shipboard friends rallied round to console me, but what could they say? "Don't cry, Jeff, he's only on a course—he'll be back in a couple of months." A couple of months! The floodgates opened wide as I was ravaged by dreadful doubts. How well, after all, did I know this man I'd married? This stranger for whom I'd crossed the ocean?

Tears were useless, of course; mopping up, I received new directions, the heart gone out of me. My husband's family were expecting me, but it was hours before the next train, so I'd be cared for by the Salvation Army in the meantime. A fatherly man in uniform stepped forward and was introduced. The rest of the brides were on the move now, boarding the train to the West—to Vancouver. Feeling like stranded flotsam cast up on this alien shore, I watched them go. My last link with home was severed.

The ladies at the Salvation Army Hostel extended hospitality, giving me my first meal in Canada, "Never tasted lemon pie before? Imagine!" A young English girl was staying there awaiting passage back to England. She was a war widow, and with her baby had come to Canada to make her home with her dead husband's parents. "It didn't work out," she told me with a sad resignation unsuited to her twenty-two years. My wobbling perspective was jolted sharply back into line; I had an unbounded future with a living, loving husband whose family was even at this moment preparing to welcome me. What did I have to get all boiled up about?

Later, breathing good wishes, the Major saw me safely aboard the train. Gathering speed, we passed into a rock-cutting from which we emerged in sight of ice-rimmed water, with a scattering of white houses climbing the tree-clad shores. Wearing coat, hat, scarf and gloves over a wool dress and heavy underwear, I suddenly realized I was sweltering. There was heat in this train and how! The conductor appeared smiling beside me and I fumbled for my ticket, but he proffered a clothes hanger. Such service! My coat removed, he lingered to chat. He produced a map and entertained me by tracing the train's route. There was more to Nova Scotia than I'd imagined.

There was a prolonged stop, bright lights in the deepening gloom revealed that this was "WINDSOR." The conductor caught my eye, "Next stop," he said. I collected my things to the accompaniment of the blaring whistle; we clattered over a long bridge and were at my destination. My legs shook as the conductor helped me down, "There they are—you'll be fine now!"

Four young people stepped forward, my brothers and sister-in-law, friendly strangers, yet not strangers. There was a short confused ride in darkness, then I was swept into a warm kitchen on a wave of excited chatter. A slender, pink-cheeked woman with eyes suspiciously bright held her arms out to me, uttering blurred words of welcome, "Come and meet dad," she said. Dad, an invalid, was the pivot of the home. "Why, you're just like your pictures," he greeted me, "You're a big girl!" "Welcome, Welcome" rippled through the house in words and laughter, in actions and eager questions—everybody talking at once.

They didn't know, either, why I'd been sent there, instead of Vancouver. "Last night they called, said you'd arrived in Halifax and would be here today, then they phoned you were going to Vancouver. At lunchtime they said there was another change of plans and you'd be coming here after all." Apparently I wasn't the only one who had a traumatic day; I'd never dreamed my arrival would throw anyone into a tizzy. I asked about my dearly beloved—"Aw, he'll get so mad to think he missed you by just a few days, he was here last week." "No, we haven't heard from him yet, there hasn't been time, he'd only get to Vancouver yesterday!" The light dawned—as new to the West Coast as I was to the East, he had to get his bearings—He still loved me! Immeasurably relieved, I began to appreciate my surroundings.

The next few days were hectic with a steady succession of callers. It was a noisy household anyway, geared to a deaf mother. Nobody ever went softly, doors slammed, visitors shouted. Dad's call-button activated a car-horn, and the phone, which rang for every number on a multi-party line, was fitted with a fire-alarm bell. This was my first experience of a party-line phone, and I simply couldn't believe it. Telephones were almost sacrosanct in England, only used when necessary and calls kept brief. Here the endless time spent on the phone and the trivialities discussed were incredible. Everybody got into the act. Whoever was handy, be it friend, casual caller or family member, answered it. People I had never heard of telephoned to welcome me, but best of all, it brought long, fervent telegrams from Vancouver—I was to go there after all—just as soon as he could find a place for me to stay.

Within a week I had the green light from Vancouver and set off on my travels again. I slept in a train for the first time, woke to a sumptuous breakfast and Montreal. Northern Ontario was a limitless land of Christmas trees. People on the train chatted to me like old friends. One man asked too many questions for my liking. He wanted to know where I'd sailed from and the name of my vessel. He didn't learn anything from me—"CARELESS TALK COSTS LIVES" (as wartime posters told us). The prairies were snow-covered, and almost as rolling, almost as interminable as the Atlantic. Then the majestic Rockies: the awesome peaks, sheer drops and frozen waterfalls.

Sunday morning and mild air . . . green grass . . . Vancouver. At last Vancouver! "Journey's end in lovers' meeting." Exchanging goodbyes with my friendly travelling companions, I left the train, claimed my luggage and stood scanning the milling throngs, my heart galloping, ready to panic, "Where is he? Where is he?" Then, as the crowds thinned, running footsteps, a flurry of blue uniform—and I was clutched, clasped, enveloped in a bear hug. "At last! At last!—I thought you'd never get here!"

The old magic blossomed again; doubts and fears vanished, the long empty months, the heart-wrenching partings, the extended travellings became worthwhile. They were all behind us. Hand in hand we wandered out into the quiet of an early Sunday morning. We got to know one another again on the shores of the Pacific Ocean, while Spring erupted around us in blossoming trees, singing birds and sunny skies—a perfect setting for the start of a second honeymoon that still goes on. We went on to have four children and live in all the eastern provinces of Canada. We are now retired and live in our chosen city of Victoria.

EPILOGUE

Through these stories we have caught a glimpse of the war brides' lives before, during and after World War II. The stories have a common thread but it is the war brides' differences that make them unique, the similarities that create sisterhood. Their sisterhood reveals a special kind of courage and camaraderie rooted in their struggle through the traumatic years of World War II.

Approximately 48,000 war brides came to Canada and were soon plunged into busy daily routines. Even as they adapted to a new country and culture, they raised their families, kept in touch with loved ones back home, worked in the community and joined organizations. The years flew by and their wartime experiences became dream-like memories that they stored away while their busy daily lives preoccupied them.

Over the years war bride groups were organized throughout Canada, and war brides who lived in close proximity to each other managed to get together now and then. As their children grew up and left home, the war brides began to have more time for them-selves and friendships with other women. They moved into a new stage of life which allowed them more time to reflect on their earlier years. As one war bride explains: "We think often of times past and old friendships that were once very important to us. We remember our childhood home, the family and the good times that were left behind."

It was in 1980, that Doris Johnson and Edith Hinecker arrived at a point in their lives when they could find the time they needed to organize the first chapter of the Vancouver Island War Brides. Doris already knew a number of local war brides in her area, and invited them to assist her and Edith in taking the necessary steps towards founding their chartered organization. With twelve founding members in the organization, Edith Hinecker became the Vancouver Island War Brides' first president, and Doris

Johnson took on the role of secretary/treasurer. The founding group was soon amazed by the dramatic results of their initial advertising campaign—they had no idea of the great number of war brides living on Vancouver Island. Inspired by the huge response, the Vancouver Island War Brides planned their first reunion for the following September.

The reunion was a resounding success with over one hundred war brides and their husbands present. After the first reunion, the Vancouver Island War Brides divided themselves into regional zones: Greater Victoria, Cowichan Valley, Greater Nanaimo, Alberni Valley and Comox Valley. In rotation, each region took on the responsibility of coordinating an annual reunion. As well, each of the individual zones organized its own monthly luncheons.

The Vancouver Island war brides enjoy friendships enriched and deepened by their common experiences. Their unique bond began when each of them made a life-altering decision to marry a foreign Allied serviceman during wartime. As they all grow older, they share not only their memories but also their problems and concerns—nurturing and supporting each other as well as celebrating their lives as war brides. These war brides truly demonstrate that sisterhood can not only cross oceans but can span a lifetime, growing in strength as the years go by.

The editors recently had the opportunity to attend the Vancouver Island War Brides' 15th annual reunion in Courtenay, BC. Fittingly entitled "Seems Like Old Times," the reunion gave us a glimpse into their past, into a time when their determined and courageous spirit filled them with a love of life which is still present today. As we observed at the reunion and as the stories reveal in this book, the war brides collectively weave together a tapestry of memories which commemorate both their diversity and unity.

Barbara Ladouceur and Phyllis Spence

ABOUT THE EDITORS

Barbara Ladouceur earned her MA in Women's Studies at the University of York in England. Most recently she has taught Women's Studies at the University of Victoria. She now resides in Vancouver as a free-lance writer and instructor.

Phyllis Spence earned her BA in psychology/sociology, and currently works with seniors in health care programs. She resides in Victoria and plans to continue recording oral histories.

The editors' belief in the importance of recording and publishing women's life stories was inspired by the Women's Studies Program they attended as mature students at the University of Victoria.